Popular Science™

DISCOVERIES
AND INVENTIONS
FROM THE LAST
CENTURY THAT
SHAPE OUR LIVES

SCIENCE

YEAR BY YEAR

Popular Science™

DISCOVERIES
AND INVENTIONS
FROM THE LAST
CENTURY THAT
SHAPE OUR LIVES

SCIENCE

YEAR BY YEAR

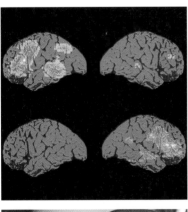

SCHOLASTIC
REFERENCE

A MARSHALL EDITION
Conceived, edited, and designed by
Marshall Editions Ltd
The Orangery, 161 New Bond Street, London W1S 2UF
www.marshallpublishing.com

First published in the U.K. in 2001 by
Marshall Publishing Ltd

First published in the U.S.A. by Scholastic Inc.
555 Broadway, New York, NY 10012

10 9 8 7 6 5 4 3 2 1

Popular science: science year by year: discoveries and
inventions from the 20th century that shape our lives today.
p. cm.
Includes index.
ISBN 0-439-28438-4
1. Science—History—20th century—Chronology—
Juvenile literature. 2. Technology—History—20th century—
Chronology. [1. Science—History—20th century—
Chronology. 2. Technology—History—20th century—
Chronology.]

Q125 .P755 2001
509.04—dc21   00-050476

Originated in Singapore by Master Image
Printed and bound in Germany by Mohndruck Gmbh

First Scholastic printing, August 2001

Consultant Editor Robert Dinwiddie
Contributors
Mark Cook, Viv Croot,
Ann Kramer, Carmine Ruggiero, Philip Wilkinson
For Scholastic
Senior Editor Virginia Ann Koeth
Art Director Nancy Sabato
For Marshall Editions
Managing Editor Scarlett O'Hara
Managing Designer Caroline Sangster
Picture Researcher Antonella Mauro
Editorial Assistance Vanessa Morgan, Elise See Tai
Production Christina Schuster
For PAGEOne
Creative Director Bob Gordon
Editors Michael Spilling, Stephen Griffin
Designers Robert Law, Tim Stansfield,
Andrew Nash, Thomas Keenes
Picture Researchers Julia Harris-Voss, Jane Moore,
Dee Robinson, Andrea Sadler
Cover Photography
Front, tl Royal Free Hospital of Medicine, Wellcome Trust;
c Ancient Art & Architecture Collection; tr Roger Ressmeyer/Corbis;
bl Charles O'Rear/Corbis; br Photodisk; Back, t Bob Battersby, Eye
Ubiquitous/Corbis; b Ancient Art & Architecture.

Contents

Special Focus Topics

Introduction

The 20th century was a period of extraordinary change in human affairs, in which the progress of technology and scientific thought played a prominent role. Many aspects of our lives today, in areas such as transportation, medicine, and communication, would not have been believed possible 100 years ago. These changes have been due to just a few crucial developments, such as the airplane (a product of the 1900s), television (1920s), antibiotics (1940s), and microprocessors (1970s). Many other developments, such as gene technology and nuclear fusion, look to be of major importance in the 21st century, although their impact up to now has been small.

Our understanding of the physical universe has also undergone some remarkable transformations. In 1900, scientists had only just grasped the idea of subatomic particles; the physical basis of heredity was a complete mystery; astronomers had no idea that other galaxies existed beyond our own. By 2000, physicists had identified over 400 types of subatomic particles, human genetic material was almost completely decoded, and the estimated number of galaxies had grown from one (our own Milky Way) to 100 billion.

In *Popular Science: Science Year by Year*, you will discover how these and many other advances came to be made—many in a series of steps over a long period of time, others as single flashes of inspiration. Here you will find such diverse stories as the invention of bubble gum, the ten-year series of events that put people on the Moon, the birth of computers, the unraveling of the structure of DNA, and the many new ways of looking inside the body. Then there are transistors, heart pacemakers, electric guitars, mobile phones, quarks, organ transplants, the "Big Bang" theory, the ozone layer, dinosaur discoveries, nuclear energy, the World Wide Web—the list goes on and on.

Today we are at the beginning of a new century and a new millennium, which will bring countless new discoveries and technological advances that will change our lives. We really have no idea what life may be like in 100 or 1,000 years' time. However, we can be sure that people will look back at the 20th century as a time when science and technology made some huge and profound leaps forward.

PHYSICS

The current thinking: electricity is caused by flow of electrons

A German physicist, Paul Karl Drude, has produced a convincing explanation of how an electric current flows in a metal wire. He proposes that the physical basis of a current is a gradual drift within the metal of tiny, charged particles called "electrons." Drude's explanation of electric current flow is remarkable because it implies that in metals, some electrons can separate from their "parent" atoms and are free to move about. Electrons are negatively charged, which also means that the real direction of charge flow in a current is from negative to positive—it was always thought to flow in the opposite direction.

The glass tube J.J. Thomson used to discover the electron. ▼

A GLANCE AT THE PAST

The electron discovered

British physicist J.J. Thomson (*above*) discovered electrons in 1897 while studying "cathode rays"– mysterious rays that could be produced in an airless glass tube by embedding electrodes at both ends and then applying a high voltage. It was known that the rays carried a negative electrical charge and were produced by one of the electrodes (the cathode). Thomson found that he could deflect the rays in an electrical field if all the air was removed from the tube. This showed that the rays were particles. Measuring the size of the deflection showed that the particles were tiny– much smaller than the smallest atoms (hydrogen atoms). Thomson had identified the first subatomic particle –the electron.

▲ *The clementine is the smallest member of the mandarin family.*

BIOLOGY

New citrus fruit developed by priest

A priest from the small seaport town of Oran in Algeria has developed a hybrid between the bitter orange and a sweet variety of mandarin orange. The new fruit, called a clementine after its discoverer, Father Clement Rodier, is proving popular with consumers because of its sweet, juicy pulp, absence of seeds, skin that can be peeled off in seconds, and flesh that easily separates into sections. Its discovery was accidental: Rodier unknowingly planted the citrus hybrid—a hybrid is the offspring of two plants of different varieties, or species—and the resulting tree yielded a fruit with a more intense flavor and juiciness than the original plants that created it.

Science News 1900

- The first hydrofoil catamaran is built by Italian E. Forlanini.

- The world's first tape recorder, which uses magnetic wire, is demonstrated at the Paris Exhibition.

- In Switzerland, Count Ferdinand von Zeppelin's Airship LZ1 makes a brief maiden flight.

ENERGY

Boom results in first offshore oil well

America's oil boom continues, with production this year surpassing one billion barrels and more than 15,000 new wells drilled. The search for oil has now extended onto the seabed, with the world's first offshore oil field near the California town of Summerland. Oil production takes place on 11 separate piers, each containing up to 20 wells. The most impressive of these piers extends over 12,000 feet (3,650 meters) into the Pacific Ocean. Unfortunately, Summerland wells are small producers. The most productive well, "Blue Goose," produces only 75 barrels a day.

Different blood types discovered

BIOLOGY

Austrian physician Karl Landsteiner has discovered that each person has a slightly different type of blood. He has identified at least three types or groups of human blood, and has called them A, B, and O. His discovery may explain why people react in different ways when given a blood transfusion, because blood from a donor—the person giving blood—may not match the blood of the person receiving it. If type A blood, for instance, is given to a person with blood type B, the serum, or clear liquid in the blood, can cause red blood cells to clump together, which can be extremely dangerous. Now, blood for transfusions can be matched correctly.

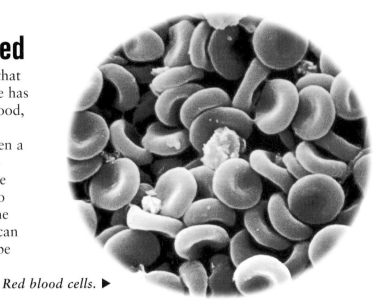

Red blood cells. ▶

▲ *Bull leaping in a fresco from Knossos, dating from 1600 B.C.*

Palace of Minotaur unearthed

ARCHAEOLOGY

The splendid palaces of Knossos, home of the legendary King Minos, have been uncovered on the Mediterranean island of Crete by English archaeologist Arthur Evans. Evans, who in 1894 purchased a site near the town of Iraklion, has realized his dream with the discovery of a five-and-a-half-acre (two-and-a-half-hectare), 800-room palace complex. The site is thought to date from between 1400 and 2000 B.C.—1,000 years before the heyday of Athens. One of the rooms has revealed a fresco of a charging bull, and other finds suggest that the ancient Minoans maintained a cult of the Bull, evidence for the ancient Greek myth of the flesh-eating, half-man, half-bull Minotaur, defeated by the Greek hero Theseus.

Max Planck's quantum theory

PHYSICS

The German physicist Max Planck has announced a startling result from his research into the foundations of thermodynamics (the study of energy and energy transfer). In a radical departure from classical ideas, Planck proposes that energy changes within systems occur in fixed discrete amounts called "quanta," which can be thought of as "packets" of energy. (Quanta is the plural of the Latin word *quantum*, which means "packet.") Planck proposes, for example, that light and radiant heat are absorbed or emitted from objects in the form of these quanta, which have specific energy values according to the type of energy. This overturns the previously accepted view that energy transfer is a continuous process. Planck's theory is believed to have far-reaching implications.

Max Planck, professor of physics and director of the Institute for Theoretical Physics at the University of Berlin. ▶

COMMUNICATIONS

Invention of radio

Working in his parents' attic in their house near Bologna, Italy, Guglielmo Marconi (*above*) sent the first radio signals in 1894. Marconi had heard about the work of the German physicist Heinrich Hertz, who in 1888 had demonstrated the existence of radio waves. When Marconi set up his apparatus, he found he could make a bell ring by sending a radio signal across the attic. He then made improvements to his equipment, and about a year later could send radio signals over a distance of 2 miles (3.2 kilometers).

COMMUNICATIONS

Transatlantic communication

Radio pioneer Guglielmo Marconi has amazed the world—he has supervised the sending of a radio signal across the Atlantic. Sitting at his receiver in St. John's, Newfoundland, the inventor picked up the signal (the letter *s* in Morse code), which came from Cornwall in southwest England. Experts are mystified by Marconi's success. Radio waves normally travel in straight lines, so the Earth's curvature should have sent the signal from Cornwall disappearing off into space long before it reached Newfoundland. But Marconi's signal did not vanish, and this fact will likely change communications forever.

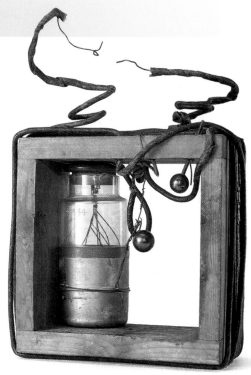

▲ *Marconi's first tuned transmitter.*

BIOLOGY

Hugo De Vries' leaps in evolution

A Dutch botanist, Hugo De Vries, proposes that changes in species occur in jumps, which he is calling "mutations." De Vries' ideas are set out in his book *Die Mutationstheorie*, in which he describes his observations and experiments with wild varieties of evening primrose. He has discovered that in the cultivation of the flowers, new forms or varieties appear randomly among a group of ordinary specimens. It is this sudden appearance of new forms that he refers to as mutations, and it is probable that they provide the variation within species that is needed for Charles Darwin's famous process of "natural selection" to drive evolution.

Guglielmo Marconi
b. 1874 d. 1937

Marconi was born into a wealthy family in Bologna, northern Italy. His father was Italian and his mother Irish. He was educated mostly at home by private tutors, but also attended the Technical Institute at Livorno for a short time. Marconi began to experiment with radio when he was 20, realizing that he could send and receive radio signals by adapting components invented by several different people, notably the German scientist Heinrich Hertz and Frenchman Edouard Branly.

FORENSICS

Telltale prints

The police at Scotland Yard in London have opened their fingerprint department. Using a simple system of classifying fingerprint patterns, the British police intend to keep comprehensive records of all convicted criminals. Fingerprinting was first used by William Hershel of the Indian Civil Service in 1877, to ensure that army pensioners in Bengal did not draw their pensions more than once. They were made to "sign" for their money by leaving an inky impression on a piece of paper. The technique was later improved by Sir Francis Galton, and developed by Edward Henry, who, as chief commissioner of the London police, has introduced the system at Scotland Yard. Fingerprints offer a sure way of identifying a person. Criminals watch out!

▲ *The ridge pattern on every human finger does not alter with age.*

Hornby constructs fun for children

ENTERTAINMENT

Frank Hornby, a bookkeeper from Liverpool, has invented a new type of toy for kids, which he's selling in little tin boxes under the name "Mechanics Made Easy." It's a construction system where standardized, preformed, reusable perforated metal parts can be attached to each other with nuts and bolts to form structures such as bridges, cranes, airplanes, and so on. The basic parts include metal strips and girders of various lengths, as well as brackets, flanges, pulleys, wheels, rods, and gears. The only tools needed to join the parts together are a simple screwdriver and wrench, and these come in the box. It looks like these kits are going to be a big hit this Christmas!

Mechanics Made Easy was ▶ later renamed Meccano®. Erector® sets, devised by A.C. Gilbert, were introduced in the U.S. in 1913, and were very similar to Meccano.

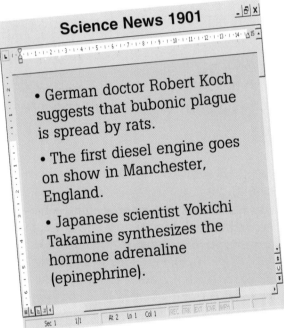

Science News 1901

- German doctor Robert Koch suggests that bubonic plague is spread by rats.
- The first diesel engine goes on show in Manchester, England.
- Japanese scientist Yokichi Takamine synthesizes the hormone adrenaline (epinephrine).

Cause of beri-beri discovered

BIOLOGY

Beri-beri is a tropical disease that occurs throughout Asia. It affects the nervous system and its name means "extreme weakness" because sufferers experience numbness, weakness, and even paralysis. Now Dutch physician Dr. Gerrit Grijns has shown that the disease is caused by the removal of a nutrient from white rice during the process of polishing. Polished white rice is a staple part of the Asian diet, and it has been suspected for some years that it might be a factor in the disease. In the 1880s, Japanese physician Dr. K. Takaki showed that if Japanese sailors ate more fruit, vegetables, fish, and meat, and less polished rice, the number of beri-beri sufferers declined.

Giraffe relative found in Africa

ZOOLOGY

Various skins, a skull, and descriptions of tracks sent back to London's Zoological Society from deepest Africa have revealed the existence of a large land animal previously unknown to science. The explorer Sir Harry Johnston has been sending these items back from the Ituri forest, an area in the northeast of Belgian Congo, where he set off two years ago to investigate rumors of a strange donkeylike animal with stripy legs. At first he thought he had discovered a new species of horse. But later Johnston stumbled across the animal's tracks, which showed that, unlike a horse, it had cloven hooves. It is now thought to be a relative of the giraffe. The Wambutti pygmies, the local people, call the animal the o'api, and European zoologists have decided to name it the "okapi."

An okapi discovered in the forests of Belgian Congo. ▶

Electric typewriters sold worldwide

The Blickensderfer company of Connecticut has produced the world's first electric typewriter. With the old-style manual typewriter, the operator had to take care to hit the keys with equal strength, otherwise the typed text looked messy and uneven. The electric typewriter takes care of this problem. By using motors to move the keys, the type bars move at the same speed each time, giving an even printout, with every letter clear and black.

▲ *Changing office life: the electric typewriter.*

The first typewriter

The first successful typewriter was produced in the 1860s by American printer Christopher Latham Scholes. Scholes sold his patents to the Remington Company, and they began to manufacture the machine in 1874. It did not catch on at first, but Remington hit on the idea of lending the typewriters to companies, who later wanted to buy them. These early machines already had a "QWERTY" keyboard layout. Scholes chose this layout to keep frequently used keys apart, slowing down the typist and preventing the keys from jamming.

▲ *Ivan Pavlov (far left) with colleagues and one of his dogs.*

BIOLOGY

Pavlov and his dogs

A Russian physiologist, Ivan Pavlov, has uncovered a fundamental type of nervous system response that he believes underlies many aspects of habitual behavior. He is calling it the "conditioned reflex." Pavlov's ideas are based on experiments in which biologically important events—such as feeding time for a dog—are accompanied by a signal, such as the ringing of a bell. After a few days, the dog begins to salivate at the sound of the bell, whether or not any food is present. Pavlov has concluded that some association must form in the dog's nervous system between the bell's sound and the idea of food. He believes this type of "learning by association" may be involved in some types of human behavior too.

Earth's atmosphere has layers

EARTH SCIENCE

French scientist Léon Teisserenc de Bort has discovered that Earth's atmosphere consists of at least two distinct layers. It seems that in the layer up to about 7 miles (11.3 kilometers) above Earth's surface, which he's calling the "troposphere," the temperature changes constantly, although there is an overall decrease in temperature with height. The temperature changes in this layer cause fluctuating weather. But above an altitude of about 7 miles, which he is calling the "stratosphere," atmospheric temperature remains relatively constant at all heights and the weather stays the same at all times. Independently, British scientists have predicted the existence of an electrified layer in the atmosphere that reflects radio waves. They call it the "ionosphere."

Science News 1902

- At Susa, Iran, a French expedition discovers tablets engraved with the legal code of Hammurabi, the earliest known set of laws.

- Sigmund Freud, Alfred Adler, and others in Vienna form the first psychoanalytical society.

- German Karl Landsteiner discovers a fourth blood group, AB.

Electricity breaks the silence

MEDICINE

The familiar ear trumpet may soon be found in the garbage can of history. An electrical hearing aid developed by Millar Reese Hutchinson looks set to make the trusty trumpet obsolete. The manufacturers claim their new "Acousticon" can amplify sound by up to 45 decibels. The technology behind this breakthrough is nothing new, as the microphone and earpiece are already found in any telephone. Sound arriving at the microphone causes a diaphragm to vibrate in time with the sound waves. As the diaphragm vibrates, it changes the microphone's resistance, generating an electrical signal. When this electricity arrives at the earpiece, it causes a speaker to vibrate, reproducing the sound at an increased volume. Thanks to electricity, "Pardon?" could become a sound of the past.

Electrical hearing ▶ aids will be smaller and more discreet than traditional trumpets.

A gasoline ▶ engine powers Booth's horse-drawn cleaner's pump.

Booth's vacuum cleans up

HOME APPLIANCES

British civil engineer Hubert Cecil Booth has triumphed with his latest invention, the vacuum cleaner. Asked to clean the carpet for King Edward VII's coronation in Westminster Abbey, he did the job in record time. Now everyone wants their carpets cleaned by a Booth vacuum cleaner. Booth's machine works by using a powerful pump to suck air and dust through a hose. A cloth filter traps the dust in a container, while allowing air to pass back out into the room. Booth's machines are now often seen on London streets, their hoses pushed through the windows of buildings to be cleaned.

Gasoline is king of the road

TRANSPORTATION

The gasoline-powered automobile is set to take over the road. Developed by Charles E. and J. Frank Duryea between 1893 and 1895, and taken up by most other motor manufacturers, they were first shown to an amazed public in 1900 at the first National Auto Show at Madison Square Garden, New York. Now automobiles with gasoline-fueled engines are more popular than their electric and steam-driven counterparts. It all comes down to hard cash. The opening up of the Texas oil fields in 1901 means that gasoline is now cheap and plentiful. Also, a fire at his Motor Works in Detroit means that one major manufacturer now uses a system of mass production to build automobiles, bringing down the costs and making automobiles affordable.

Good-bye steam! ▶ Gasoline-powered automobiles are here to stay.

X rays discovered

Wilhelm Conrad Röntgen (*above*) remained a little-known academic until a chance observation led him to discover the X ray in 1895. His most famous experiment involved placing his wife's hand between the X-ray source and a photographic plate, producing the first permanent X ray of the human body. The ability of X rays to reveal structures inside a living body captured the public's imagination and made Röntgen a household name. For his discovery, Röntgen was awarded the first Nobel Prize for physics in 1901.

MEDICINE

X rays used to attack tumors

In medicine, X rays have proved to be not quite as useful as initially predicted, with many pioneers suffering terrible burns from exposure to them. However, physician George Perthes has discovered that X rays can be used to reduce the size of cancerous tumors. Perthes' method involves concentrating the X-ray dose on the tumor by placing the X-ray source directly above it. If Perthes is correct, X rays will give doctors a powerful new tool in the fight against cancer.

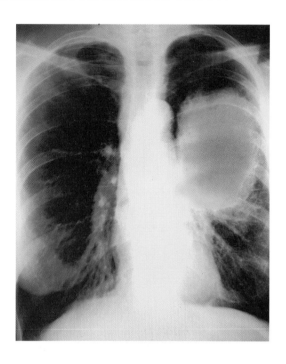

▲ *X rays, now used to fight cancer, unmask a living body's internal structure.*

BIOLOGY

The key to heredity

In his paper, *The Chromosomes Theory of Heredity,* American student Walter Sutton has explained why children of the same parents are different. It has long been thought that "chromosomes," seen in the nuclei of living cells, play a part in heredity. Sutton proposes that in most cells, chromosomes occur in pairs, but sex cells—egg and sperm cells—contain only one chromosome from each pair. He suggests that chromosomes contain strings of hereditary factors, called "genes," and that in most cells these exist as pairs. He argues that, during the formation of a sex cell, only one gene is taken from each pair. In this way, each sex cell receives a different mix of genes.

▲ *Chromosomes in cell nuclei occur in pairs.*

◀ *A cool idea—air-conditioning makes life more comfortable.*

ENGINEERING

Cold comfort in summer

Hot, sticky rooms may be a thing of the past. American engineer Willis Haviland Carrier has invented the world's first effective "air-conditioning" unit. But its first use is to keep paper cool. A Brooklyn printer, who could not print color images because heat and humidity were affecting his paper, commissioned Carrier to find a solution. Carrier came up with a cooling unit that sucks humid air in through a filter, passes it over coils containing chilled salty water, then redirects the cool air back into the room.

Doctors record heart's electricity

Seeing your heartbeat could soon be as routine as checking your pulse. Every time your heart beats, you feel a pulse of blood, but what you cannot feel is the tiny amount of electricity that also passes through you. A Dutch physician, Willem Einthoven, has developed the "string galvanometer" to measure the heart's electricity. To do this, electrodes are placed on the hands and feet—any electricity produced by the heart is then measured through the movement of a fine quartz string. The string's position is photographed several times during each heartbeat. By examining the photographs in turn, a trace can be made showing the heartbeat's electrical signature. Einthoven has found features common to all heartbeat traces and changes in these can be identified.

To examine the heartbeat, the patient's hands ▶
and a foot are placed in troughs containing a
conducting solution.

Science News 1903

- The first geothermal electric power station is built in Italy.

- In Britain, Bertrand Russell publishes *The Principles of Mathematics*, an outline of a program for basing math on pure logic.

- The American Ford Motor Company sells its first "Model A" auto to a doctor in Detroit.

Headache cure goes on sale

The German pharmaceutical company Bayer is marketing a new pain-relief drug under the trade name "Aspirin."

The drug was synthesized by a Bayer chemist, Felix Hoffmann, six years ago, when he was looking for a remedy to relieve his father's arthritis. It is rumored that Aspirin—or acetylsalicylic acid—can also cure headaches. A related compound, sodium salicylate, has been used for over 25 years as an anti-arthritic but often irritates the stomach.

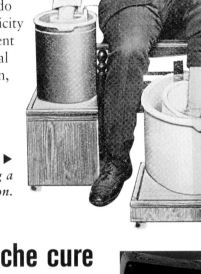

▲ *Aspirin is related to a substance called salicin, found in the bark and leaves of willow trees.*

The Wright stuff

December 13, Kitty Hawk, North Carolina: Orville and Wilbur Wright have just made the first flight in a powered, heavier-than-air machine. The brothers, who own a bicycle shop in Dayton, Ohio, made important modifications to the basic design of the machine built, but not successfully flown, by American astronomer Samuel Pierpoint Langley. The Wrights' greatest invention is the aileron, a movable wing flap that allows the pilot to control the balance of the wings during flight. They also built a lightweight engine for their biplane, *The Flyer*, and tested the result in a home-made wind tunnel.

▲ *On its first flight*, The Flyer, *with Orville Wright at the controls, flew for 12 seconds, traveling just 120 feet (37 meters).*

Tiny killers

Yellow fever was proven to be spread by the bites of mosquitoes of the genus *Aedes* only as recently as 1900. Studying a yellow fever epidemic in Cuba under the guidance of Dr. Walter Reed, British doctor James Carroll allowed mosquitoes that had fed on victims of the illness to bite him. His suspicions were proved when he soon developed the fever. He survived, only to die a few years later from yellow fever-induced heart disease. Earlier, in 1897, British physician Ronald Ross proved that malaria was spread by mosquitoes of the genus *Anopheles*.

MEDICINE

Army surgeon wipes out malaria in Panama

United States Army surgeon Colonel William Gorgas has developed such effective measures for controlling mosquitoes that both yellow fever and malaria are being wiped out in the region where the Panama canal is being built. Construction by the French company De Lesseps began in 1880, but ceased by 1889 following earthquakes and the deaths of 20,000 workers from disease. The United States acquired the Canal Zone last year, and Gorgas has tackled the disease problem by draining the lakes used by mosquitoes for breeding, and by separating the ill from the healthy workers.

▲ *Colonel William Gorgas.*

HOME APPLIANCES

A smoother, safer shave

The new razor blades are selling in the millions. Wisconsin salesman King Camp Gillette invented the safety razor and blade back in 1895, responding to a challenge from his boss: "Invent something that will be used once and then be thrown away." Gillette came up with the safety razor, with its thin, throwaway steel blade. It doesn't need sharpening and is less likely to cut the skin than the old-style "cutthroat" razor. Many scoffed when Gillette said he was selling something you could use and throw away, but the disposable blade has caught on.

◀ *Some 90,000 Gillette razors have been sold this year!*

MEDICINE

Useful new local anesthetic

German chemist Albert Einhorn has recently synthesized a new compound to be used as a local anesthetic—a substance that will block pain signals within a region of the body when injected close to a nerve supplying that region. He's calling the compound procaine hydrochloride. Dr. Einhorn had been looking for a replacement for the substance most often used for local anesthesia at the present time, cocaine, which is now recognized to be addictive and poisonous to the nervous system. Procaine (soon to be available in the United States under the trade name Novacaine) seems perfect. It is nonaddictive, four to six times less toxic than cocaine, has a shorter duration of action, and is easier to synthesize and sterilize. In the future it may be used for painless tooth extraction and other minor surgery, as well as pain relief during childbirth.

Science News 1904

- In Russia, the Trans-Siberian Railway, linking Moscow to the Pacific coast, is completed.

- Frenchman Leon Guillet develops the first stainless steels.

- New York tea and coffee merchant Thomas Sullivan invents the tea bag—it is made of hand-sewn silk!

Nerves, nerves, nerves

BIOLOGY

Spanish physician Ramon y Cajal, Professor of Anatomy at Madrid University, has published a major work on the structure of the nervous system in humans and vertebrates. Cajal describes how the nervous system is made up of billions of individual nerve cells. Each nerve cell has a threadlike projection from it, and bundles of these threads, or fibers, form nerves. Cajal has been studying the nervous system for more than 20 years. His big breakthrough came in 1887, when he used a new technique of staining nerve tissue before placing it under a microscope. Individual nerve cells appeared immediately, proving the physician's theory. His work explains how nerve cells receive and send information.

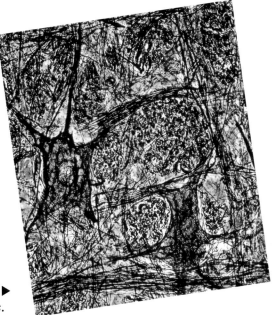

Some nerve cells and ▶ their projecting fibers.

▲ *Fleming's valve, based on Edison's light bulb.*

Fleming develops first diode

ELECTRONICS

Englishman John Ambrose Fleming, who has worked closely with Italian Guglielmo Marconi, inventor of the radio, has patented the first vacuum tube, or diode, nicknamed the "Fleming valve." This new device consists of a sealed vacuum tube containing two metal electrodes, and a metal plate in front of a heated wire, or filament. The diode acts just like a valve, forcing electricity to flow in one direction only, rather than flowing backward and forward alternately. In this way, it converts alternating current (AC) to direct current (DC) and can be used to detect radio waves.

With the introduction of the taxicab, anyone can travel in style. ▶

Taxi! Cabs boost auto production

TRANSPORTATION

Now anyone can ride in style. Louis Renault, founder of the Renault Automobile Company, has won a contract to supply Paris with taxicabs. His workshops have expanded to cope with building 1,200 automobiles a year (in its first year the company made only six). Renault's cabs are gasoline-powered cars, and fitted with meters so that it is possible to figure the distance the cab has gone and the fare. New York has had taxicabs since 1898, but they are electric and not fitted with meters.

MEDICAL IMAGING

Röntgen's discovery of X rays made headline news in 1896. In the first few years of the twentieth century, the public was fascinated by the prospect of seeing through clothing and flesh. They flocked to demonstrations where volunteers, flooded with X rays, showed their bones and internal organs. An estimated three million X-ray photographs were taken in 1901. But X rays offered more than high entertainment. They were the first in a series of new imaging technologies that would transform our ability to see inside the body.

Beneath the skin

A German physicist, Wilhelm Röntgen, was awarded the first Nobel Prize for physics in 1901 for his work on X rays. His most famous early X-ray photograph showed the bones in his wife's hand. He created this image by persuading his wife to put her hand between a vacuum tube and a sheet of photographic film. A 15-minute exposure created the world-famous photo. Mrs. Röntgen is said to have shuddered when shown the X ray of her own skeletal hand, seeing it as a premonition of death.

▲ *Röntgen's X ray.*

Wilhelm Röntgen

Wilhelm Röntgen (*above*) made his discovery when he was experimenting with vacuum tubes. Röntgen noticed how a fluorescent screen near a cardboard-covered vacuum tube glowed in a blacked-out laboratory. After tests, he realized the glowing was caused by a new type of energy, which he called "X rays."

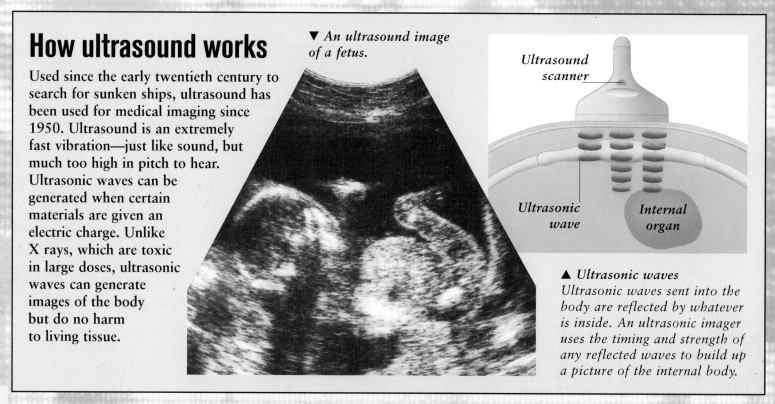

How ultrasound works

Used since the early twentieth century to search for sunken ships, ultrasound has been used for medical imaging since 1950. Ultrasound is an extremely fast vibration—just like sound, but much too high in pitch to hear. Ultrasonic waves can be generated when certain materials are given an electric charge. Unlike X rays, which are toxic in large doses, ultrasonic waves can generate images of the body but do no harm to living tissue.

▼ *An ultrasound image of a fetus.*

Ultrasound scanner

Ultrasonic wave

Internal organ

▲ **Ultrasonic waves**
Ultrasonic waves sent into the body are reflected by whatever is inside. An ultrasonic imager uses the timing and strength of any reflected waves to build up a picture of the internal body.

1953
Ultrasound is first
used to show a
breast cancer.

1967
Lauterbur proposes
magnetic resonance
imaging (MRI).

1972
Godfrey Hounsfield
devises the CT
scanner.

1977
The first MRI scan
of a human is
taken.

1985
The first medical
PET-scan images
are available.

Contrast X rays

X rays are superb for showing
abnormalities in bones but not as good
for showing the body's soft organs and
blood vessels. Mostly, X rays pass
straight through these tissues. From
1905 to 1962, a whole series of
techniques were devised for introducing
radiopaque substances (fluids that
would block X rays) into soft organs
and ducts before X-raying them. These
"contrast" X-ray techniques allowed
the organs to be visualized. In 1962
coronary arteriography, or angiography,
was introduced and has proved
extremely useful in heart-disease
diagnosis.

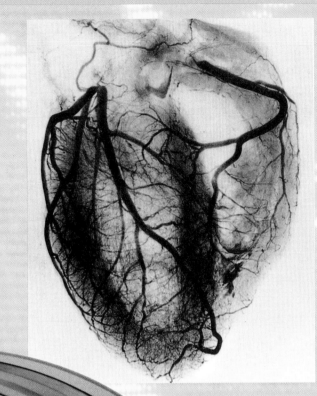

◀ *In this coronary
angiogram, many
of the blood vessels
supplying the heart
muscle can be seen.
This is because a
radiopaque
substance was
introduced into
the blood vessels
before the X ray
was taken.*

Computer-aided X rays

Computers have been used to enhance
X-ray imaging since the 1970s. If many
different X-ray images are taken of the
body, a computer can assemble them into a
combined, overall picture. One of the most
successful computer-enhanced X-ray
techniques is called the CT (computerized
tomography) scan. To make a CT scan,
X rays of a body part are taken at many
different angles. A computer combines all
the images to produce cross-sections of the
body part.

▼ *Inside a CT tube
The patient lies in an
X-ray machine that
completely circles the
body. Detectors in the
machine send data to
a computer, which
then forms an image.*

Radioactive pictures

A positron emission tomography (PET) scan
detects traces of a radioactive substance that
is injected into a patient's blood. This
substance, called a "marker," emits particles
the PET scanner can detect. Some parts of
the body absorb more of the marker than
others. The PET scanner uses this to
monitor the functioning, as well as to study
the structure, of body parts.

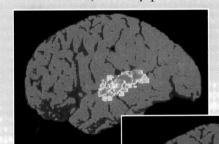

▶ *Brain scans
These two PET
scans show
some activity
(red and yellow
areas) concerned
with word recognition and speech
in a region of the brain called the
temporal lobe. In the lower scan,
the activity has spread into the
more central parietal lobe.*

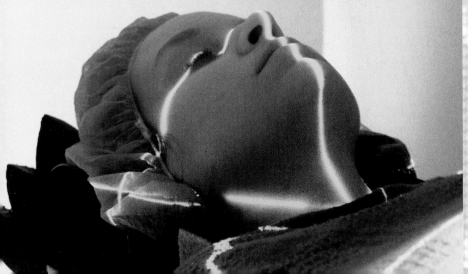

19

PHYSICS

Albert Einstein's special theory of relativity

▼ *Albert Einstein, whose special theory of relativity has impressed the scientific world.*

Dr. Albert Einstein, a 26-year-old working in the Swiss patent office in Berne, has impressed the scientific world with his "special theory of relativity." The theory is based on the idea that the velocity of light remains constant, whatever the relative motion of its source and an observer. The theory has amazing implications. It states, among other things, that mass increases and time passes more slowly when an object is traveling close to the speed of light.

BIOLOGY

Chromosomes determine sex

A few years ago, Clarence McClung proposed that an unpaired "X" chromosome (a carrier of inherited information) in body cells was involved in determining sex. Now, U.S. biologist Nettie Stevens has shown that two copies of the X chromosome are present in female cells, but one is inactive. Male cells contain one X chromosome and a tiny "Y" chromosome. Stevens's findings offer a convincing explanation for how sex is determined. Females pass an X chromosome on to all their children via their eggs. Males have two types of sperm cells: Some contain an X chromosome and combine with eggs to form females; others contain a Y chromosome and produce males.

Four human chromosomes. ▶

EARTH SCIENCE

Meteorite made huge crater

Philadelphia mining engineer Daniel Barringer has produced convincing evidence that a massive crater in Arizona was caused by the impact of a meteorite (rock from space) many thousands of years ago. Previously, a meteorite was rejected as the cause, because there was insufficient evidence of meteoritic material buried beneath the crater. Instead, the crater was thought to have a volcanic origin. But Barringer has discovered that the crater's rim contains chunks of meteoritic iron randomly mixed in with the ejected rock. He argues that if this meteoritic material had fallen at a different time than when the crater was formed, it would be present in a separate layer from the rock.

◀ *The Arizona crater is nearly one mile (one-and-a-half kilometers) wide.*

Safety glass developed for automobile windshields

MATERIALS

Automobile manufacturers are striving to make driving more comfortable. Thanks to glass windshields, motorists are no longer buffeted by high winds. But glass windshields easily break, showering the auto and its occupants with deadly fragments. Now a Frenchman has provided a solution: Eduard Benedictus, artist and part-time chemist, has developed a new "safety glass." The new glass consists of a sheet of celluloid sandwiched between two sheets of ordinary glass. The addition of plastic gives enhanced flexibility—safety glass bulges rather than shatters on impact. Should the windshield break, the shattered glass sticks to the plastic rather than flying off in splinters.

▲ *Windshields give automobiles added luxury but frequently shatter, injuring driver and passengers.*

Science News 1905

- In America, George W. Crile performs the first direct blood transfusion.

- After working on exhaust silencers for automobiles, Hiram Maxim, German inventor of the machine gun, invents a silencer for the gun.

- The German navy launches its first U-boat submarine.

Cause of syphilis identified

MEDICINE

German zoologist Fritz Schaudinn and a colleague, dermatologist Erich Hoffmann, have discovered the bacterium that causes the hideous, disfiguring venereal disease syphilis. The organism has been named *Spirocheta pallida*, and it belongs to a group of bacteria called spirochetes. It is a curious, threadlike organism, visible only under a microscope. It has recently been confirmed that syphilis can be transmitted from mothers to babies as well as by sexual intercourse. At the moment, there is no known effective treatment—mercury has been tried as a cure for years but is not very effective and is very toxic. At least the identification of the causative organism gives greater hope that a cure may one day be found.

Giant dinosaur named

PALEONTOLOGY

A species of giant, meat-eating dinosaur whose fossilized bones were unearthed three years ago in Hell Creek, Montana, has been named *Tyrannosaurus rex* by Henry Osborn, curator of the Department of Vertebrate Paleontology at the American Museum of Natural History in New York City. The name means "ruling tyrant lizard." The bones were discovered by the famous "fossil hunter" Barnum Brown in rock strata indicating that the dinosaur is tens of millions of years old. It is 47 feet (14 meters) long, and in life it must have weighed some eight tons (seven metric tonnes)—it had massive hind legs, short arms, two-fingered hands, and a long tail. The skeleton will be mounted and displayed in the Museum of Natural History.

T. rex is notable for its huge head—its jaw is four feet (1.2 meters) long and its serrated teeth six inches (15 centimeters) long. ▶

1906

A GLANCE AT THE PAST

Edison's phonograph

The American inventor Thomas Edison (above) made the first sound recording in 1877. His "phonograph" used a sheet of tinfoil wrapped around a rotating metal cylinder. Sound waves, focused through a funnel, made a steel needle press a bumpy groove into the foil as the cylinder rotated. When the needle was run along the groove a second time, its vibrations roughly reproduced the original sound.

ENTERTAINMENT

Automatic entertainer is a big hit in Chicago

The Automatic Machine and Tool Company of Chicago is marketing a novelty music machine called the "John Gabel Automatic Entertainer." Americans have long been accustomed to nickel-in-the-slot machines that play a tune. Louis Glass first attached a coin slot to one of Thomas Edison's phonographs in 1889. Glass's enterprising effort proved that people would pay to hear recorded music in bars—even though the customers had to hold listening tubes to their ears to hear the tune. The Automatic Entertainer uses the newer flat 10-inch (25-centimeter) discs, and allows the customer to choose from a list of 24 different discs. The machine is worked by turning a crank handle. But the music is still not able to rise to a volume that will effectively entertain a crowded saloon bar.

▲ *Instant entertainment with the Automatic Entertainer.*

FOOD

Kellogg's corn flakes

Will Keith Kellogg has founded a company to market a healthy breakfast called "corn flakes." The rolled and toasted wheat and corn has been developed by Will Keith's brother John Harvey Kellogg, a physician at Battle Creek Sanitarium in Michigan. The Kelloggs believe that their cereal will replace the traditional fried breakfast.

The new cereal is made from ▲ flaked, toasted wheat and corn.

◀ *The Royal Navy's HMS Dreadnought is the fastest, largest warship on the high seas.*

MILITARY TECHNOLOGY

New era on the high seas

Britain, the world's greatest maritime power, has sparked an unprecedented arms race by launching the *Dreadnought*, the most powerful battleship the world has ever seen. Fast-moving, protected by 11-inch (28-centimeter) thick armor, and carrying 10 massive 12-inch (30-centimeter) guns, the new ship is designed to render all existing naval vessels obsolete. *Dreadnought* is the brainchild of Admiral Sir John Fisher. Fisher argues that the Royal Navy can only maintain its superiority at sea by embracing the most up-to-date technology. Other world powers, including Britain's chief rival, Germany, are rapidly preparing plans for their own super-battleships. The resulting naval race is bound to be expensive, and seems likely to increase international tensions.

Radioactivity —a history

Radioactivity was discovered by French physicist Antoine-Henri Becquerel in 1896, when he found that a photographic plate left close to a piece of uranium had become heavily fogged. In 1898, Marie and Pierre Curie (*above*) showed that another element, thorium, had a similar effect, and coined the term "radioactivity" to describe the phenomenon.

EARTH SCIENCE

Rocks dated using radioactivity

Massachusetts-born radiochemist Bertram Boltwood has worked out how to measure the age of certain rocks from the amount of radioactivity they contain. It is known that radioactive chemical elements decay at a fixed rate into other elements. Boltwood has found that radioactive uranium slowly decays to a stable, nonradioactive form of lead. He has proposed that if a rock was first formed containing some uranium, the ratio of its lead to its uranium must gradually rise over time. Therefore, by measuring this ratio, the age of the rock can be estimated.

▲ *Bertram Boltwood, whose pioneering work has enabled the age of rock samples to be estimated.*

ENGINEERING

New lamps available

Incandescent tungsten filament lamps have gone on sale in the United States. The bulbs, which contain filaments made of tungsten, will replace the carbon filament lamps used since the 1870s. Carbon is very brittle, and a longer-lasting filament material has been sought for a long time. Tungsten was the obvious choice, but it is only recently that scientists could convert the metal into a wire that can be used as a filament.

▲ *Tungsten filaments have an extremely high melting point of 6,170°F (3,410°C).*

MEDICINE

Reaching new depths

Thanks to Oxford academic John Scott Haldane, the Royal Navy has smashed the world diving record, reaching depths of 180 feet (54 meters). Haldane has built the first air pump to deliver enough breathable air to protect divers from the crushing water pressure found at these extreme depths. Returning too quickly to the surface is hazardous, as divers can suffer extreme pain, paralysis, and even death—a condition known as "the bends." These symptoms are caused by nitrogen gas forming tiny bubbles in the body's tissues. Haldane has developed a system of staged decompression to prevent this—divers can rise quickly at first but must slow down as they near the surface.

◀ *A diver prepares to plumb the depths. Haldane's twin developments have opened our oceans for exploration.*

A GLANCE AT THE PAST

Early autos

The first gasoline-powered automobile was made in 1885 by German engineer Karl Benz, who developed his own version of the gasoline engine and used it to power a three-wheeled carriage. However, the prototype of today's car was developed in France by René Panhard and Emile Lavassor in 1891, when they mounted a Gottlieb Daimler gasoline engine in the front of their vehicle. Until 1898, when Louis Renault invented the drive shaft, engine power was transferred to the drive wheels via a chain, as on bicycles.

TRANSPORTATION

Ford's production line paves the way for autos for all

Determined to corner the market and to produce cars that more people can afford, Henry Ford has adapted and improved the mass production method pioneered by Ransom Eli Olds. Parts are manufactured in separate workshops and wheeled into the main factory so that workers can put the cars together. It takes just over 12 hours to build each car. Ford produces two versions of his Model T, selling for $850 and $825 respectively. It's still not cheap, but Ford is working on ways to cut costs.

▲ *The Model T Ford, available in "any color as long as it's black."*

MEDICINE

Skin testing for tuberculosis

French physician Claude Mantoux has developed a method for establishing whether someone is suffering from tuberculosis (consumption), or has previously been infected with the causative bacterium. The method involves injecting tuberculin—a sterile extract from the bacterium—just under the top layer of the skin. Later, if redness and swelling appear at the site of the injection, it indicates that the person either has active tuberculosis or has been exposed to it in the past. If there is no reaction, the person has never been infected or exposed. One day, the test may be used to decide whom to vaccinate against the disease.

Mount Wilson Observatory. ▼

ASTRONOMY

Telescope focuses on stars

A new telescope—currently the largest in the world—has started operating at the Mount Wilson Solar Observatory in southern California. The telescope is of the reflecting type—at its heart is a mirror some five feet (one-and-a-half meters) in diameter, which has taken three years to grind and polish. The observatory was originally established in 1904 by George Hale to study solar phenomena. However, the new telescope will be used for photographing and analyzing the light from distant stars, star clusters, and nebulae (indistinct smudges of light in the heavens), and for measuring distances to other kinds of celestial objects.

New type of crane is a towering achievement

ENGINEERING

A new type of crane is likely to transform the world's construction sites. Developed in England, the tower crane has a steel framework that can be made in sections at a factory and put together at the construction site. It occupies only a small space, which makes it ideal for crowded city centers, but can also be mounted on rails, allowing it to move the length of a large building. A long, working arm, or jib, allows loads to be lifted great distances. Tower cranes are already being developed for other uses in the construction industry—for example, by building a pair of supports so that the crane can straddle the width of a large lock on a canal.

A tower crane working ▶ on the construction of the Panama canal.

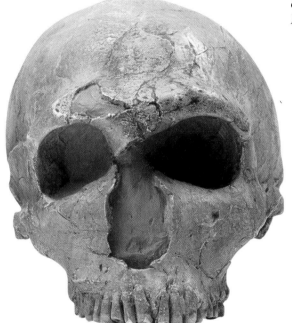

◀ *Neanderthal man had features somewhat different from humans.*

Neanderthal man reconstructed

ANTHROPOLOGY

French academic and anthropologist Pierre-Marcellin Boule has reconstructed the most complete specimen of a Neanderthal skeleton yet discovered, at La Chapelle-aux-Saints in France. Boule has concluded that *Homo neanderthalensis*—who would have walked the Earth 50,000 years ago—was more ape than human. Anthropologists have puzzled over the identity of Neanderthal man since bones were first discovered in the Neander Tal (meaning "valley") in Germany, in 1856. Boule's study concludes that the Neanderthal is a separate species and not a direct ancestor of humans.

New transparent wrapping material

MATERIALS

A Swiss chemist, Jacques Brandenberger, has patented a process for making a thin, flexible, but strong transparent material that he's calling "cellophane." Brandenberger has been working on the industrial process for making cellophane from wood pulp for several years. His career as an inventor started, quite literally, by accident. Seated at a restaurant one day, he saw a fellow diner accidentally spill wine all over the tablecloth. Brandenberger decided to develop a thin transparent material that could be applied to tablecloths to make them waterproof. He tried spraying liquid viscose (a cellulose product) onto cloths, but the viscose made them too brittle and inflexible. However, he noted that the coating peeled off to give a strong clear film, and immediately realized its potential as a wrapping material. Brandenberger is hoping to sell lots of his cellophane to wealthy people needing an unusual wrapping paper for luxurious gifts.

Science News 1908

- The Geiger counter, a device for measuring radioactivity, is invented by German physicist Hans Geiger.

- A tractor with moving treads is developed in California by the Holt Company.

- Harvard dropout Hugh Moore invents the watercooler and paper cups.

25

THE AUTOMOBILE

The history of the automobile has been one of gradual evolution rather than revolution. During the first decade of the twentieth century, cars evolved from motorized versions of the carriages once drawn by horses into a practical means of transportation.

The basic layout of the modern car was set early on: the engine in the front of a four-wheeled machine and all the passengers facing forward. Later, the introduction of the pressed-steel body made cars stronger and easier to produce.

Better cars

At the beginning of the twentieth century, many innovations helped to make cars more reliable and safer. Air-filled tires replaced solid rubber to improve comfort and road-holding. A wheel was introduced to control steering; previously, a long rod called a tiller was used for steering but many motorists had been killed or hurt by sudden tiller movements. By 1902, drum brakes provided a safer way to stop a car.

▲ *A Ford production line.*

Henry Ford

From 1910, Henry Ford (*right*) applied mass production to automobile building. Ford saved money by buying materials in bulk and cut production time by giving employees just one task to perform as the cars moved swiftly through the factory. Soon copied by other manufacturers, his techniques cut the cost of new cars, bringing them within reach of many more people.

◄ *Wealthy families often employed a chauffeur to drive their cars—and to carry out the many repairs and adjustments that were needed.*

1912	1929	1937	1959	1970s
A British company builds the first car with a steel body.	General Motors introduces synchromesh transmission.	The Volkswagen Beetle® is launched in Germany.	The Mini is launched by the British Motor Corporation.	Unleaded gasoline is introduced to reduce air pollution by lead.

How the four-stroke engine works

Most internal-combustion engines have a number of cylinders placed side by side. The up-and-down motion of the pistons is converted to a circular motion of the crankshaft via connecting rods. Power from the engine is transmitted from one end of the crankshaft. Because each piston moves up and down four times during its operating cycle, the engine is called a four-stroke engine. Each cylinder fires in turn to even out the power delivery and usually the two outer cylinders move up when the two in the middle are moving down.

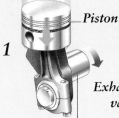

Induction stroke ▶
The piston moves down the cylinder and the inlet valve opens to let in the air-and-fuel mixture.

Inlet valve

Piston

1

Exhaust stroke
The exhaust valve opens and the piston moves back up the cylinder to force out the burned gas. ▼

Exhaust valve

Crankshaft

Spark plug

2

▲ *Compression stroke*
Next, the inlet valve closes and the piston moves up to compress the mixture.

3

◀ *Power stroke*
A spark plug in the top of the cylinder ignites the mixture, which expands rapidly, pushing the piston down.

4

▲ *Head restraints prevent injury.*

Safe driving

By the 1970s, public concern at the number of road deaths led to important advances in car safety. Crumple zones that absorb the energy of a crash, safety cages, seat belts, and air bags were all introduced to protect passengers. Technology such as traction control and antilock brakes meant that cars were less likely to have accidents in the first place.

The urban car

Developed by Swatch and Mercedes-Benz, the Smart Car is a two-seater designed for use in crowded cities. It is so short that it can be parked in a narrow street with its nose to the sidewalk, causing no more obstruction to traffic than a regular car parked sideways. The car has an economical engine and easily replaceable body panels. Sales of the vehicle commenced in Europe in 1998.

A Smart Car. ▲

27

The age of planet Earth

The realization that Earth must be extremely ancient—and that fossils several hundred million years old could exist—first surfaced in 1830 with the publication of *The Principles of Geology*, by a Scottish geologist, Charles Lyell (*above*). The book argued that Earth must be very old to have reached its currently observable state, given the slowness of geological processes. Lyell suggested that Earth is 240 million years old, but this is now thought to be a considerable underestimation.

PALEONTOLOGY

Amazing collection of fossils found in the Rockies

The American paleontologist Charles Walcott has stumbled upon an amazing collection of fossils in British Columbia—the largest find of perfectly preserved fossils from any era. They have revealed what life was like in Earth's seas hundreds of millions of years ago in what is known as the Cambrian era. Walcott spotted the fossils in a block of hard shale (later called the Burgess Shale) while he was making his way across a high ridge in the Rockies. The wide variety of creatures in the sea at the time suggests that a structured food web had already evolved.

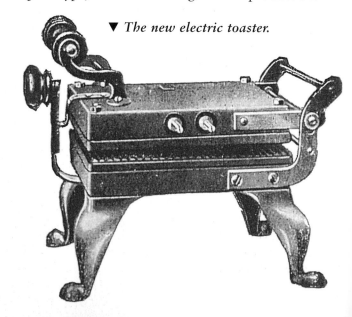

▲ *Around 80 different species have been found within the Burgess Shale.*

Motors now ▶ *make boating easier.*

TRANSPORTATION

Hello motor, good-bye oars

A distant ice cream has inspired Norwegian-born American engineer Ole Evinrude to develop an outboard motor for boats. Evinrude has long been fascinated by the internal combustion engine. Three years ago, he and his fiancée Bess Cary were picnicking on an island. The day was hot and Bess wanted an ice cream. To meet her wishes, Evinrude made the five-mile (eight-kilometer) round-trip in a rowboat, making him realize that boats, too, would benefit from a gasoline-powered motor. A year later, he tested his prototype, and it has since gone into production.

▼ *The new electric toaster.*

HOME APPLIANCES

The toast of U.S. kitchens

Would you like hot buttered toast without the bother of holding a toasting fork in the fire? Then the new electric toaster, marketed by the General Electric Company of Schenectady, New York, is for you. The toaster has a heating element made of wires that glow when plugged in. All you do is lay the bread over the wires and sit back. When one side is brown, you turn the bread over, and your toast is done. The toaster's main drawback is that you have to keep an eye on the toast and be ready to remove it before it burns. But, in spite of this problem, the toaster still seems likely to catch on.

Blériot flies the English Channel

Aviation history was made on July 25 when French inventor Louis Blériot made the first successful heavier-than-air flight across the English Channel. He set off from a cliff top near Calais, France, at about five A.M. in a monoplane of his own design, the *Blériot XI*. Despite poor weather, he landed near Dover, England, about 37 minutes later. Powered by a three-cylinder engine, the monoplane has a wingspan of 25½ feet (7.8 meters) and achieved a speed of roughly 25 miles (40 kilometers) per hour.

Four years ago, ▶ *Louis Blériot opened the first aircraft factory near Paris, France.*

Science News 1909

- In the U.S., the A.G. Spalding Company introduces the first rubber-coated sports shoes.

- Yugoslav Andrija Mohorovicic realizes that Earth's crust overlies a denser mantle below the surface.

- American chemist Leo Baekland has produced the world's first plastic, Bakelite®.

A new scale to measure acidity and alkalinity

Sren Peter Srensen, a Danish chemist, has devised a new scale for expressing acidity or alkinity of any chemical solution in water. The scale is called the "pH" scale and runs from 0 to 14. Neutral solutions (neither acidic or alkaline) have a pH of 7, while strong acids such as sulfuric acid have a pH in the range of 0 to 2. At the other extreme, strong alkalis such as caustic soda have a pH of 14. The pH of a solution is a measure of its concentration of hydrogen (H^+) ions. The term pH means "potential for hydrogen."

Wings on water–the first hydrofoil

Realizing that wings create lift as they pass through air, Italian Professor of Engineering Enrico Forlanini wondered if they would behave the same way in water. He applied them to a boat to see if it would "fly" across the water. The wings are called "foils," from a Greek word meaning "turn aside," since they push water aside as the boat moves forward.

Forlanini put his theory into practice and built a hydrofoil on which the foils are arranged like ladder rungs. He tested it successfully, reaching a speed of 38 knots. He took Alexander Graham Bell for a ride, and Bell was so impressed he bought a license to develop Forlanini's ladder foil system.

▼ *The hydrofoil "flies" on water; its winglike foils lift the main hull out of the water, reducing drag.*

Development of the telephone

Alexander Graham Bell's telephone (*above*) had a diaphragm (membrane) that vibrated when you spoke into it. The diaphragm was set up near an electromagnet so that when it moved there was a change in the magnetic field and the electric current. The varying current was sent along the telephone line and a similar apparatus turned it back into speech at the other end. Later phones worked in the same way as Bell's, but were connected more efficiently with more lines and better exchanges.

COMMUNICATIONS

Telephones take the United States by storm

Millions of homes in the United States now have a telephone, making it easy for people on different sides of the country to speak to each other almost immediately. Since the telephone was invented by Alexander Graham Bell in 1876, many improvements have been made. Telephone lines and manual exchanges now connect towns and cities all over America. Some places even have automatic exchanges, allowing the user to dial a number directly without having to call the operator first.

▲ *Telephone a friend today.*

MEDICINE

Cause of typhus discovered

Typhus is a disease that has killed millions of people. Although there is no known cure for epidemic typhus, American doctor Howard Ricketts has discovered what causes the disease and how it is transmitted. Ricketts and his assistant Russell Wilder have shown that the causative agents are tiny organisms like small bacteria and that body lice spread them from person to person—the unusual organisms have been found in the bodies of both typhus victims and lice.

Alexander Graham Bell
b. 1847 d. 1922

Born in Scotland, Alexander Graham Bell began his working life as an elocution teacher, working especially with deaf children. He later moved to the United States where he trained teachers of the deaf. It was through this work that Bell became interested in acoustics, the science of sound, and began to look at ways of transmitting sound using electricity.
By March of 1876, he realized that he could transmit speech in this way, and the idea of the telephone was born.

TRANSPORTATION

Airman takes off from ship

On November 14, American civilian pilot Eugene B. Ely persuaded naval authorities to let him take off from the deck of the USS *Birmingham*, currently moored in Hampton Roads, Long Island. A special 83-foot (25-meter) wooden ramp was built on the bow of the cruiser. Ely flew his 50-horsepower Curtiss biplane (which he had put together from the wrecks of two previous machines), almost plunged into the water, but landed safely on Willoughby Spit. Since the pioneering flight by the Wright Brothers in 1903, the military has been unable to see any use for aircraft in conflict, but Ely's stunt may change their minds by proving that aircraft carriers are possible. Coincidentally, Frenchman Henri Fabre has this year built the first "seaplane"—an airplane that can take off and land on water.

▲ *Eugene B. Ely takes off from the deck of the USS* Birmingham.

Pure gold

Ernest Rutherford's ideas on the atom are based largely on an experiment carried out in 1909 by Hans Geiger (*above*), and Ernest Marsden. During the experiment, alpha particles were fired at a thin gold foil. Some particles passed right through, but a few in every 10,000 bounced back at various angles, suggesting that they were striking something within the gold atoms. Rutherford concluded that the alpha particles would bounce back in this way only if all the positive charge in a gold atom, and therefore almost all the mass, were concentrated in a small central nucleus some 10,000 times smaller than the entire atom.

PHYSICS

Ernest Rutherford proposes the structure of the atom

British physicist Ernest Rutherford has come up with a new proposal for the structure of atoms. He believes that each atom contains a tiny, compact, positively charged region at its center that he's calling the nucleus. He further proposes that electrons move around at some distance from the nucleus while the remainder of each atom consists of empty space. The previously accepted model for atomic structure, which was proposed by J.J. Thomson, held that electrons were embedded within a nebulous sphere of positive charge, like raisins in a raisin pudding.

Ernest Rutherford. ▲

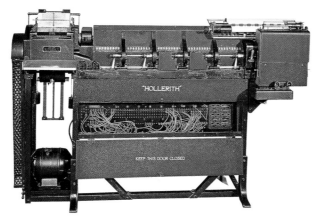

▲ *Dr. Herman Hollerith invented the electrically powered tabulating machines.*

COMPUTERS

You can count on this!

Britain has recently joined a growing list of countries using tabulating machines to count their populations. The machines count and store information using punched cards. The data from each household are changed into a series of holes punched into a small card. Up to 10,000 cards can be produced by an operator in a single day. As each card passes through the tabulator, metallic pins detect the individual holes and clocklike counters display the results.

ARCHAEOLOGY

Incan mountaintop hideaway discovered

Machu Picchu—the ancient mountain hideaway of the Incan kings—has been discovered high in the Peruvian Andes. Sandwiched between the peaks of Machu Picchu and Huayna Picchu, American Hiram Bingham stumbled upon the city after a long hike through the jungle. Yale professor Bingham—who was in search of the fabled city of Vilcabamba, the last refuge of the Inca kings—has made one of the great archaeological finds of the century. After a difficult climb along jungle-covered slopes, a local Indian led Bingham to a series of forest-covered terraces; upon closer inspection, the site revealed royal tombs and magnificent temples.

▼ *Machu Picchu is thought to date from the fifteenth century A.D. The city has sheer cliffs on three sides of the site.*

1912

A GLANCE AT THE PAST

The first electric locomotive

The world's first main line railroad to use electric locomotives was the American Baltimore and Ohio, in 1895. The locomotive (*above*), which had four motor-driven axels, drew electric current from a rigid overhead line. Although this was the first electrically powered railroad, there had been earlier developments. In 1879, a small three-horsepower electric engine, designed by Werner von Siemens, hauled 30 passengers along a 600-yard (549-meter) line at the Berlin Exhibition.

TRANSPORTATION

Diesel trains take to the tracks in Germany and Switzerland

The first diesel locomotives are now being built in both Germany and Switzerland. Sulzer—the manufacturer in Switzerland—is producing diesel locomotives that weigh 85 tons (77 metric tonnes), with a horsepower of 1,200. The diesel engine is more powerful than the gasoline engines used in electric trains and is based on the engine patented by German engineer Rudolph Diesel in 1892.

▲ *Diesel trains signal the beginning of the end for steam.*

COMMUNICATIONS

The first portable typewriter

Few inventions have changed the way we write as much as the typewriter. But typewriters are large, heavy, and cumbersome. Many people, from clerks to journalists, are clamoring for a machine that they can take anywhere with them. The Corona company has come up with the answer—the first portable typewriter. The mechanism is slimmed down, so that the case is smaller than in older models, but it works in the same way, with each key joined to its type bar by a lever and a metal linking rod. And it weighs a fraction of earlier machines.

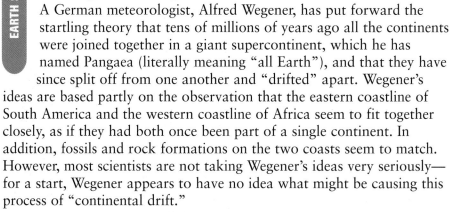

EARTH SCIENCE

Were the continents once joined in a giant supercontinent?

A German meteorologist, Alfred Wegener, has put forward the startling theory that tens of millions of years ago all the continents were joined together in a giant supercontinent, which he has named Pangaea (literally meaning "all Earth"), and that they have since split off from one another and "drifted" apart. Wegener's ideas are based partly on the observation that the eastern coastline of South America and the western coastline of Africa seem to fit together closely, as if they had both once been part of a single continent. In addition, fossils and rock formations on the two coasts seem to match. However, most scientists are not taking Wegener's ideas very seriously—for a start, Wegener appears to have no idea what might be causing this process of "continental drift."

◀ *This map shows how "continental drift" might have occurred.*

Filtered coffee in the home

HOME APPLIANCES

Everyone will soon be able to enjoy filtered coffee at home. German housewife Melitta Benz has begun manufacturing her own line of coffee filters, which she has named Melitta® filters. She invented the process in 1908, when she lined a can with absorbent paper, punched holes in the bottom of the can, placed fresh coffee in it, poured boiling water over the coffee, and then let the water drip through. The result—perfect coffee. The following year, she exhibited her filter coffee pot at the Leipzig trade fair, and is now likely to make a fortune.

▲ *Grounds for good taste—filtered coffee in the home.*

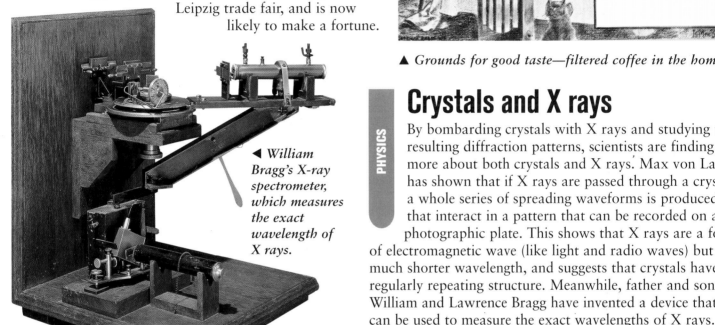

◀ *William Bragg's X-ray spectrometer, which measures the exact wavelength of X rays.*

Crystals and X rays

PHYSICS

By bombarding crystals with X rays and studying the resulting diffraction patterns, scientists are finding out more about both crystals and X rays. Max von Laue has shown that if X rays are passed through a crystal a whole series of spreading waveforms is produced that interact in a pattern that can be recorded on a photographic plate. This shows that X rays are a form of electromagnetic wave (like light and radio waves) but of much shorter wavelength, and suggests that crystals have a regularly repeating structure. Meanwhile, father and son William and Lawrence Bragg have invented a device that can be used to measure the exact wavelengths of X rays.

Races timed electrically

ELECTRONICS

A revolutionary way of timing races has been tried at this year's Stockholm Olympic Games. The method uses a combination of an electric timer and high-speed photography. The timer can give results that are accurate to within one-tenth of a second, while the photograph enables officials to see who is ahead in a close race. At the moment, this method of timing is only an experiment. The old method, with times taken by a group of judges holding stopwatches, is still used to record the official results. But the new method will likely be used widely in the future.

Science News 1912

- American Elmer Ambrose Sperry develops gyrostabilization, a way of reducing roll in ships.

- American Sidney Russell invents the heating pad, later to become the electric blanket.

- French doctor Gaston Odin claims that he has isolated a microbe that causes cancer.

◀ *A new method of timing races was tried out at this year's Olympic Games in Stockholm.*

Arthur Korn's images

German professor Arthur Korn created the first fax machine in the early 1900s. It used a process Korn called "telephotography," in which an image (like the one above of the German Crown Prince) was broken down into a signal that was then sent along a wire and decoded at the other end. Any original, a picture or writing, could be broken down and faxed in the same way.

The ▶ *Woolworth Building, which cost $13.5 million—Woolworth paid for it in cash!*

COMMUNICATIONS

The facts about Belin's portable fax machine

At last, scientists have come up with a simple method of sending a picture from one place to another along a telephone line. The invention is the brainchild of Frenchman Edouard Belin. Although based on the work of Arthur Korn, it is a significant improvement. With Korn's fax, the process of wrapping the image around a drum and scanning was manual; Belin's scanning process is automatic and far more reliable. Newspaper editors are already looking at the system as a possible method for transmitting stories and pictures.

▲ *Belin's fax machine.*

EARTH SCIENCE

The ozone layer is discovered

French physicist Charles Fabry has discovered a layer in the upper regions of the Earth's atmosphere (the stratosphere) that protects life on the planet's surface by absorbing harmful ultraviolet radiation from the Sun. Fabry has established that the substance that absorbs the radiation is ozone—a rare atmospheric gas, the molecules of which each consist of three oxygen atoms. Fabry discovered the ozone layer by means of an instrument he developed with the help of colleague Alfred Pérot.

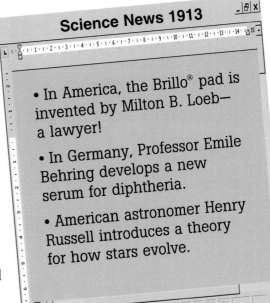

Science News 1913

- In America, the Brillo® pad is invented by Milton B. Loeb— a lawyer!

- In Germany, Professor Emile Behring develops a new serum for diphtheria.

- American astronomer Henry Russell introduces a theory for how stars evolve.

ENGINEERING

The height of technology

At 792 feet (241 meters), New York's Woolworth Building is the tallest in the world. With demand for office space in the crowded centers of many U.S. cities at a premium, skyscrapers like this are appearing in many places. They look impressive from the outside, with their soaring spires and stone decoration, but their real secret is in the hidden structure. This consists of a strong steel frame that can be erected quickly and supports the building's walls, windows, and floors. This means that the walls, although covered in stone, can be light and thin because they do not have to hold up the weight of the building.

Rolling off the assembly line

Henry Ford is still intent on bringing automobiles to the masses. He has modernized his factory at Highland Park, Michigan, introducing a moving assembly line. The automobile bodies move slowly along a conveyor belt and workers at each side add the necessary parts. This streamlining brings manufacturing time down to 98 minutes per car and cuts costs substantially. Ford is now able to sell one of his Model Ts (nicknamed "Tin Lizzies") for $400. It has become the cheapest automobile on the market.

Ford's assembly ▶ line has greatly improved automobile production, making motoring for all a possibility.

Henry Ford
b. 1863 d. 1947

Born at Greenfield, Michigan, Henry Ford produced his first gasoline-fueled car in 1893. He founded his own company in Detroit six years later and then set up the Ford Motor Company in 1903. He aimed to make the car available to everybody and revolutionized the manufacturing process to produce vehicles cheaply. In 1908, Ford produced the Model T, which was the world's first popular, mass-produced automobile.

Gas-filled lightbulbs are a bright idea

American chemist Irving Langmuir, of General Electric, has found a way of extending the life of lightbulbs and making them shine more brightly. He has invented a gas-filled, coiled tungsten lamp bulb. Vacuum tungsten filament bulbs have been available for a few years, but at high temperatures tungsten from the filament evaporates and condenses against the cooler sides of the bulb, causing the bulb to "blacken" and grow dim. Evaporation also weakens the filament, shortening the life of the bulb. Langmuir has found that by filling the bulb with an inert gas—nitrogen—the process of evaporation slows down. His tungsten bulb also uses a coiled filament, which reduces heat loss and evaporation, thereby increasing the life and efficiency of the lightbulb even further.

Bohr modifies structure of the atom

Danish physicist Neils Bohr has offered a modified version of the atomic structure first proposed in 1911 by Ernest Rutherford. Bohr has made Rutherford's model of the atom fit with the quantum theory of Max Planck and Albert Einstein. In Bohr's atom, electrons move around in fixed orbits at different distances from the atomic nucleus, and each orbit is associated with a particular energy state. An electron can move or "jump" from one orbit to another, and when it does, it absorbs or emits a small, fixed amount (a quantum) of energy in the form of radiation. If an electron jumps from one orbit to another that is closer to the nucleus, it must emit a quantum of energy equal to the difference of the energy states of the two orbits. These little energy packets equate with Einstein's small particles or "photons" of light.

▲ *Nitrogen-filled lightbulbs extend the life of the bulb as well as increasing the brightness.*

1876	1878	1881	1889	1891
Bell patents the telephone, beating Gray by two hours.	*The first telephone directory published in New Haven, CT.*	*Bidwell constructs a device to send photos by telephone wire.*	*The first public coin-operated telephone is set up, in the U.S.A.*	*Strowger patents the first automatic telephone exchange.*

TELEPHONES

At the beginning of the twentieth century, telephones were clustered in small regional networks. Long-distance calling improved in 1906, when Lee De Forest invented the "electron tube." This was an electric amplifier—a device that could boost the signal flowing through a wire. Telephone ownership mushroomed from 1910 to 1920. In the United States alone the number of telephones grew from 7 to 16 million. The majority were owned by businesses that needed to keep in touch. Most domestic users were happy to rely on the occasional use of a publicly available line.

◀ *Alexander Graham Bell.*

Calling long distance

On January 25, 1915, telephone pioneer Alexander Graham Bell in New York spoke to his colleague Thomas Watson in San Francisco at the opening of a record-breaking long-distance line. Their telephone signals were boosted along the line by three "vacuum repeaters," based on De Forest's technology. Around 130,000 telephone poles held up the 2,500 tons (2,250 metric tonnes) of copper wire that connected the callers.

Early exchanges

Although the first automatic telephone exchanges were installed around 1900, around half of them, in Europe and the United States, continued to rely on human operators until the mid-1930s. Workers in a manual telephone exchange put one caller through to another by connecting wires into a large bank of sockets called a switchboard.

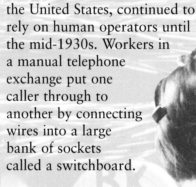

By 1910, most ▶ telephone operators were women.

100 percent

Amazingly, over the last century, the telephone network maintained "100 percent backward compatibility." In other words, no telephone since Bell's time has ever become obsolete. If you had the right connector, for example, you could still plug this 1920s candlestick telephone into the network and call anyone in the world. Backward compatibility is essential. One phone user may have the latest technology but still need to keep in touch with less well-equipped callers.

1915	1948	1964	1965	1999
The world's first transcontinental call is made, in the U.S.A.	The world's first fully automatic cellular phone service debuts.	AT & T unveils the PicturePhone, a videophone.	A satellite carries public telephone messages for the first time.	The first cellular videophones go on sale.

◄ A push-button phone.

Wrong number

Dialing errors increased dramatically when push-button phones arrived in the 1960s. In response leading phone companies designed a standard push-button phone. It had the right size and angle of keys to minimize errors.

Microwave phones

Cellular phones have replaced connecting wires with microwave signals. The latest generation of cellular phones can send text messages and small pictures and can even connect to the Internet. Test models already exist that can carry compressed video so you can see your friends "on the move."

◄ A videophone.

How a phone network works

The international phone network provides many routes for getting data from one place to another. In this example, a message sent by a fax machine (1) first goes to a local telephone exchange (2), then via a cable or by a microwave (ultra-high frequency radio) link to an international exchange (3). Next, it is routed via satellite or an undersea cable to another country, where it reaches the receiving fax machine (4) via another local exchange.

▼ Cell-phone network
Linked into the international phone network shown here is a cell-phone network (5). The network is split into a mosaic of cells, each with a transmitting/receiving antenna linked to an exchange (6). Individual users communicate via their local cell-phone antenna and one or more exchanges. The antennas are usually placed in high spots so signals aren't obstructed by buildings.

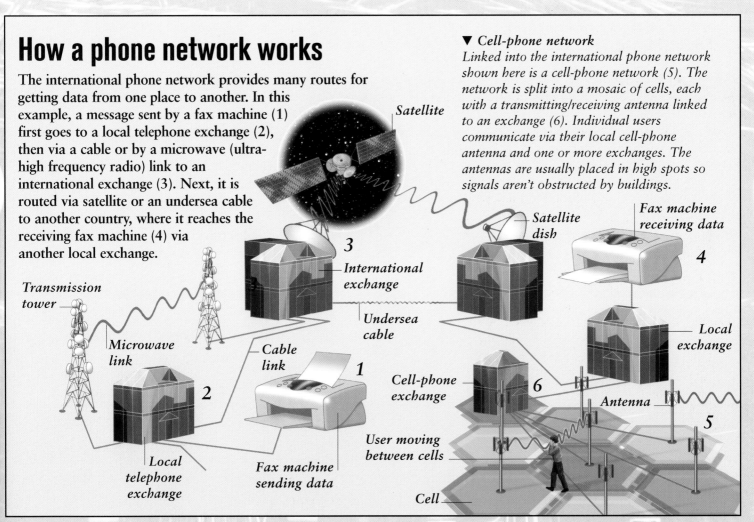

Satellite

Transmission tower

Microwave link

Cable link

Satellite dish

Fax machine receiving data

3

International exchange

Undersea cable

4

2

1

Local exchange

Local telephone exchange

Fax machine sending data

Cell-phone exchange

User moving between cells

6

Antenna

5

Cell

Spiral structures

The spiral structures or nebulas present in the heavens were first photographed between 1898 and 1900 by an American astronomer, James Edward Keeler (*above*). Working at the Lick Observatory, Keeler took photographs of tens of thousands of objects that appeared to be just nebulous clouds of gas within the Milky Way. He observed that a spiral shape is the most common type among these objects. (Other structures are elliptical or have no specific shape.)

ASTRONOMY

Mystery spirals in the sky

A disagreement is developing about the "spiral nebulas" seen as smudges of light scattered in the night sky. Many astronomers believe that these are clouds of finely divided material forming part of our galactic system of stars, the Milky Way. Others, such as Heber D. Curtis of the Lick Observatory in California, think they are vast collections of stars, or "island universes," many thousands of light years outside the Milky Way.

▲ *This spiral nebula is located in the constellation of Ursa Major.*

Science News 1914

- The first modern-style sewage treatment plant opens in Manchester, England.

- In Cleveland, Ohio, red and green traffic lights are used for the first time.

- American biochemist, Edward Kendall isolates the main hormone made by the thyroid gland, thyroxine.

COMMUNICATIONS

Showing the cost of war

As thousands march off to fight in the Great War, news from the battlefront reaches the public at great speed. Widespread use of radio means that information can be beamed instantly from the front to the world's major cities, and these stories are backed up by news that comes via the telegraph. Photographers are also going to the battlefields, and their images provide appalling evidence of the hard life the soldiers lead in the trenches. All this means that ordinary people are better and more rapidly informed about this war than any previous conflict, and are becoming more aware of the terrible human cost of trench warfare.

ENGINEERING

Canal links Atlantic to Pacific

The Panama Canal is open at last. Ships no longer have to make the 7,000-mile (11,270-kilometer) trip around South America to get from the Atlantic to the Pacific Ocean. They simply sail through the 40-mile (64-kilometer) canal from one shoreline to the other. Work originally started in the 1880s, but was abandoned by 1889 because of disease, difficult terrain, and financial problems. The present canal is the result of a further 10 years of hard construction work.

◀ *The first ship to make the eight-hour passage through the Panama Canal on August 15.*

MILITARY TECHNOLOGY

Underwater menace terrorizes Atlantic shipping

German submarines, known as "U-boats," are terrorizing Allied shipping in the Atlantic Ocean. With the development of the periscope and self-propelled torpedo, they have emerged as one of the most revolutionary developments in sea warfare. On May 7, the Cunard liner *Lusitania* was torpedoed with a loss of 1,400 civilian passengers. To try to block economic aid to Great Britain, German submarines have sunk 850,000 tons (770,950 metric tonnes) of shipping in 1915 alone. The destructive capabilities of the submarine were first demonstrated in 1914, when a U-9 sank three British armored cruisers with an ease that shocked the British Admiralty.

▲ *The sinking of the* Lusitania *has led to calls for the United States to end its policy of neutrality and enter the war on the Allied side.*

A GLANCE AT THE PAST

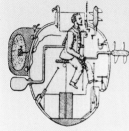

History of the submarine

The first successful submarine was built in 1620 by Dutchman Cornelius Drebbel, who designed a wooden submersible vehicle that carried 20 men at a depth of 65 feet (20 meters) in the Thames River in England. In 1775, U.S. engineer David Bushnell invented the *Turtle* (*above*), an egg-shaped submarine that carried one man. The *Turtle* was the world's first combat submarine. Driven by two hand-operated propellers, the *Turtle* was used by Sgt. Ezra Lee in an unsuccessful attempt to attach a mine to a British ship in New York harbor in 1776. The invention of the self-propelled torpedo in 1870 offered submarines the ultimate weapon. These underwater missiles are launched from the bow or stern and steered toward their targets by signals from the submarine.

At last!—glass that can take the heat

MATERIALS

Glass is not the strongest of materials; a sudden change of temperature results in it shattering. This is due to the glass expanding on heating and contracting on cooling. Changing the temperature too quickly places too much stress on the glass, causing it to shatter. But now researchers C. Sullivan and W.C. Taylor at Corning Glass in the United States have developed Pyrex®, a glass that expands by only a third as much as ordinary glass, reducing the stress and making it much more resistant to heat.

▲ *The fruit fly is a fast-breeding organism that is ideal for studying heredity.*

Theory of heredity developed

BIOLOGY

Through his studies of fruit flies, American zoologist Thomas Hunt Morgan has explained some of the fundamental mechanisms by which inherited characteristics are passed from one generation to the next. The detailed conclusions are published in his recent book, *The Mechanism of Mendelian Heredity*. Morgan started working on heredity in 1907, after discovering the work of geneticist Gregor Mendel. The fruit fly has been used to test the validity of Mendel's laws. One of Morgan's most important discoveries is that certain hereditary characteristics tend to be passed collectively from one generation to the next. He believes this is because the genes for those characteristics are located on the same chromosome.

Filterable viruses

A virus is intermediate between a living and a nonliving thing. First identified in the 1890s, viruses were originally called "filterable viruses," because they were small enough to pass through filters that bacteria could not. In 1892, it was shown that filtered sap from tobacco plants affected by mosaic disease (*above*) could transmit the disease to other tobacco plants. In 1898, the agent that causes hoof-and-mouth disease in cattle was similarly shown to be a virus.

BIOLOGY

Life-forms that eat bacteria discovered

French-Canadian microbiologist Félix d'Hérelle has discovered infectious agents that can apparently prey on and destroy bacteria. He suspects that these agents are a type of tiny life-form, similar to the "viruses" that have been shown to cause a number of plant and animal diseases. D'Hérelle has decided to call these agents bacteriophages, or "bacteria-eaters." He stumbled upon them while in Paris, studying bacteria that cause dysentery. D'Hérelle noticed clear spots (areas free of bacteria) on gelatin cultures of the bacterium. Subsequently he happened to mix a filtrate of the clear areas with a culture of dysentery bacteria. The bacteria were quickly destroyed, indicating that the filtrate contained bacteria-eaters.

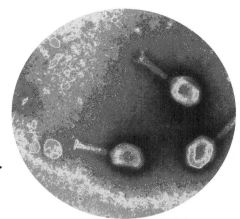

▲ *Félix d'Hérelle has suggested that viruses such as this bacteriophage might be used to combat bacterial infections.*

CHEMISTRY

Chemicals bond

American chemist Gilbert Newton Lewis has made a major contribution to our understanding of atoms. In particular, he has described chemical bonding—the way in which atoms link together to form chemical compounds. Every atom contains a nucleus. Arranged around the nucleus, in layers or shells, are negatively charged particles called electrons. Lewis has noticed that an atom with eight electrons in its outermost shell is very stable. He has also noticed that, to achieve this stability, atoms transfer or share electrons with other atoms, forming what he describes as "chemical bonds."

Science News 1916

- In the United States, windshield wipers are used in cars for the first time.

- Artificial detergents are developed in Germany in order to preserve fats for soap manufacture.

- In the United States, Jones Wister patents a rifle for shooting around corners, to be used in trench warfare.

AGRICULTURE

The farmers' friend

In Detroit a blacksmith named August Fruehof has built the first tractor-trailer, a truck with a detachable cab containing a gasoline-fueled engine. The cab can be hitched onto a variety of trailers or other farm equipment, making it extremely versatile and hard working. The invention means that small farmers now need only one vehicle to work their land.

◀ *Tractors prove to be a timesaving device for farmers.*

Dive, dive, dive!

MILITARY TECHNOLOGY

The British Royal Navy has developed an explosive device to combat the German U-boat threat to their Atlantic merchant shipping. Called "depth charges," the weapon consists of canisters filled with explosives that can be rolled off a ship. The canisters can be detonated at a preselected depth by means of a hydrostatic valve. The shock waves from the explosion are usually enough to loosen the submarine's joints and damage some of its equipment. So far in 1916, 1.2 million tons (1.1 million metric tonnes) of British merchant shipping has been lost to the U-boats, compared with the destruction of only 22 U-boats.

◀ *Depth charges are dropped from the stern of a ship.*

First electric washing machine

HOME APPLIANCES

At last, a machine to take the drudgery out of wash day! For several decades now there have been simple "washing machines," consisting of a wooden box in which you placed the clothes and water. The trouble was, you had to turn the heavy box by hand. Now manufacturers are starting to fit electric motors to their machines. You only have to fill the container with clothes and warm water, turn on the machine, and the motor does the rest. When the wash is finished, you wring the water out of the clothes using the hand rollers—simple!

◀ *Electricity is used to drive this formerly hand-operated washer. The electric motor is mounted underneath the tub.*

The Tank Mark I is armed with either two side-mounted naval guns, or four Vickers machine guns. ▶

Tanks attack

MILITARY TECHNOLOGY

On September 15, German infantry at the Battle of the Somme were surprised by the sight of 24 armored, track-laying vehicles trundling toward their trenches. Called the "tank" by their crews, the British army hopes that this curious weapon will help break the stalemate on the Western Front. Designed and developed by William Tritton and W.G. Wilson, the tanks have proved difficult to combat, with infantry fire bouncing off their half-inch (10-millimeter) frontal armor plating. While some trenches were overrun, the attack was not an unqualified success: mechanical problems and the thickly churned mud stopped 25 of the 49 tanks participating, while many became stuck in enemy trenches.

The material of a thousand uses

Born in 1863, Leo Baekeland (*above*) achieved success as both a chemist and entrepreneur. His first breakthrough came in the 1890s with "Volex," an improved photographic paper. He eventually sold the rights for one million dollars. Not content with this, Baekeland then set out to produce a cheap insulator for the electrical industry. Reacting phenol with formaldehyde, he developed not only an excellent insulator but also a moldable plastic, Bakelite. Bakelite became known as "the material of a thousand uses."

MATERIALS

Plastic transforms household goods

Rolls Royce is going to launch another innovation to its new cars—this time it is not to be found in the engine but on the gear shift. The gear shift's handle will be made from Bakelite®, the world's first totally synthetic plastic. Ten years ago, Dr. Leo Baekeland discovered that under the right conditions the reaction of phenol with formaldehyde produced a hard, solid plastic. When heated, this plastic can be molded into any number of different objects. Once a mold has been created, the component can be mass-produced millions of times. Since its discovery, Bakelite has been used mainly as an insulator for electrical products, but now this versatile material looks as if it will revolutionize household goods.

▲ *Mass-produced plastic goods, such as this flask, are set to flood the market.*

BIOLOGY

Jumping genes

American biologist Harold Plough has shown that when sex cells (sperm and egg cells) are formed in animals, the paired chromosomes in their precursor cells line up with each other and exchange genetic material just before they divide. This process is called "crossing-over." One chromosome from each pair comes from each parent, allowing organisms to pass on a mix of their paternal and maternal genes.

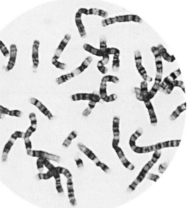

▲ *Paired chromosomes line up and swap genetic material.*

COSMOLOGY

Gravitational oddity

German physicist Karl Schwarzschild has produced a mathematical description of how space and time would be altered and warped within the vicinity of a large "point mass"—that is, a mass compressed into an infinitely small volume. The description is actually a solution to some complex equations concerning the nature of gravitational fields proposed in 1915 by Albert Einstein. Schwarzschild's calculations explain how anything straying to within a certain distance of a point mass would be sucked into it and crushed. Fortunately, no objects of this type have so far been identified in the universe.

Karl Schwarzschild
b. 1873 d. 1916

Karl Schwarzschild was born in Frankfurt, Germany, and studied at Strasbourg and Munich. By 1901 he was professor of the astronomical observatory at Göttingen. In 1909 he was appointed director of the astrophysical observatory at Potsdam. He performed his work on "point masses" and their gravitational effects while serving in the German army on the Russian front in 1916. His findings from this work did not become well known until after his death.

Lead poisoning linked to paint

MEDICINE

Medical authorities in the United States have established that children are being poisoned in their homes by lead, particularly lead in paints. For some years, people have perceived "white lead," which could be tinted a variety of colors, to be the best protective coating for both the interior and exterior of homes. Families have used lead paint not only on their walls, but also on their cribs, toys, woodwork, and furniture. Unfortunately, infants and toddlers routinely place things in their mouths as a part of normal development—and so become chronically poisoned. This leads to nervous-system disorders, slowed growth, and behavioral and learning problems. Acute poisoning can even kill a young child. Several European countries have now banned the use of white lead interior paint. The question is—will the United States follow suit?

▲ *Poor households suffer the highest risk of lead poisoning.*

Science News 1917

- The world's longest steel cantilever bridge, the Quebec railway bridge spanning the St. Lawrence River, is completed.

- Dutch astronomer Willem de Sitter suggests that the universe must be expanding.

- In the United States, Clarence Birdseye discovers that foods can be preserved by freezing.

The world's largest telescope

ASTRONOMY

A new reflecting telescope (one that uses mirrors rather than lenses) has been installed at the Mount Wilson Observatory in southern California. Now the world's largest, it is fitted with a 100-inch (2.5-meter) diameter mirror, notable for its support system—the mirror floats on a pool of liquid mercury. This takes most of the weight off the bearings on which the telescope rotates as it is pointed at different areas of the sky, so reducing friction. The telescope is named the Hooker Telescope in honor of a local businessman, John D. Hooker, who provided funds for construction of the mirror. The grinding of the mirror and design of the mount, clock drive (mechanism for rotating the telescope), and dome were daunting tasks—and transporting the parts up Mount Wilson by mule and truck was a combination of ingenuity, brute force, and determination.

Tests for color blindness

BIOLOGY

Japanese ophthalmologist Dr. Shinobu Ishihara has devised a test for diagnosing various forms of color vision deficiency—also known as "color blindness." The test consists of a series of plates, each comprising a group of colored dots. People with normal color vision see figures or patterns within the dots, whereas color-blind people see different figures or no pattern at all. A total inability to see colors is extremely rare—most people with color vision deficiency merely confuse certain shades of red and green or see some colors as gray. These problems are much more common in men than women. It should now be possible for doctors to detect color blindness in childhood.

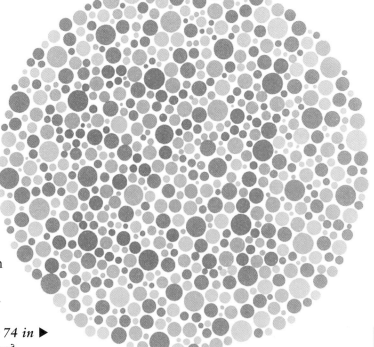

Most people see the number 74 in ▶ green spots—what do you see?

1918

A GLANCE AT THE PAST

Boolean algebra

In the 1850s English mathematician George Boole (*above*) developed an abstract system of logic now called Boolean algebra. This system of algebra is binary in nature as it is based on only two numbers: 1 and 0, commonly thought of as "true" and "false." The three most basic operations in Boolean algebra are AND, OR, and NOT. These operations are all any machine requires to perform calculations along with other logical operations. Boolean algebra is basic to the design of all digital technology up to, and beyond, the year 2000.

COMPUTERS

The birth of the binary computer

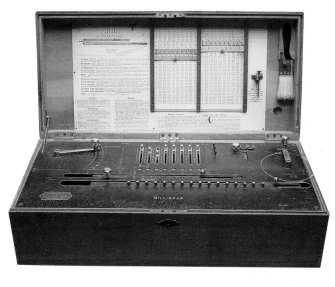

▲ *An early adding machine.*

Picture an electrical machine that can perform complex calculations in a fraction of a second. If such a machine were ever built, it would probably use the "binary" system— a way of representing numbers as sequences of 1s and 0s. The binary system would be suitable because "1s" and "0s" could be represented by the presence or absence of electrical currents in parts of its circuitry. Now two Frenchmen, Bloch and Abraham, have built a device that could make such a machine possible. It's a small electrical circuit that is capable of generating the type of "on" or "off" signals needed.

ASTRONOMY

How big is the Milky Way?

The U.S. astronomer Harlow Shapley, of the Mount Wilson Observatory in California, has made the first accurate estimate of the size of the galaxy (also known as the "Milky Way") and where its center lies. Until now, most astronomers have assumed Earth lies near the center of the galaxy, but Shapley reckons the center lies some 50,000 light years (or 5.8 thousand billion miles—9.3 thousand billion kilometers) away, in the same direction as the constellation of Sagittarius. Overall, this implies that the galaxy is at least 120,000 light years across, which is about 10 times bigger than previously thought.

Harlow Shapley. ▶

Science News 1918

- Henry Ford, the American automobile manufacturer, mass-produces tractors.

- German engineers begin to manufacture the first all-metal plane.

- Czech chemist Jaroslav Heyrovsky begins to develop polarography, a system for measuring ions in a solution.

PHYSICS

The first mass spectrograph

English physicist Francis Aston has constructed the first mass spectrograph. So called because it can be used to measure the masses of atoms or electrons, it works by passing a beam of charged particles through an electromagnetic field that separates particles of different masses. This produces a spectrum of masses, which can be recorded on a photographic plate. Aston's invention follows from the work of English physicist J.J. Thomson.

Yellow traffic light introduced

TRANSPORTATION

Even though motor cars have only been on the streets for 10 years or so, traffic is becoming so thick that new safety measures are needed in the more heavily populated cities. Red and green stop/go traffic lights already exist, but in Great Britain, a new system that includes an yellow light (for caution) has now been introduced in between the red/green sequence. This discourages cars from crashing into each other at intersections, and gives pedestrians time to cross the road.

◀ *Go! Traffic signals at Ludgate Circus in London.*

The first electric clocks

HOME APPLIANCES

Henry Ellis Warren, an electrical engineer from Ashland, Massachusetts, has made a breakthrough in timekeeping. He has begun producing the world's first practical electric clocks. The clocks contain an electromagnet that makes a pendulum swing. Clocks like this are accurate, do not run down, and, most important of all, never need winding. People have built electric clocks before, but with the spread of electricity more and more people will buy Warren's clocks.

▲ *An electrically driven clock with a glass dome. Electric clocks will probably become popular in public places.*

"Big Bertha" booms

MILITARY TECHNOLOGY

At 7:16 A.M. on a cold March morning, an enormous explosion rocked Paris. It was assumed that the detonation was caused by an aircraft bomb. It was late in the afternoon, after a shell had landed every 15 minutes, that Parisians realized the explosions were caused by a huge Howitzer gun, firing from 74 miles (119 kilometers) away, well behind German lines. "Big Berthas," as the guns came to be known, are a sensational new development in long-range artillery. The guns were moved by rail behind the front line, and an intermittent bombardment of Paris continued for a further 140 days. In this crucial year of the Great War, the German military is seeking to prove to the world their superior technical capabilities.

Big Bertha's two-part retractable ▶ barrel weighs 138 tons (125 metric tonnes); its 8-inch (20-centimeter) shell travels 92 miles (148 kilometers) in 176 seconds.

General relativity

Einstein completed his general theory of relativity, or theory of gravitation, in 1915. He had been working for four years on the mathematical problems presented by the theory (which is separate from—and more complex than—the special theory of relativity published in 1905). The general theory deals with gravitation and proposes a four-dimensional model of the universe, in which space and time form a continuum. In this continuum, a large mass can "bend" space in such a way as to cause a gravitational effect.

PHYSICS

Einstein's theory demonstrated

Proof has been obtained from observations taken during a recent total solar eclipse that Albert Einstein's general theory of relativity, or theory of gravitation, is correct. Measurements made during the solar eclipse by the British astrophysicist Arthur Eddington showed that light from distant stars lying close to the Sun's position in the sky was bent, making the stars appear in slightly incorrect positions. The deviations were exactly as predicted by Einstein, proving his theory correct.

▲ *The eclipse was observed off the coast of Cameroon on May 29.*

ENERGY

Propeller turbine powers factory

A modern-day answer to the water wheel looks set to meet our increasing power demands. Water turbines were originally developed in the last century, but they had only limited use because they required very high water pressure. Six years ago Austrian engineer Viktor Kaplan developed a novel propeller turbine that promised increased efficiency by allowing each propeller blade to turn on its axis. The first turbine of this sort has now been installed in a textile factory in Velm, Austria.

Large water turbines can generate plenty of power.

Albert Einstein
b. 1879 d. 1955

Born in Ulm, Germany, Einstein studied physics in Zurich. In 1901 he became a Swiss citizen. While working at the Swiss patent office in Berne, he developed his special theory of relativity, and in 1914 was appointed a director of the Kaiser Wilhelm Institute for Physics in Berlin. He won the Nobel Prize for Physics in 1921, but when the Nazis came to power in Germany in 1933, he took refuge first in Great Britain and then in the United States. He died in April 1955.

PHYSICS

Rutherford smashes atoms

The British physicist and atom expert, Ernest Rutherford, has succeeded where alchemists have failed for thousands of years—in changing one type of atom into another. Rutherford recently announced the results of experiments in which he bombarded nitrogen atoms with alpha particles—highly energetic particles obtained from radioactive sources. The alpha particles smashed into the nuclei (central regions) of the nitrogen atoms with such force that they knocked out protons—tiny, positively charged particles—and at the same time changed the nitrogen atoms into oxygen atoms. Physicists are saying that this "nuclear reaction" heralds a new era of atomic research. The experiment also proves that protons are parts of atomic nuclei.

Up, up, and away

Transatlantic flights may soon be commonplace. In July, the British airship R 34 achieved the first two-way crossing of the North Atlantic. It set off from Edinburgh, Scotland, on July 2, and arrived at Long Island, New York, four days later. On board was a crew of 30, one of whom had to parachute to the ground to help anchor the great airship. Subsequently, the R 34 made the return flight, arriving in Norfolk, England. The first flight in stages across the Atlantic took place in May when six Americans commanded by Albert Read flew from Newfoundland via the Azores to Lisbon, Portugal. In June, British pilots Alcock and Brown made the first nonstop transatlantic flight.

◀ *Transatlantic pioneer—the R 34 airship.*

Short waves, long distances

Radio experts have discovered a way of sending broadcast programs over long distances. Radio travels in waves, which form repeating curves like ripples on water. The wavelength of a radio signal is the distance from the peak of one ripple to the next, and scientists classify radio waves according to their length: long, short, and even shorter "very high frequency" waves. They have discovered that short waves are ideal for long-distance broadcasting. Frank Conrad of the Westinghouse Company has sent a shortwave program from a radio station in Pittsburgh to one in Cleveland, some 100 miles (160 kilometers) away. Using a more powerful transmitter, American engineers then sent a broadcast that was picked up across the Atlantic, 3,500 miles (5,633 kilometers) away, in Great Britain.

◀ *Onlookers gather around as experts carry out field experiments in sending signals by radio.*

Humans did not evolve from apes

A distinguished British anatomist, Frederick Wood Jones, says that humans cannot have evolved from great apes as has previously been supposed. Instead, he argues that both humans and apes evolved millions of years ago from a common mammalian ancestor, which is now extinct. His views are based on detailed examinations of the skeletons and embryological development of both humans and other primates. Great apes exhibit many unique anatomical features. If humans had evolved from apes, some traces of these features would be expected in human skeletons and embryos, but in fact no trace can be found.

Science News 1919

- The Rotochamber, a T-shaped combustion chamber, is built by English engineer Harry Ricardo.

- Tea bags made from gauze are produced for the catering trade by Joseph Krieger in the United States.

- The pop-up electric toaster is patented in the United States by Charles Strite.

AIRCRAFT

The early pioneers of flight were often designer, builder, test pilot, and businessman rolled into one. Aircraft design was frequently a combination of basic science and guesswork.

Gradually a more scientific approach was used in design and construction. As the manufacturing companies grew, they were able to employ specialists in mathematics, aerodynamics, and engineering to develop aircraft prototypes (test versions), and professional test pilots to put these prototypes through their paces.

Junkers Ju 52. ▼

The Wright pioneers

Wilbur and Orville Wright succeeded in their quest for powered flight because of their methodical approach. Realizing that they had a lot to learn, they studied the flight of birds and the theory of flight. They tested their ideas in a homemade wind tunnel and built gliders in which they learned about control and piloting. On December 17, 1903, their hard work paid off as Orville took their plane, *The Flyer*, into the air for the first time.

▲ *The Wright brothers' plane.*

◄ *An AT&T De Havilland airliner.*

The birth of the airline

It was the development of large, reliable aircraft during World War I that led to international airlines. After the war, airplanes were used to ferry officials between London and Paris for the peace talks. Soon the first civilian service began. In 1919, the first international airline passenger flew to Paris in an AT&T (Aircraft Transport and Travel Ltd) De Havilland DH4.

1919	1939	1947	1966	1976
First direct transatlantic flight by Alcock and Brown.	The first jet-powered aircraft takes to the air in Germany.	The Bell X1 rocket plane breaks the sound barrier.	The first vertical take-off and landing jet aircraft enters service.	The first scheduled supersonic airliner goes into service.

Heavier than air

The corrugated metal skin of the *Junkers Ju 52* gave it great strength. Although in the early 1930s the wooden biplane was still the most popular design, pioneers like Junkers in Germany showed that it was possible to build strong metal airplanes that did away with the mass of wires and struts that had become the norm. By the end of the decade, aircraft made of metal, with a retractable undercarriage and powerful engines, had started to make biplanes look out-of-date.

Taking advantage of the latest materials to reduce structural weight and using the most powerful engines ever made, the A3XX will carry its passengers in cabins on two levels. ▼

How a jet engine works

A jet engine pushes out fast-moving hot gas to propel it forward. Air is drawn into the engine and compressed by a series of spinning blades called a compressor. The air is then mixed with fuel and burned in a combustion chamber. As the hot gas leaves the combustion chamber, it turns another set of blades called a turbine. It is the turbine that powers the compressor. This simple type of jet engine is called a turbojet. A turbofan is a type of jet engine that has a fan attached to the front of the compressor. Most of the air that passes through the fan goes around the outside of the main part of the engine. Turbofans are quieter and more fuel-efficient than turbojets.

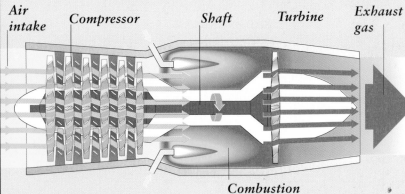

Air intake   Compressor   Shaft   Turbine   Exhaust gas

Combustion chamber

▲ **The compressor**
Between the spinning blades of the compressor is a series of non-moving stator blades. These help to smooth out the air flow.

▲ **Thrust**
As the exhaust gas is expelled, it pushes the engine in the opposite direction.

◄ *Computerized cockpit.*

▲ *Turbofan engines.*

Super Jumbo

The world's airports are stretched to the limit. With landings every two minutes and restrictions on night operations, there is simply no room to fit in any extra flights. That is why Airbus® is building the *A3XX* "Super Jumbo," which will carry 1,000 passengers.

A GLANCE AT THE PAST

Music goes on air

The first radio signals containing both speech and music were sent by Reginald Fessenden (*above*) in 1906. Former university professor Fessenden had built his own transmitter in Massachusetts. He combined his signal generator with a microphone so that the radio waves sent out varied with the voice of the operator. Soon radio operators on ships along the coast were picking up Fessenden's signals and the idea of "broadcasting" radio signals to many listeners at once became a reality.

COMMUNICATIONS

1,000 people hear first regular broadcast

Regular radio broadcasting has begun in the United States. The Pittsburgh radio station KDKA, which is operated by the Westinghouse Corporation, announced the news of the election of Warren Harding to the presidency on November 2. Around 1,000 people are thought to have heard the broadcast on their radio receivers. Now KDKA is sending out regular broadcasts at the same time each day.

▲ *The Pittsburgh radio station KDKA now broadcasts regularly.*

MILITARY TECHNOLOGY

The "Tommy" gun developed in the United States

A new, continuous-firing hand weapon, called the "Tommy" gun after its designer U.S. Army officer John T. Thompson, has been developed in America. The Tommy gun is the latest and most technically impressive innovation in infantry firepower, following the world's first submachine gun—the MP18, or Bergmann Muskete—developed in Germany two years earlier. Weighing almost 10 pounds (4.4 kilograms) and firing .45-caliber ammunition, the Tommy gun can take either a circular drum that holds 50 rounds, or a box that holds 20 or 30 rounds. After the limitations of the heavy machine guns that dominated the Great War, Thompson hopes that his gun will revolutionize infantry warfare by allowing foot soldiers greater mobility.

◀ *British Secretary of War Winston Churchill* (left) *examines the new submachine gun.*

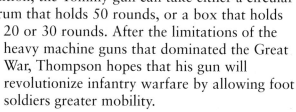

ENTERTAINMENT

Movies make tracks

The problem of combining sound with movies may have been solved. Until now, the favorite way has been to play a phonograph record as the movie is shown. This method can be quite convincing, but it is easy for the sound and picture to get "out of sync." The new sound track places the sound right on the film in the form of an optical pattern. The pattern varies with the different sounds and is "read" by a device in the projector as the film is shown. Because it is printed in exactly the right place, it cannot get out of sync during projection.

Early hormone discoveries

Hormones are chemical "messengers" released into the bloodstream by organs or endocrine glands. They stimulate the body to do certain things. Adrenaline, for instance, helps the body to deal with stress. In 1902, William Maddock Bayliss (*above*) and Ernest Henry Starling discovered secretin, the first known hormone. It is produced by glands in the wall of the intestine. By 1905, Bayliss and Starling began to call these chemical messengers "hormones," from a Greek word meaning "to rouse to activity."

MEDICINE

Insulin extract provides hope for diabetics

In research using dogs, Canadian physicians Frederick Banting and Charles Best have managed to isolate the hormone insulin, which will help to treat people suffering from diabetes. Insulin is a hormone produced by the pancreas, which helps body cells to absorb energy-giving glucose. However, in people suffering from diabetes, the pancreas does not produce enough insulin, so that blood sugar levels rise alarmingly, often leading to death. Banting and Best artificially created diabetes in dogs by tying off their pancreatic ducts. They isolated insulin from cells produced by the pancreas and injected it into the dogs, which were cured.

▲ *Frederick Banting, one of the scientists who has isolated the hormone insulin.*

BIOLOGY

Pearls get cultured

A new industry is developing in Japan—the culturing of pearls. Natural pearls are accidents of nature, formed when a tiny irritant finds its way into an oyster shell. The oyster cannot expel the object, so in defense it secretes layers of a substance called nacre around the intruder, forming the pearl. Now a method has been developed for artificially provoking oysters to produce pearls. A mother-of-pearl bead is introduced into an oyster. Over a period of one to three years the oyster deposits layers of shiny nacre around the bead.

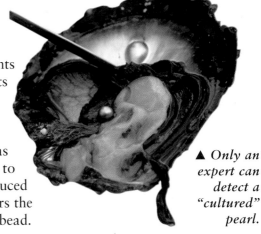

▲ *Only an expert can detect a "cultured" pearl.*

MEDICINE

Using inkblots as a diagnostic tool

In his book *Psychodiagnostik*, the Swiss psychiatrist Hermann Rorschach has described a novel method for analyzing the mental state of people with various psychiatric or psychological problems. The method relies on asking the subject to describe what, if anything, he or she sees in each of a standardized set of black-and-white and colored inkblots. There are no "right" or "wrong" answers. Rorschach claims that a person's responses provide insights into his or her attitudes, conflicts, emotions, relationship with parents, sexual orientation, creativity, level of initiative, ability to relate to other people, and so on. Opinions are currently divided on the validity of the test.

◄ *Each blot in the test has two halves, which are almost mirror images.*

Detecting objects underwater

By 1916, British, American, and French scientists had developed a system for detecting underwater objects first invented by Paul Langevin (*above*). It sent out sound waves that rebounded against an object, sending back an echo. The system was called asdic (Anti-Submarine Detection Investigation Committee).

OCEANOGRAPHY

Scientists to research the ocean

Germany is to use a relatively new invention to carry out the first complete investigation of the physical structure and water circulation of the Atlantic Ocean. Asdic, which was developed in order to detect icebergs and submarines, is a device that sends out sound waves below the water. These hit submerged objects and are reflected back as echoes that are picked up by a microphone-like listening device.

▲ *Germany's research vessel,* Meteor, *will pioneer the new asdic technology.*

ARCHAEOLOGY

A tomb full of "wonderful things"

On November 22, the tomb of the Egyptian boy-king Tutankhamen was discovered by the British archaeologist Howard Carter in the Valley of the Kings, near Luxor, Egypt. The tomb has remained undisturbed since the pharaoh's death in 1323 B.C. A stunning collection of over 5,000 precious objects was buried with the young pharaoh, whose embalmed corpse was surrounded by a complex system of jeweled mummy cases and coffins. Carter found the tomb after discovering a sunken stairway. After drilling a hole in the sealed entrance, he was dumbstruck by the riches beyond. When asked by his patron, Lord Carnarvon, if he could see anything, Carter is reported to have said: "Yes, wonderful things."

◄ *Beds, chairs, stools, vases, weapons, clothing, and this gold funeral mask were found in Tutankhamen's tomb.*

ASTRONOMY

What a couple of stars!

A Canadian astronomer, John Plaskett, has discovered a remarkable double star system (two stars orbiting each other) thousands of light years distant from Earth. Double stars are common in the Milky Way galaxy, but what distinguishes Plaskett's twosome is their sheer size—both stars are larger than any other star ever observed. Plaskett found that each of the luminous, blue-colored stars is about 90 times larger than the Sun. However, despite their size, the stars are barely visible to the naked eye because they are so far away. Even with a good telescope they appear as a single point of light; only by analyzing their light emissions was Plaskett able to work out that there were two stars present.

A GLANCE AT THE PAST

History of vaccination

The first vaccination was performed in 1796 by the English physician Edward Jenner. Noting that milkmaids who had contracted the mild disease cowpox never contracted smallpox, Jenner removed some material from a milkmaid's cowpox pustule and scratched it into the skin of an eight-year-old boy. The boy then contracted cowpox. Later, Jenner injected the boy with smallpox and the disease failed to develop. During the late 19th century, following research on disease organisms by the French chemist Louis Pasteur (*above*) and the German bacteriologist Robert Koch, many new vaccines were developed against infectious illnesses such as anthrax, rabies, and tetanus.

MEDICINE

Tuberculosis vaccine developed

Albert Calmette, a microbiologist at the Pasteur Institute in Lille, France, and veterinarian Jean Guérin have tested a vaccine for one of the world's foremost killer diseases, tuberculosis. The new vaccine is called BCG (Bacillus Calmette-Guérin) and is prepared from an artificially weakened strain of the bacterium that causes tuberculosis in cattle. The vaccine produces a mild infection that greatly increases resistance to serious forms of tuberculosis. The vaccine is usually injected into the upper arm. After 6–12 weeks a small pustule develops, which heals, leaving a small scar.

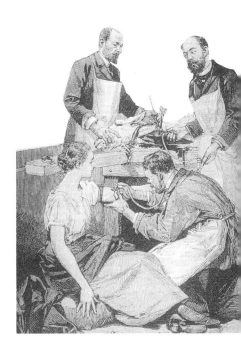

▲ *The tuberculosis vaccine is already administered in France.*

ENTERTAINMENT

A new way to look at the heavens

In Munich, Germany, they have an exciting new way of looking at the stars. It is called a planetarium, and it works by projecting an image of the night sky onto a dome above a specially designed dark room. The Munich planetarium's projector, made by the Carl Zeiss Company of Jena, Germany, casts a picture of the stars onto a dome 33 feet (10 meters) in diameter. As the projector turns, viewers watch transfixed as the stars move in their course across the heavens. Professor Walther Bauersfield demonstrated the planetarium at a special conference at Munich's Deutsches Museum. Experts and public alike were enthusiastic, but the projector has now been sent back for some final adjustments.

The planetarium projector. ▶

HOME APPLIANCES

New "Zippers" are creating a stir

B.F. Goodrich, the rubber goods company, has put in an order for 150,000 "hookless sliding fasteners" for a new type of rubber boot they are making. The fasteners consist of two rows of teeth on cloth tapes (which can be sewn to the edges of the item to be fastened), together with a slider that will interlock the teeth for fastening or disengage them for unfastening. Because of the *z-z-zip* sound they make, Goodrich is intending to call the fasteners "Zippers." The device was originally designed for the Universal Fastener Company in 1913 by Swedish engineer Gideon Sundback as a simplified version of a "Clasp Locker," patented in 1893 by U.S. inventor Whitcomb Judson. Judson's fasteners never really caught on, but Zippers look set to be a resounding success.

HOME APPLIANCES

It's time for the self-winding watch

Have you ever forgotten to wind your watch and then ended up late for an appointment? If so, this new invention may be just the thing for you. John Harwood, a London watchmaker, has invented a wristwatch that winds itself. Inside the case is a weight that swings as the wearer moves around, rewinding the main spring of the watch as it does so. Harwood's watch is not yet available, but discussions with various manufacturers in Switzerland are said to be under way.

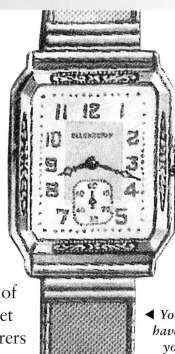

◀ *You'll never have to wind your watch again!*

A brief history of time

The first watches appeared in the early 16th century. They were like little clocks and had tiny movements made entirely by hand, which made them expensive luxury items. But in 1868 a Swiss watchmaker, Georges Frederic Rosskopf, worked out how to simplify watch movements so that they could be produced more cheaply. In the late 1880s, wristwatches began to appear. They were highly popular with women, because, unlike the early watches, they did not need to be kept in a special pocket.

COMMUNICATIONS

Radio on the go

The Zenith Corporation of Chicago has produced the world's first portable radio. Zenith was founded by two radio amateurs who loved to make their own equipment. But they soon realized that most people do not want to build their own radio sets from a kit of components. So the new Zenith® radio is sold ready-made. With no extra parts to plug in, the radio is completely self-contained.

◀ *Portable radios work even when you carry them around.*

MEDICINE

Electrocardiograph invented

This year's Nobel Prize for Medicine has been awarded to a Dutch physiologist for his discoveries regarding the electrical properties of the heart. Willem Einthoven has developed the electrocardiograph, a tool that doctors can use to record the electrical pulse that accompanies each heartbeat. Recordings of the heart are made through electrodes attached to the patient's limbs and chest. Over 30 years, Einthoven has been able to successfully diagnose patients suffering from different forms of heart disease, irregularities in heartbeat, high blood pressure, and even thyroid disease.

◀ *Willem Einthoven, inventor of the electrocardiograph.*

Science News 1924

• The world's first intercity highway, the 30-mile- (48-kilometer-) long Milano-Varuse Autostrada, opens in Italy.

• In the United States, Celluwipes, disposable handkerchiefs later called Kleenex®, are introduced.

• U.S. frozen food pioneer Clarence Birdseye founds the General Seafoods Company.

New resin used for tableware

MATERIALS

While not having the catchiest of names, urea-formaldehyde resin looks set to enter our homes in many different forms; as an adhesive, a coating, and a hard-wearing solid. The two building blocks of this material, urea and formaldehyde, have found useful service in their own right. Urea is commonly used as a fertilizer, while formaldehyde solution is used to sterilize surgical instruments and preserve pathological specimens. The versatile resin is prepared by heating the two components in the presence of ammonia. The end product is a polymer that can be used as an adhesive or as a protective coating for clothes. If this resin is then mixed with wood fiber it transforms into a hard, heat-resistant solid.

▲ *The moldable solid resin is ideally suited to mass production, and is likely to be used for an increasing number of household objects.*

◄ *The moving-coil loudspeaker.*

The first moving-coil loudspeaker

ENTERTAINMENT

The sound coming out of our gramophones is about to get better, thanks to the new moving-coil loudspeaker. The speaker has three main parts—a coil of wire, a strong magnet, and a cone made of stiff paper. The coil is placed in the magnetic field, the area of force around the magnet, and is fitted so that it can move quickly backward and forward for short distances. One end of the coil is attached to the center of the paper cone. When an electric current is applied to the coil, it interacts with the magnetic field, making the coil move and the cone vibrate. The cone's vibrations produce audible sounds. Early experiments show that the loudspeaker's sound can be clearer and more faithful to the original than that produced by the horns normally attached to gramophones. Another advantage of the loudspeaker is that it can be made in a small, more convenient form than traditional sound-reproducers such as horns.

How to keep them down on the farm

AGRICULTURE

The International Harvester Company has introduced the Farmall tractor—set to become a boon for all farmers. Its name describes its function, as it can do almost all the work needed to run a farm—plowing, planting, cultivating, and harvesting. The front wheels are much smaller than those at the back, and are set close together so that the tractor can be driven between crops sown in rows. Its small wheels also make it much more maneuverable and allow the driver to make sharper, tighter turns. It is the first all-purpose tractor and is high enough off the ground to pull a cultivator through crops, unlike preceding gasoline-fueled models.

◄ *A turn for the better—the new tractor.*

The history of the camera

The first photographs were taken in 1816 by French pioneer Joseph Nicéphore Niépce. Niépce's camera was a simple light-proof wooden box containing a lens to focus the image and a plate of metal coated with light-sensitive chemicals. People continued to use similar cameras, with glass or metal plates, for much of the 19th century. But in 1888, George Eastman of Rochester, New York, introduced the Kodak®, a small, cheap camera that took photographs on a roll of flexible film. The Kodak was simple to use and brought photography to ordinary people for the first time.

COMMUNICATIONS

Leica® is liked by amateurs and pros alike

The Leica camera uses small-format film on a 36-exposure roll. ▼

Cameras have just become smaller and more reliable. The German company, Leitz, has launched the Leica, a high-quality camera that can be carried with ease and is simple and fast to use. You don't need a tripod and there is no clumsy leather bellows—the user focuses by turning a metal ring on the lens. There are also simple settings to control exposure, so that the camera can take photographs in different lighting conditions.

ANTHROPOLOGY

Missing link found in South Africa

Australian-born South African anthropologist Raymond Dart has identified a new kind of human ancestor. Christened *Australopithecus africanus* by Dart, the discovery was based on the examination of the fossilized skull of a child at Taung, South Africa, excavated last year. The specimen is calculated to be two to three million years old, and provides a crucial missing link in the evolutionary chain linking apes and humans. The discovery has totally revised assumptions about the origins of humankind, which were previously thought to be in Asia. However, Dart's claim that the genus of hominid would have had a posture and teeth similar to modern humans—despite its small, ape-sized brain—has been met with hostility by other anthropologists.

▲ *The skull found at Taung.*

◄ John Logie Baird and his television equipment that is based on a device created by German inventor Paul Nipkow.

COMMUNICATIONS

First TV picture

Television is born! The idea that moving pictures can be sent across the air like radio signals is the brainchild of Scottish inventor John Logie Baird, who has just given the first demonstration of television to members of the Royal Institution in London. Baird believes that he has solved the problem of how to break up a moving image into small segments that can be transmitted. His equipment uses spinning disks to split the picture up into a series of lines. Baird's TV pictures are very blurred, but already some scientists are predicting that a more sophisticated, electronic scanning system will give better results.

Importance of iron in red blood cells discovered

BIOLOGY

Important research with dogs shows that we need iron in our diet to ensure good health. American pathologist George Hoyt Whipple took blood from dogs so that they artificially developed anemia, a blood disorder in which the production of red blood cells falls below normal. Whipple put the dogs on varying diets to find out whether different foods affected the formation of red blood cells. He noticed that the dogs that ate liver, which is rich in iron, formed red blood cells more quickly than those that did not. Red blood cells are made in the bone marrow and, from his research, Whipple has concluded that iron must play an important part in their formation.

▲ *Iron-rich foods help form red blood cells more quickly.*

Pauli develops his "exclusion principle"

PHYSICS

The Austrian physicist Wolfgang Pauli has developed an important law, called the "exclusion principle," that defines the possible energy states of electrons within atoms. Pauli's proposals tie together quantum theory (which states that energy changes can take place only in small discrete steps) and the known characteristics of the atoms of particular elements. Pauli says that every electron in an atom has an energy level or "quantum state" that can be defined by four numbers called quantum numbers. Three of these numbers define the region (called the orbital) that the electron occupies in the atom.

The fourth number defines a property of the electron called its "spin," which can have either of two values. Central to Pauli's proposals is the "exclusion principle" itself, which states that no two electrons in the same atom can have the same quantum state. Consequently, a maximum of two electrons (with different spins) can exist within any atomic orbital. This has far-reaching implications regarding atomic structure and the groupings of different chemical substances in the periodic table of elements.

Science News 1925

- The new sport of waterskiing begins to sweep across the United States.

- Canadian Arthur Sicard develops the snowblower, a machine for clearing snow.

- American astronomer Vernon Slipher determines the speeds at which 41 nebulas (galaxies) are moving away from Earth.

▲ *Wolfgang Pauli.*

First freeway opens in New York

TRANSPORTATION

As the number of automobiles rapidly multiplies, traffic engineers in New York have come up with a new way to deal with the flow. The Bronx River Parkway dispenses with intersections and provides entrances and exits instead, allowing traffic to merge seamlessly, with as few holdups as possible. To help with proper lane usage, a line of trees and shrubs has been planted down the center, dividing the north and south lanes.

ENTERTAINMENT

You ain't heard nothing…yet!

Popular singer Al Jolson is to make a movie that will feature the sound of his voice. Entitled *The Jazz Singer*, the film is set to be the first talking movie to be shown in movie theaters across the United States. Producers are confident that they have at last found a way of keeping the sound and pictures synchronized together, although they say that camera operators have to work in thickly padded boxes so that the noise of the camera does not get recorded on the sound track. Movie buffs say that the days of the silent cinema are over. Soon every movie will feature sound.

▲ The Jazz Singer, *due to be released next year.*

A GLANCE AT THE PAST

The history of the movies

People began to experiment with movie-making in the 1880s and 1890s. With these early systems, like Edison's Kinetoscope (*above*), a movie could only be watched by one person at a time. But in 1895 the Lumière brothers opened the world's first public cinema in Paris. At once, people realized that a new form of entertainment was born, and silent films became popular throughout Europe and America.

HOME APPLIANCES

Toast pops up

Minnesota mechanic Charles Strite is transforming the toaster. Strite has realized that many people are frustrated with their electric toasters—there is no way to see when the toast is done, so it often gets burned. In Strite's toaster, you push a slice of bread into a slot, where it rests between two heating elements. Both sides of the bread are toasted at once, and after a set time a spring sends the toast popping back out of the slot. The device has a clockwork timer to ensure the correct toasting time, so burned toast should soon become a thing of the past. Strite plans to sell his invention under the brand name "Toastmaster®," so remember to look for it in the shops soon.

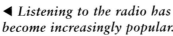

◀ *Listening to the radio has become increasingly popular.*

Science News 1926

• American aviators Richard Byrd and Floyd Bennett make the first airplane flight over the North Pole.

• Aerosol sprays are invented by Norwegian scientist Erik Rotheim.

• In the United States, Edward Lee Thorndike develops tests for measuring intelligence.

COMMUNICATIONS

Radio is booming

Listening to radio broadcasts is becoming one of the world's favorite pastimes. Many people have crystal sets—receivers that use a crystal to detect radio waves and have a pair of headphones for listening. In Great Britain alone, almost two million crystal sets have been sold and the business is still booming. Great Britain also has one of the best broadcast systems. Listeners are impressed by the variety of programs produced by the British Broadcasting Corporation, with broadcasts ranging from news and weather forecasts to serious music and light entertainment. Program-makers in other countries are following suit, aiming to provide entertainment for all tastes.

Royal tomb discovered

ARCHAEOLOGY

Following painstaking excavations, British archaeologist Leonard Woolley has uncovered a treasure-filled cemetery at Ur, Iraq, dating from 2,600 B.C. The contents of the graves suggest that Sumerian royalty was extremely wealthy, with gold statues of the city's moon god, Nanna, golden figures of animals and plants, as well as gold helmets, weapons, and precious stones. The find also shows evidence of human sacrifice. Woolley first discovered the site as far back as 1922, but he wanted his men to gain more practical excavation experience before attempting to unearth the cemetery. Woolley has therefore been highly praised for his cautious excavation methods.

◄ *Chariots and Sumerian infantry carrying spears decorate a musical instrument found at Ur.*

First liquid-fuel-propelled rocket

TRANSPORTATION

American physicist Robert Hutchings Goddard has revolutionized rocket science by using liquid propellant. Previous rockets were fueled by gunpowder and drew oxygen needed for ignition from the atmosphere. This made them unpredictable. Goddard's rocket uses controllable amounts of liquid fuel (gasoline) and liquid oxygen. The liquids are stored in two separate tanks and pumped into a combustion chamber where they mix and are ignited. On March 16, Goddard ran his first successful trial using a rocket that was 15 feet (4.5 meters) tall. It climbed 41 feet (12.5 meters) into the air and reached a maximum speed of 60 miles (97 kilometers) per hour.

Robert Hutchings Goddard has revolutionized the rocket. ▶

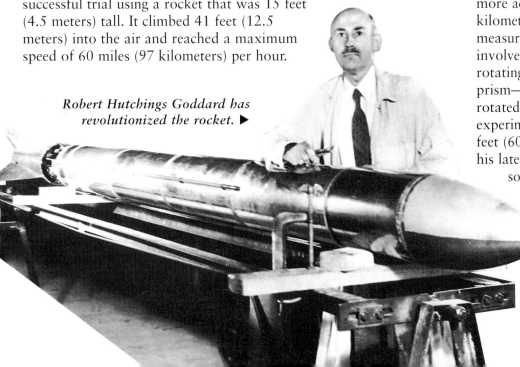

New value for speed of light

PHYSICS

The U.S. physicist Albert Michelson, who first measured the speed of light over 45 years ago (when he stated its value at 186,243 miles or 299,910 kilometers per second) has come up with a new value, which he believes is much more accurate, of 186,173 miles or 299,796 kilometers per second. As with his original measurements, Michelson's method has involved bouncing a light beam via a rotating prism to a mirror, then back to the prism—and detecting how far the prism has rotated in the interim. In his original experiment, he placed the mirror some 2,000 feet (609.6 meters) from the prism; but in his latest experiments he has placed them some 22 miles (35 kilometers) apart, on the peaks of two mountains (Mt. Wilson and Mt. San Antonio) in California. Before conducting the experiment, he measured the distance between the two peaks to an accuracy of less than one inch (2.5 centimeters).

ELECTRIFICATION

The electrical supply in your home is available at the flick of a switch to power everything from lights to television sets. But in the 1920s most homes in Europe and America did not have electricity. Homes still used gas or oil for lighting and burned fuel for heating and cooking. By the early 1950s, however, most used electricity for lighting and to power a host of labor-saving devices.

The public demand for electricity began in the late 1870s with the invention of the incandescent electric lightbulb. In the United States, only a few hundred households were supplied at first. Today it is the rare home that does not have electricity.

▲ *Thomas Edison.*

Thomas Edison

U.S. engineer, inventor, and businessman, Thomas Alva Edison brought electricity to the people. When he invented an electric lightbulb in 1879, he looked for ways of delivering electricity so that people could use his invention. Edison's teams of engineers devised electrical generation and distribution systems.

Electric streetcar

The streetcar is like a bus that runs on rails. The first U.S. streetcars date from the 1880s. By the 1900s, electric streetcars were a popular means of transportation amid the horse-drawn traffic of many U.S. cities. The use of streetcars declined with the arrival of fast-moving cars and buses.

▲ *A streetcar was powered by a motor supplied with electricity from an overhead power line. This example is from the 1920s.*

Modern conveniences

The spread of domestic electricity during the 1920s led to a boom in the sale of labor-saving appliances. The first customers were rich people who bought the new gadgets for their servants to use. As the price of the appliances came down, sales increased, encouraged by the new electricity-generating companies. By the 1950s, a typical kitchen in America or Europe had an electric toaster, kettle, refrigerator, and washing machine. Reliable, safe, and efficient electric stoves were available for the first time.

1928
Joseph Schick invents the electric razor.

1933
In Great Britain, an automatic electric teamaker goes on sale.

1955
In the U.S.A., the first electric deep freezers are marketed.

1962
Squibb starts manufacturing electric toothbrushes.

1967
The first microwave ovens for home use are introduced.

Supplying electricity

Power plants generate our electricity. Most burn fossil fuels—coal, oil, or natural gas—or use nuclear energy to generate steam. The steam turns a turbine that drives a generator. The electrical supply from the power plant is carried long distances at high voltages through thick cable. In the country, these cables are suspended from towers, but in towns and cities, the cables are buried underground. Electricity is usually supplied as alternating current (AC), which is easily "stepped down" to smaller voltages.

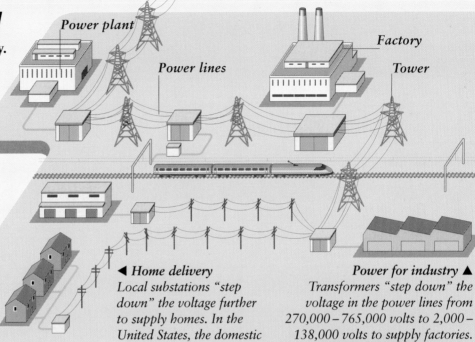

Power plant

Power lines

Factory

Tower

◀ *Home delivery*
Local substations "step down" the voltage further to supply homes. In the United States, the domestic voltage is 110 or 220 volts.

Power for industry ▲
Transformers "step down" the voltage in the power lines from 270,000 – 765,000 volts to 2,000 – 138,000 volts to supply factories.

Urban electrification

The fashionable kitchen of the 1950s was full of electrical appliances aimed at making the housewife's job easier. ▼

During the early 1900s, there were hundreds of electrical suppliers, each delivering electricity at a different voltage. By the 1920s, power supplies were standardized and organized for the benefit of communities. In city streets, gaslights were gradually replaced by electric lamps. By the 1930s, almost 70 percent of homes in the United States had electricity, and by the 1960s, this figure had risen close to 100 percent.

Seen from space, ▶
cities reveal themselves at night by the electric light they produce (the white areas).

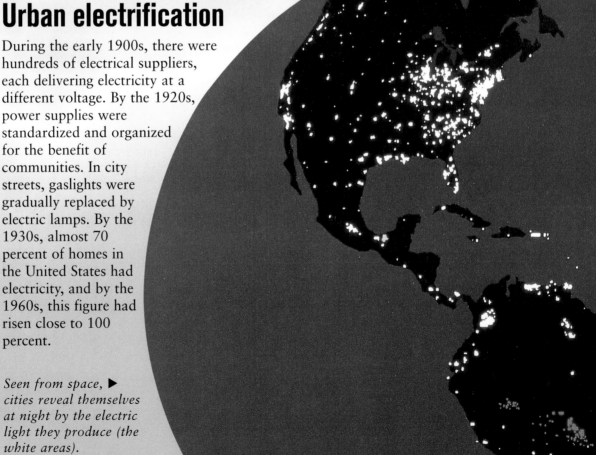

Wave-particle duality

The radical idea that particles such as electrons and protons also have some of the properties of waves (such as the ability to be diffracted) was first proposed by the French physicist Louis-Victor de Broglie (*above*) in 1923. De Broglie also showed how the wavelength associated with a particle could be calculated from the particle's momentum. In 1929, he was awarded the Nobel Prize for Physics for his work on the phenomenon, which has been termed "wave-particle duality."

PHYSICS

Electrons can behave like waves

American physicists Lester Germer and Clinton Davisson have proved that it is possible to "diffract" electrons, which shows that electrons can behave like waves as well as particles. Diffraction is the spreading out of a wave when it passes through an opening. The scientists' experiment involved firing electrons at a crystal of nickel. The pattern of radiation that emerged could only have been created by overlapping waves—so they concluded that gaps between layers of atoms in the crystal were diffracting the electrons as though they were waves.

▲ *Ring pattern resulting from electron-beam diffraction.*

PHYSICS

Heisenberg's "uncertainty principle"

A German physicist, Werner Heisenberg, Professor of Theoretical Physics at the University of Leipzig, has proposed a highly radical idea regarding the nature of matter. He says that at the subatomic scale events cannot be measured, or predicted, with any certainty. This conflicts with traditional physics, which maintains that complete predictability is possible, given enough data. Heisenberg calls his idea "the uncertainty principle." Formally, it states that as one of a pair of properties is known with greater accuracy so the uncertainty in the measurement of the other becomes greater. For example, it is impossible to specify both the position and momentum of an electron at the same time.

◀ *Tape recorders look set to replace the old wire recorders.*

COMMUNICATIONS

Tape is a sound idea

American inventor J.A. O'Neill has just improved the magnetic recording process with the introduction of the first tape recorder. Engineers have known how to record sounds using magnetism ever since Valdemar Poulsen of Denmark patented a machine to make recordings on steel piano wire in 1898. In the wire recorder, sound was picked up by a microphone connected to an electromagnet. This magnetized the steel wire in a pattern that followed the varying sound received by the microphone. Poulsen's invention has not been much used, partly because the technique of making recordings directly onto disks has proved so successful. O'Neill's machine, which works like the wire recorder, may prove more useful.

Science News 1927

- In the United States, Richard Drew invents cellophane tape, now familiar as Scotch® tape.

- The Holland Tunnel, linking New York and New Jersey, opens in the United States.

- American pilot Charles A. Lindbergh makes the first nonstop, solo flight across the Atlantic in 33 hours.

HOME APPLIANCES

Rolex's waterproof wristwatch

Long-distance swimmer Mercedes Gleitz has emerged from the sea in triumph—and not just because she has made it across the English Channel. Those who looked closely could see that Gleitz was wearing a wristwatch, and the salt water had not ruined its movement. Her watch is an Oyster®, and it was given to her by Hans Wilsdorf, who developed it for the Rolex Company. The Rolex Oyster is the world's first waterproof timepiece. Now people all over the world, especially those who like to swim or who work at sea, are keen to try the new watch from the Swiss company.

The Rolex Oyster is the world's first waterproof watch. ▶

ANTHROPOLOGY

Flint spearheads point the way

The discovery of finely crafted flint spearpoints embedded in the bones of a bison known to have been extinct for 10,000 years has offered conclusive evidence that Native American cultures existed in North America as far back as the Ice Age. The find was made near the town of Folsom, New Mexico, by an expedition of American archaeologists, and resolves long-standing differences of opinion about when the first humans arrived in North America. Previously, it was thought that Native American culture was only two or three thousand years old.

Other artifacts, including scrapers, knives, and blades, have also been found. The find indicates the existence of a Paleo-Indian people who hunted now extinct big game in the central plains region of North America.

▼ *The "iron lung" allows a patient to breathe and helps prolong his or her life.*

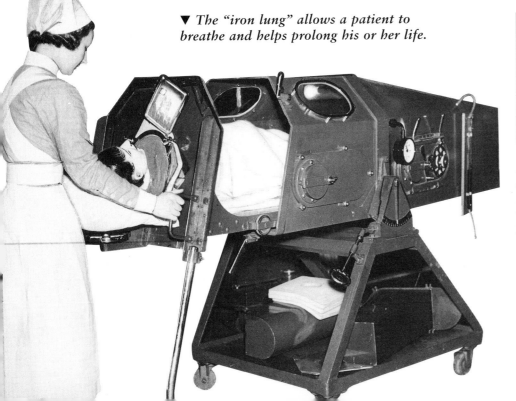

MEDICINE

First "iron lung"

Each year thousands of children are diagnosed as having polio. In its most extreme form, polio can leave patients unable to breathe at all. In 1925, Philip Drinker, an American, began searching for a suitable treatment to prevent these deaths. Today, a device christened the "iron lung" assists the breathing of those patients who can no longer breathe unaided. The patient is sealed inside an airtight chamber, with only the head exposed. The pressure inside the chamber is then lowered and raised, forcing the patient's lungs to expand and deflate. The first clinical trials are set for this year.

The first Zeppelin

Airships or dirigibles—rigid balloons that can be steered—were first developed in 1852 by French engineer Henri Giffard. in the 1890s, Count Ferdinand von Zeppelin greatly improved the design and began developing streamlined dirigibles, known as Zeppelins. He launched his first Zeppelin in 1900. It consisted of a light, cylinder-shaped metal frame covered with cloth, and contained a number of hydrogen-filled gas bags to provide lifting force.

TRANSPORTATION

Zeppelin completes return flight to United States

Zeppelin airships can now cross the Atlantic. ▼

Wealthy passengers have been traveling through the air in rigid airships since 1910, but now the Graf Zeppelin has successfully completed the first-ever transatlantic flight by a lighter-than-air aircraft. It took off from Friedrichshafen, Germany, and safely touched down in New Jersey, United States, four days, 15 hours, and 30 minutes later. Zeppelins are housed in special movable hangars, so that they can be taken out safely, no matter which way the wind is blowing.

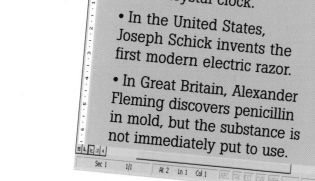

Science News 1928

- Canadian-born Warren Marrison and American J.W. Horton develop the first quartz crystal clock.

- In the United States, Joseph Schick invents the first modern electric razor.

- In Great Britain, Alexander Fleming discovers penicillin in mold, but the substance is not immediately put to use.

FOOD

Bubble gum's in the pink

Walter Diemer, a 23-year-old accountant at the Fleer Gum Company, has invented a new type of chewing gum that can be blown into bubbles—and the Philadelphia-based company will be selling it this Christmas under the brand name Dubble Bubble®. Diemer was actually playing around with gum recipes in his spare time when he discovered a product that seemed more stretchy than regular gum. His demonstration gum was bright pink, because that was the only coloring at hand when he was making it—and now it seems that the marketed product is going to be in the same eye-catching shade.

MEDICINE

Sticking point

Skin is the largest organ in the human body and your main barrier against the outside world. This barrier frequently succumbs to cuts. Until now, bandaging even the smallest wound required the painstaking cutting of adhesive tape and cotton gauze to create the dressing. This time-consuming process has been eliminated by the development of Elastoplast®, a ready-made adhesive plaster. Elastoplast is purchased as a long roll with squares of cotton gauze already attached to the adhesive tape. To give extra protection, the top surface is covered in creoline, a tough fabric made from horsehair. All that is required is that you cut a strip to the required size and then place it over the wound.

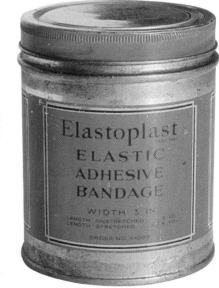

While it may never save lives, Elastoplast will certainly revolutionize first aid. ▶

"Red shift" explained

When a light-emitting object moves away from an observer, the peaks and troughs of the light waves appear to the observer to be slightly more spread out or "stretched" than if the light source was stationary. In other words, the light's wavelength appears to increase. For visible light, an increase in wavelength is equivalent to a shift toward the red end of the light spectrum, or in short, a "red shift." It was Hippolyte Fizeau (*above*) who first explained the implications of red shift in terms of astronomical observation in 1848.

The yo-yo is said ▶ to have been introduced to the United States from the Philippines just a few years ago by a man named Pedro Flores.

ASTRONOMY

The universe is expanding

American astronomer Edwin Hubble has produced convincing evidence that the universe is expanding—at a very fast rate. From his study of nebulae (galaxies separate from our own), he noted that light coming from these galaxies revealed a phenomenon called a "red shift," an alteration in the wavelength of the light, indicating that nearly all of them are moving away from us at high speed. Hubble has noticed that the more remote a galaxy is the faster it appears to be receding. Therefore, all the galaxies must be moving away from us and from one another, and so the universe is expanding.

▲ *From his study of galaxies, Hubble has discovered that the universe is expanding.*

ENTERTAINMENT

The yo-yo is introduced

A new toy is sweeping America—the "yo-yo." It's a simple wooden disk, about two inches (five centimeters) in diameter, with a deep groove that (almost) splits the disk into two halves. A string loops around a central axle that connects the halves. To operate the toy, the string is wound around the axle, the free end is held securely, and the disk is dropped or thrown. With practice, it can be made to bounce up and down along the string, and even perform tricks, to which enthusiasts are giving names, such as "the sleeper" and "walking the dog."

COMMUNICATIONS

BBC starts TV broadcasts

The British Broadcasting Corporation (BBC) has transmitted its first television broadcast from its station 2LO. In March, Scottish inventor John Logie Baird showed BBC officials his latest television equipment. Baird's pictures were far from perfect, but they were impressive enough for the BBC to give Baird the use of a transmitter. Since the first program went on air on September 30, the few who own a television set have been amazed at the results.

Because Baird only has one transmitter, he cannot yet broadcast sound and pictures simultaneously. ▶

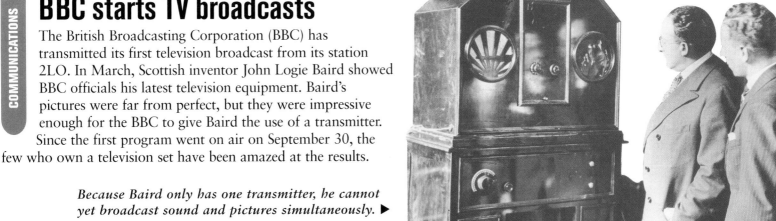

1845
Reinforced concrete is invented.

1851
Crystal Palace is built in London, England.

1856
A quick and cheap way of manufacturing steel is invented.

1875
A successful formula for window glass is developed.

1885
The first metal-framed skyscraper is built in Chicago.

STRUCTURAL MATERIALS

The Industrial Revolution had spread from Great Britain to Europe and North America by the early 1800s. Industrial methods produced new building materials such as iron girders and plate glass. Building parts could be assembled in the factory and then joined to similar pieces on site. London's Crystal Palace was built in this manner in 1851.

By the 1880s, stronger, lighter steel and the invention of the electric elevator paved the way for the New York skyscrapers of the 1920s.

◀ *The Eiffel Tower.*

Top of the world

The Empire State Building was built incredibly fast. More than 3,000 construction workers took only 58 weeks to build its 102 stories. At one point they finished 14 stories in 10 days. At 1,250 feet (381 meters) high when completed in 1931, the Empire State was the world's tallest building. It held this record until 1973.

The Empire State Building, New York City. ▶

Iron giant

The iron-and-steel Eiffel Tower was erected in 1889 for the Paris Exhibition. At 984 feet (300 meters) tall it was nearly double the height of the world's previous tallest structure. The tower was a celebration of nineteenth-century high technology with its intricate skeleton on display. It was originally designed to last for only 20 years, but in the year 2000, thousands of visitors continued to take elevators to the top of the Eiffel Tower every day.

How skyscrapers work

A skyscraper is built around a steel or concrete frame that acts like a skeleton to support the building. Horizontal beams and girders and vertical columns support the walls, roof, and floors. The building must also resist horizontal forces. Strong winds can buffet it with forces greater than its own weight.

▶ *Skeleton frame*
Steel columns and girders spread the load throughout the building.

Column

Girder

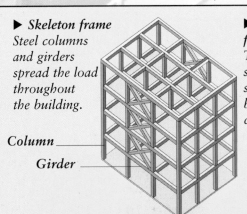

▶ *Cable-hung frame*
The floors are supported by steel cable and by a central concrete core.

Concrete floor

Steel cable

Concrete core

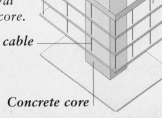

Concrete home

U.S. architect Frank Lloyd Wright completed the house known as Falling Water in 1936. Wright mixed the traditional and the modern. He combined wooden frames and stone with steel, glass, and concrete to create pleasing designs that blended with their surroundings. His work was a great influence on twentieth-century architects.

◀ *Falling Water.*

▲ *The Pompidou Centre, Paris.*

Plastic Eden

Plastics, unlike most building materials, are entirely artificial. Since the 1950s and 1960s, plastics have been used to make beams and struts, roof and wall panels, and even windows. Modern plastics are long-lasting but readily disposable. Bubbles made out of sheets of ETFE (ethyltetrafluoroethylene) were used in the world's largest greenhouse at the Eden Project, Great Britain. The ETFE provides good insulation, is lightweight, transmits light, and is nonstick (so any bird droppings that fall on it are washed away by the next rain).

Inside out

The Pompidou Centre, Paris—completed in 1977—is a high-tech building of glass, steel, and concrete. An outer steel frame supports it and the services (such as electric cabling and air ducts), walkways, and escalators are on the outside, too, creating a large, open space inside. Each floor is the size of two soccer fields with movable partitions. The building contains a design center, art galleries, and a library.

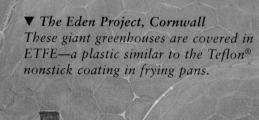

▼ *The Eden Project, Cornwall*
These giant greenhouses are covered in ETFE—a plastic similar to the Teflon® nonstick coating in frying pans.

1930

Polymer pioneer

Born in 1881, Hermann Staudinger (*above*) developed the study and synthesis of polymers while working at various universities in Germany from 1908 onward. Polymer molecules are made up of thousands more atoms than ordinary molecules. For example, a polymer molecule such as the plastic polythene is made up of as many as 7,500 atoms. Staudinger received the 1953 Nobel Prize for Chemistry for his work in creating these giants among molecules.

MATERIALS

Inventor turns waste into gold

Waldo Semon has developed a novel synthetic plastic from what was previously just a waste product. Working at the chemical giant B.F. Goodrich, Semon experimented with several synthetic organic polymers, including polyvinyl chloride (PVC)—a hard solid with little commercial value. The process that Semon has developed turns PVC into a hard-wearing, moldable plastic. Another vinyl polymer looks set to make an equally big impact—polystyrene can be produced as a hard plastic and also as a light foamlike solid.

▲ *The new plastics may be used for household goods.*

ASTRONOMY

Pluto is discovered

Clyde Tombaugh, a 24-year-old astronomy assistant at the Percival Lowell observatory in Flagstaff, Arizona, has discovered a new planet. It is to be named Pluto, after the Greek god of the underworld. Tombaugh is part of a team set up by the American astronomer Percival Lowell to search for the cause of irregularities in the motions of two other planets—Neptune and Uranus. Tombaugh discovered Pluto by comparing photographs of the same region of sky taken several days apart. In this way he was able to identify a dim and distant planet moving against a fixed background of stars in the constellation of Gemini.

▲ *Pluto (see arrows) as it appeared within the constellation of Gemini in February 1930.*

ENGINEERING

Chrysler Building is world's tallest

New York's most stunning skyscraper has just been completed. It is the 77-story Chrysler Building, headquarters of the famous car company, and is the world's tallest building yet, at 1,046 feet (319 meters) high. Designed by William van Alen, the Chrysler Building is a masterpiece of the Art Deco style. The greatest surprise was the tower's pointed spire, which was made in secret inside the building and hoisted to the top at the last minute.

◀ *The "secret" spire's last-minute appearance instantly made the Chrysler Building taller than the nearby Bank of Manhattan.*

▲ A cross-section of a tree: a new way of dating.

ARCHAEOLOGY

A date with tree rings

A new scientific way of dating the past, known as "dendro-chronology," has been developed through examining tree rings. Over the last 10 years, American archaeologist Andrew Douglass has shown how tree rings can be used to date archaeological material. By piercing a tree through to its center and removing a plug of wood, Douglass was able to examine tree rings of consecutive, overlapping ages. Tree rings indicate climatic variations of seasonal rainfall and temperature. By counting and measuring tree rings, the number of annual growths in an area can be counted. These can then be matched to the ring patterns of timbers collected from the area, and a date can be established. Douglass developed the principles of tree-ring dating after examining timber beams and roofs from Indian pueblo settlements in Arizona and New Mexico.

PHYSICS

Weird particle predicted

The Austrian physicist Wolfgang Pauli has predicted the existence of a bizarre new type of fundamental particle. The particle is thought to form during certain types of change in the nuclei of atoms. It has little or no mass, no charge, moves around at high speed, and, as yet, there is no known method for detecting it. Pauli thinks its existence accounts for various differences in a type of radioactive decay called beta emission. In this type of decay, the nucleus of an atom emits a particle called a beta particle (which is known to be an electron). Beta particles are emitted with a range of different energies, but it also known that in each beta emission the total energy released is always the same. Pauli believes the new type of particle must be emitted simultaneously with each beta particle and carry a variable amount of energy with it.

◄ The new machine can also be used for slicing cakes.

Science News 1930

• The telescopic umbrella is invented by Hans Haupt in Germany.

• English engineer Frank Whittle patents the Turbojet engine. Its thrust is created by exhaust gases.

• In the United States, Dr. Vannevar Bush constructs a large electro-mechanical calculator.

FOOD

The best thing is sliced bread

At last we can enjoy evenly sliced toast and bread for sandwiches. An American jeweler, Otto Frederick Rohwedder, has finally perfected a bread-slicing machine that not only slices bread but also wraps it immediately after slicing so the sliced loaf stays moist and fresh. Rohwedder first developed his bread-slicing machine in 1912, but at that time was unable to keep the slices together successfully, which meant that the bread became stale. By 1928, he had overcome the problem with a machine that both sliced and wrapped. Now bakers in Michigan are selling the presliced loaf. Coincidently, Rohwedder's invention came only two years after the development of a pop-up toaster.

Compound microscopes

The true microscope was invented around 1590, when eyeglass-makers began to make instruments that used the greater magnifying power that you get when you put two or more lenses together. The first people to do this were Hans and Zacharias Jensen of Holland. During the following centuries, improvements in lenses, and different ways of combining them, led to instruments that produced clearer images and better magnifications. All these instruments are known as compound microscopes, because they have more than one lens.

ENGINEERING

First crude electron microscope invented

Scientists will soon be able to examine the tiniest particles. This is the prediction of those who have seen the electron microscope, the latest invention of Max Knoll and Ernst Ruska in Berlin. For years, scientists have known that it would be impossible to see very tiny objects with an optical microscope because of the limitations of light itself. Knoll and Ruska have found a way of using a stream of electrons to replace light in a microscope and produce images of the smallest of subjects. They predict that it will soon be possible to build microscopes that can produce images of the cell structures of plants, tiny details of the bodies of insects, and even smaller creatures.

ASTRONOMY

White dwarf stars

The Indian-born astrophysicist, Subrahmanyan Chandrasekhar, has described the nature of white dwarf stars—extremely hot but small stars that appear to exist throughout our galaxy. White dwarfs are formed when stars about the size of the Sun reach the end of their lives. Before it dies, a star of this type swells into a red giant but then sheds 90 percent of its mass. Energy production ceases in its core, and the star then shrinks, becoming extremely compressed—a single teaspoonful of white dwarf weighs more than 3,000 pounds (1,350 kilograms). A white dwarf then gradually fades until it becomes a cold, lifeless, black dwarf.

▲ *An illustrated cross section of the first electron microscope.*

COMMUNICATIONS

Flash! Bang! Wallop!

Until now, anyone who wanted to take a photograph indoors had two options—hold the camera shutter open for minutes on end, or use explosive flash powder, a mixture of powdered magnesium and an oxidizing chemical. Unless the subject is completely still, opening the shutter for long periods produces blurred photographs. Flash powder, however, is messy, inconvenient, and dangerous. The answer is the flashbulb, which keeps the explosive mixture contained, cutting out the danger and mess. The new flashbulbs were introduced last year in Germany, and are now being sold in many places in Europe and America.

Photographers are enthusiastic about the new bulbs. ▶

ENGINEERING

Now the Empire State Building is the world's tallest

New York's latest skyscraper, the Empire State Building, has overtaken the Chrysler Building as the world's tallest. It is 1,250 feet (381 meters) tall, and from the topmost floor (102), you can see 78 miles (125 kilometers) in clear weather.

The most amazing thing about the building is how quickly it has been built. It took little more than 18 months to complete, with up to 38 five-man teams riveting together the seemingly endless supply of steel beams that were delivered to the site by a special railway. Workers risked their lives balancing on beams hundreds of feet in the air, and altogether 14 men were killed in accidents during the building's construction.

A construction worker on the Empire State Building balances on a steel girder while signaling to a colleague. ▼

CHEMISTRY

Freon® 12 introduced

American engineer Thomas Midgley has developed a new chemical to be used as a coolant in refrigerators and air conditioners. Known commercially as Freon 12, it is the first chlorofluorocarbon, or CFC, so-called because it contains chlorine, fluorine, and carbon. Until now, the gases used in refrigerators were ammonia and sulfur dioxide, both of which smelled terrible and were highly poisonous; a leak was very dangerous. So far, Freon 12 seems to overcome this problem—it is colorless, odorless, nontoxic, and nonflammable.

PHYSICS

A hair-raising invention

A Massachusetts Institute of Technology student, Robert Van de Graaff, has invented a device for generating static electricity at very high voltages. The generator uses a moving band of insulating material, passing over rollers, to accumulate a static electric charge on the surface of a hollow metal sphere. The electric potential of the sphere can be raised to several million volts—however, the device produces a fixed and relatively low current. It is thought that these generators will be used to supply the high energy needed for particle accelerators or "atom smashers" that are much in demand by institutions engaged in research into nuclear physics.

◀ *Touching an electrically charged Van de Graaff generator will make your hair stand on end.*

The first balloons

Practical ballooning was born in 1783 when Jacques Etienne and Joseph Michel Montgolfier made the first hot-air balloon from paper-lined silk. In September, in the presence of Louis XVI, a duck, a rooster, and a dog made the first "manned" ascent. A month later, Pilâtre de Rozier, the king's historian, made the first true manned flight. In December, French physicist Jacques Charles ascended in a hydrogen balloon. Two years later, American doctor John Jeffries and Jean-Pierre Blanchard ballooned across the English Channel in two hours.

TRANSPORTATION

First human enters the stratosphere

One year after his first record-breaking ascent to 51,762 feet (15,781 meters), the Swiss-born Belgian physicist Auguste Piccard has gone aloft once again, using the balloon he built in 1930. The secret of his success is the revolutionary spherical aluminum cabin, pressurized within to maintain sea-level conditions, and a recycled air supply system. This year, Piccard built a new cabin using the same principles and added a radio, so he can maintain contact with the ground. On August 18, he made a second ascent, breaking his own record by reaching 55,132 feet (16,200 meters).

LE MAGNIFIQUE EXPLOIT DU PROFESSEUR PICCARD

▲ *Piccard is not interested in records—he wants to get as far above Earth as possible in order to study cosmic rays.*

A recent ▲ photograph of Venus, Earth's nearest planetary neighbor.

ASTRONOMY

Venus's suffocating atmosphere

An astronomer at the Mount Wilson Observatory, California, Dr. Theodore Dunham, has discovered that the atmosphere of Venus consists mainly of carbon dioxide (CO_2)—the suffocating gas that on Earth is a waste product of animal and plant respiration and the burning of fossil fuels. The discovery is a surprise to many astronomers who previously believed that Earth and Venus had similar atmospheres. Dunham (with colleague Walter S. Adams) made the discovery when he found some unusual features in the spectrum of light radiation from Venus. Dunham demonstrated that the same spectrum could be reproduced on Earth by passing light through a long pipe containing compressed carbon dioxide. This indicated the presence of CO_2 in Venus's atmosphere, under much higher pressures than exist in Earth's atmosphere.

COMMUNICATIONS

Music on the move…but at a price

Now motorists can have music while they drive—the German company Blaupunkt has introduced the world's first automobile radio, the AS5 or "Autosuper." To pick up a signal, Blaupunkt engineers ran a series of wires across the roof of the auto and along the running boards. The wires are connected to the radio itself, a large unit that is stowed away in the trunk. The driver turns the radio on and off with a control unit on the steering wheel. Many drivers like the idea of Blaupunkt's invention, but few are likely to be rushing out to buy one: The radio costs around one-third of the price of a small automobile.

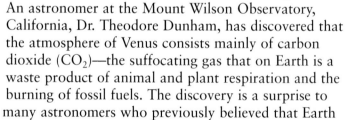

◄ *Automobile radios promise to take the boredom out of long journeys.*

It's clear that TV pictures will improve

Television pictures are set to get clearer with a new electronic TV system. At its heart is a camera developed in Great Britain by the EMI Company and based on research by Russian-born inventor Vladimir Zworykin. The camera uses a device called an iconoscope tube, which contains many small cells that can detect different light levels. The varying light levels are changed to different levels of electrical current, and the receiver converts these varying currents into a picture. The result is an image made up of far more "lines," and this means crisper, clearer pictures on our TV sets.

◄ *The new television camera's iconoscope tube. Experts are predicting that electronic scanning will eventually take over from the mechanical system.*

Science News 1932

- The parking meter is invented by Carlton Magee. It will be installed in Oklahoma City in three years' time.

- Scientists in the United States announce the development of a vaccine against yellow fever.

- Edward Lewis finds part of the jaw of a primitive primate, *Ramapithecus*, in India.

New particles discovered

U.S. physicist Carl Anderson has discovered a new subatomic particle that is identical, in all respects but one, to an electron—the difference is that it carries a positive electrical charge. The existence of the particle, to be called a "positron," was first predicted in 1928 by the British physicist Paul Dirac. Anderson discovered the positron among the breakdown products of cosmic rays—highly energetic particles emanating from space. Its discovery proves the existence of antimatter—particles that are "mirror images" of more familiar particles and that will annihilate their opposite numbers to produce pure energy. In a separate development, the British physicist James Chadwick has discovered a fundamental particle, present in nearly all atoms, that carries no electrical charge. This particle is to be called the "neutron."

Carl Anderson with the apparatus in which he tracked down the positron.►

Physicists split the atom

British physicist Sir John Cockcroft and Irish physicist Ernest Walton have smashed the nucleus of a lithium atom into two parts—they have literally "split" the atom. They have built a machine that accelerates protons (positively charged subatomic particles) to extremely high speeds. Recently they have been using this "particle accelerator" to bombard lithium atoms with protons. The nucleus of a lithium atom itself consists of three protons and four neutrons. When an accelerated proton smashes into a lithium nucleus, the resulting combination (four protons and four neutrons) is unstable and splits into two alpha particles, each consisting of two protons and two neutrons. Alpha particles are identical to the nuclei of helium atoms, so, effectively, the atom-smashing turns one chemical element (lithium) into another (helium).

The history of vitamins

Vitamins are chemical substances found in our food, which are needed for growth and good health. The body cannot produce most of them. In 1906, English chemist Frederick Hopkins (*above*) was the first to suggest that many foods contain "accessory factors," substances apart from such things as fats and proteins that are essential for health. In 1912, Polish–American biochemist Casimir Funk called these substances "vitamines" (vital amines) later known as vitamins, and isolated vitamin B1 in unpolished rice.

BIOLOGY

Vitamin C is synthesized

Swiss chemist Tadeus Reichstein has become the first to produce a vitamin synthetically in the laboratory, and his artificial form of vitamin C is identical to the natural one. In 1928, biochemist Albert Szent-Gyorgyi found that capsicums were rich in vitamin C. In 1932, American Charles Glen King isolated vitamin C from lemon juice. It has long been thought that citrus fruits can help treat scurvy, a vitamin C-deficiency disease.

◀ *The chemical structure of vitamin C contains atoms of carbon (blue), oxygen (red), and hydrogen (white).*

▲ *Audiences like drive-in movies because they can go out without having to dress up.*

Science News 1933

• The first all-electric, automatic tea-maker, the Teasmade, is introduced in Great Britain.

• A carbonated drink, 7 Up®, formerly called Lithiated Lemon, is marketed in the United States.

• British chemist R.O. Gibson has created a new plastic, polythene, from ethylene gas.

ENTERTAINMENT

World's first drive-in movie theater opens

Richard Hollingshead, of Camden, New Jersey, has opened the world's first drive-in movie theater in his home town. Hollingshead built the drive-in after he had tried out the idea by showing a film from the driveway of his own home. But his commercial drive-in is a far cry from his original home-movie setup. It features a screen measuring 30 by 40 feet (9 by 12 meters) and a fan-shaped parking lot with spaces for 400 cars in eight rows. Many people are keen on the drive-in idea. Plans are under way to build drive-in movie theaters in other cities in the United States.

ZOOLOGY

Last Tasmanian wolf dies in zoo

One of the most remarkable animals known to science, the thylacine, or Tasmanian wolf, is thought to have become extinct. What is believed to have been the last wild thylacine was shot in 1930, and the last known captive animal died this year at a zoo in Hobart, the capital of Tasmania. Despite its appearance, the thylacine was neither a species of wolf nor a dog, but a type of marsupial. Its resemblance to dogs and wolves was a result of what scientists call convergent evolution, in which similar features develop separately in different species. The thylacine evolved into a form comparable to members of the dog family because it filled much the same ecological niche in Australia as true dogs do in their environments.

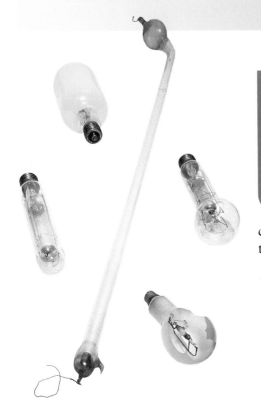

Mercury-vapor lamps introduced

ENGINEERING

The use of electric lighting continues to spread. Since the early 1900s, chemists have experimented with passing electricity through vapors and gases, such as neon, rather than filaments, particularly for display purposes. As early as 1901, Peter Cooper-Hewitt began to market a mercury-vapor lamp, and now high-intensity mercury-vapor lamps are being introduced. Mercury's spectrum contains no red, so such lamps tend to produce bluish light that is rich in ultraviolet rays.

◄ *Mercury-vapor lamps produce a bluish light.*

"Heavy water" is produced

CHEMISTRY

American chemist Gilbert Newton Lewis has separated "heavy water" from the ordinary kind at the University of California, soon after the discovery of deuterium by Harold C. Urey. Deuterium is an isotope of hydrogen: An isotope is an atom of an element that has a different mass from the standard atom of the element. Heavy water, also known as deuterium oxide, or D_2O, is similar to ordinary water, but instead of two hydrogen atoms each molecule contains two atoms of deuterium, which weighs twice as much, making each molecule 10 percent heavier than an ordinary water molecule. This makes heavy water behave in a slightly different manner: It freezes at 38.88°F (3.82°C) rather than 32°F (0°C) and it boils at 214.56°F (101.42°C) rather than 212°F (100°C.) In every 7,000 parts of ordinary water there is one part heavy water. Lewis and his team found a way to distill the heavy water from the ordinary kind by exposing it to hydrogen sulfide gas, which attracts the deuterium atoms.

▲ *Heavy water behaves slightly differently than the regular sort.*

Come fly with me

TRANSPORTATION

On February 8, the airline company Boeing unveiled the prototype of its first passenger airliner, the 247. It has an all-metal streamlined airframe, monoplane wings spanning 74 feet (22.6 meters) two Pratt & Whitney nine-cylinder radial engines and a retractable undercarriage. This revolutionary design allows it to fly at 180 miles (290 kilometers) per hour, with a maximum speed of 200 miles (322 kilometers) per hour. It carries up to 10 passengers and two pilots, and can fly for 800 miles (1,297 kilometers) without refueling. Later this year, in July, the rival Douglas company launched its own passenger carrier, the DC 1. The battle of the airlines is under way.

▲ *The revolutionary Boeing 247.*

BIOLOGY

X-ray image of a protein obtained

For the first time, an image has been made of a protein—one of many mysterious substances believed to play a key role in the body. The protein is pepsin, a substance thought to be involved in breaking down food in the stomach. However, the image is not an ordinary photograph taken through a microscope but something altogether different—an X-ray image made using the technique of X-ray crystallography. It has been obtained at a special X-ray crystallography unit at the University of Cambridge, by the Irish-born physicist John Desmond Bernal, and a student, Dorothy Crowfoot.

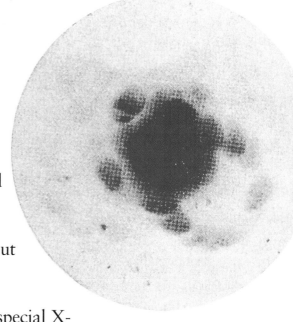

▲ *The first image (of a copper sulfate crystal) made by x-ray crystallography.*

ASTRONOMY

How neutron stars are formed

For some years, astronomers have been puzzled by the occurrence, in distant galaxies, of spots of light that for a few weeks appear to become many millions of times brighter than normal. Now two scientists at the California Institute of Technology, Fritz Zwicky and Walter Baade, have developed a convincing theory to explain the phenomenon. They believe that the points of light are large stars that have exploded at the end of their lives, releasing vast amounts of matter and energy, and they have termed these exploding stars "supernovae." They have further predicted that, after the stars explode, their remains collapse into very strange objects indeed, called neutron stars. These objects are so compressed that most of their individual atoms have collapsed, each atom's protons and electrons squeezing together to form neutrons.

OCEANOGRAPHY

Record dive in a bathysphere

After three seasons diving in their bathysphere, American writer, naturalist, and explorer William Beebe and adventurer Otis Barton have descended a half mile (800 meters) into the ocean depths around Nonsuch Island near Bermuda. It is the deepest any human being has ever ventured, and they stayed down for five minutes. The bathysphere, designed and funded by Barton, is made of cast iron, with 18-inch (45-centimeter) thick walls and 7-inch (15-centimeter) thick, fused quartz windows. It is painted black inside to make it easier to observe the luminous fish living in the depths. The bathysphere has its own oxygen and electricity supplies.

◀ *This artist's impression of the bathysphere appeared in a national newspaper.*

ENTERTAINMENT

Pinballs tilt but don't flip

One of the latest pinball machines. ▶

Pinball machines are cropping up everywhere—and in technical terms they are improving all the time. Most new pinball tables have legs and backboards, battery-operated "kickers," lights on the playing area and backboard, and bells on a few models. People have realized they can manipulate the game to their advantage by shaking, tilting, and banging the machine. So, recently, new tilt-sensor mechanisms have been introduced to prevent cheating—an early model involves a ball on a pedestal that will fall off when the machine is moved around too much, so ending the game. Also, electricity will likely replace batteries as a power source for the machines.

PHYSICS

Artificial radioactive isotope

French physicists Frédéric and Irène Joliot-Curie (the daughter of the famous Polish-born physicist Marie Curie, who is still alive) have succeeded in creating the first artificial radioactive isotope—a radioactive form of phosphorus. Working at the Radium Institute at the University of Paris, they have been bombarding atoms of nonradioactive elements with alpha particles (energetic helium nuclei; double pairs of protons and neutrons). As a result, they have succeeded in producing new, artificial, radioactive isotopes of phosphorus and other light elements (every chemical element can exist in different forms called isotopes that have different numbers of neutrons in their nuclei). The phenomenon is known as induced radioactivity. Because these substances give off radiation, it is believed they could be of tremendous use in medicine, medical and biological research, and industry.

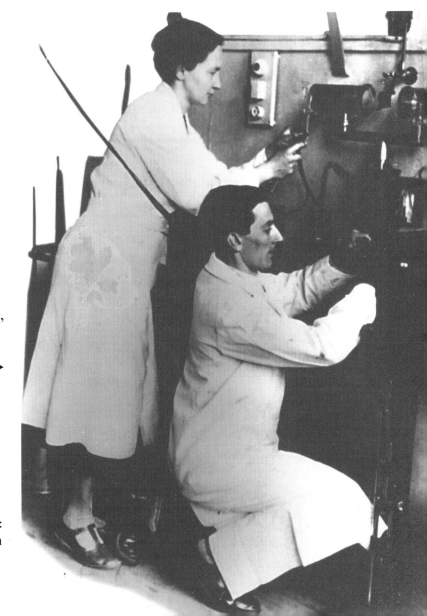

Frédéric and Irène Joliot-Curie at work in Paris. ▶

HOME APPLIANCES

A fan-tastic idea!

Fans have been around for years, moving the air around and producing a cool breeze in warm weather. But now there's a new idea. Attach a fan that is blowing outward to a window and it will suck stale air out of the room. These new extractor fans are set to be popular wherever smells build up: busy kitchens in restaurants, public toilets, and even kitchens in the home.

1935

A GLANCE AT THE PAST

Early color photography

Since the early 1900s, photographers have known that to take color pictures you need to find a way of making a material sensitive to the primary colors. One of the earliest attempts was the Autochrome process, perfected in 1907. This used a glass plate coated with tiny grains of potato starch, dyed red, green, or violet. The color in the photographs was not accurate compared with the results (*like that shown above*) of using a Kodachrome monopack.

COMMUNICATIONS

Color photography for all

Kodak, the makers of cameras and film, have come up with a new film called Kodachrome®. Previously, researchers thought that color photography would need three different colored films, which would be combined together to make a full-color picture. But Kodachrome is a monopack system, in which three layers of emulsion, each sensitive to a different primary color, are all found on the same film. Kodachrome is already becoming popular among amateur filmmakers as a 16-millimeter motion picture film.

▲ *Kodak is manufacturing a version of Kodachrome for still photography, producing transparencies.*

Sir Malcolm Campbell, whose car, Bluebird, has broken the land speed record. ▼

TRANSPORTATION

Land speed record broken

On September 3, British racing driver Malcolm Campbell broke the world land speed record for the eighth time to set an amazing new world record. Driving his famous car, *Bluebird*, at the Bonneville Salt Flats in Utah, he achieved an average speed of 301.129 miles (494.5 kilometers) per hour, the fastest officially clocked land performance. Six huge tires, 3.28 feet (1 meter) in diameter, smooth for minimum resistance, and a supercharged 8-gallon (36.5-liter) V12 Rolls-Royce R engine enabled his car to reach such an astonishing speed. This version of *Bluebird* (Campbell calls all his cars *Bluebird*) is more than 28.1 feet (8.6 meters) long and was built in Campbell's workshops at the Brookland track in Great Britain. It still uses some parts from his first 1927 *Bluebird*, namely the front axle, brake drums, and part of the chassis.

EARTH SCIENCE

Richter introduces scale

The American seismologist Charles Richter and his German-born colleague Beno Gutenberg have introduced a new scale for measuring the absolute strength of earthquakes. It is to be called the Richter scale, and it runs from 0 for the weakest earthquakes through to 9 or more for the strongest—there is no theoretical upper limit, although the largest earthquakes ever experienced to date would fall somewhere between 8.5 and 9 on the scale. The Richter scale is arranged so that each increase of one unit on the scale represents a tenfold increase in the magnitude of the quake—so, for example, a quake measuring 6 on the scale is 10 times stronger than one measuring just 5, and releases about 31 times more energy.

▲ *Many Americans prefer to drink their beer from cans.*

Beer gets canned

FOOD

Food in cans has been around for a long time, but now Americans can drink their beer out of cans. The Krueger Brewing Company of Newark, New Jersey, is the first to make beer available in cans. The company test-marketed its Cream Ale in canned form in January of this year and it has been enormously successful. A survey shows that at least half of the Americans asked prefer to drink their beer this way. Canning as a method of preserving cooked foods for future use was developed in France early in the nineteenth century. It spread quickly through Europe and the United States. Early cans were made of glass and tin; these were later replaced by steel cans, mass produced in the United States since the late 1840s.

Science News 1935

- Parking meters are introduced in Oklahoma City, charging one nickel per hour.

- The first commercial electron microscope becomes available in Great Britain.

- Methane and ammonia are discovered on large planets by German astronomer Rupert Wildt.

Amazing Technicolor®

ENTERTAINMENT

At last! The first full-length feature film shot with the Technicolor system has been released. *Becky Sharp*, starring Miriam Hopkins and Sir Cedric Hardwicke, shows that Technicolor is the most reliable of the many color movie systems developed in recent years. Technicolor uses a camera that shoots three images at the same time—one in each of the primary colors. The three images are then printed onto a single strip of film, which also contains the sound track. Technicolor cameras produce such good results that many people in the movie business predict that this system will become the standard for color films.

◄ *Technicolor cameras deliver good results but are complex and expensive.*

Hitler now realizes that he can tape broadcasts so that they can be repeated later. ▼

Hitler tapes broadcasts

COMMUNICATIONS

Germany's leader Adolf Hitler is well aware of the power of the media. Even before he came to power, his words were heard on the radio, and now the Nazi leader is taping broadcasts. He is using the latest German technology—a lightweight recording tape pioneered by companies AEG Telefunken and I.G. Farben. The tape is made of plastic and is coated with iron dioxide. It is very thin, so great lengths can be wound on to a single spool. This means that very long broadcasts can be taped without changing spools. The material can also be cut easily, so mistakes can be edited out.

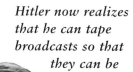

Early guitars

The guitar's ancestor was the lute, an ancient stringed instrument invented in the Arab world. By the eighteenth century, guitars were being made in Europe. Their simple construction and light weight made them popular, especially with singers who wanted to accompany themselves. But the guitar was not a loud instrument, and could easily be drowned out in a band. A group of Californians, Beauchamp, Rickenbacker, and Barth, overcame this problem in 1931, by adding a pick-up to make the first electric guitar (*an example is pictured above*). Rickenbacker went on to design the first solid-body electric guitar, which was made from Bakelite®.

ENTERTAINMENT

Electric-acoustic guitar goes on sale

The American Gibson Company has introduced its ES-150 electric guitar. There have been electric guitars before, but the Gibson is the first electric guitar to be widely praised by players. Perhaps this is because a musician, Alvino Rey, helped design the pick-up—the specialized microphone that converts the string's vibrations into an electrical signal that can be amplified. Jazz guitarist Charlie Christian is already testing out the instrument, and predicts it will give the guitar a bigger, louder role in music.

◀ *The Gibson ES-150 electric guitar; the first to be praised by guitarists.*

HOME APPLIANCES

First upright Hoover®

Since 1908, when William H. Hoover began to make vacuum cleaners, the words "Hoover" and "housework" have been inseparable. Now the Hoover company is going from strength to strength with its new upright vacuum cleaner, the Model 925. Unlike previous vacuum cleaners, which were heavyweights that looked more at home in a factory than a house, the new Hoover is light and attractive. Many of the working parts are made of lightweight magnesium alloy, and the motor casing is an elegant molding made of Bakelite. Yet the Hoover is still strong and has a large dust bag, to cope with the biggest cleaning jobs. Hoover hopes it will clean up with the Model 925.

ENGINEERING

World's tallest dam completed

After five years' building work, the Hoover Dam is complete. At 726 feet (221 meters), it is now the world's tallest dam, its structure a stunning sight on the Colorado River between Arizona and Nevada. It is an arch-gravity dam, a type that uses its special curved shape to push the massive weight of the water behind it into the banks of the river. The dam plays many roles—it both controls flooding on the river and produces hydroelectricity. In addition, there is a vast 115-mile (185-kilometer) long reservoir behind the dam, a source of water for drinking and land irrigation that promises to supply areas as far away as southern California.

◀ *The Hoover Dam, the world's tallest.*

History of the suspension bridge

In a suspension bridge, the roadway is hung, or suspended, from cables. The cables are supported by towers and anchored to the banks on either side of a river. This type of bridge was used by the Chinese during the sixth century but later became popular in the nineteenth century, when engineers realized that they could use materials such as brick and iron chains to cross huge, previously unbridgeable, spans. Notable early suspension bridges are England's Clifton Suspension Bridge (*above*) in Bristol, the first metal suspension bridge, which spans the Merrimac River in Massachusetts, and New York's Brooklyn Bridge, which pioneered the use of steel wire for the cables and set the style for suspension bridges in the twentieth century.

ENGINEERING

Golden Gate Bridge is completed

With a main span of 4,200 feet (1,280 meters), San Francisco's Golden Gate Bridge is the world's longest to date. Its pair of steel towers, which rise 745 feet (227 meters) above the water, also make it the tallest. Building the bridge was not easy. The job has taken some five years, and the problems encountered included building a huge watertight structure to allow one of the foundations to be laid on the seabed. The bridge carries a six-lane highway and two footpaths connecting San Francisco with Marin to the north.

▲ *The Golden Gate Bridge, which cost around $35 million.*

ANTHROPOLOGY

"Peking man" gets a head

Following years of extensive excavations at the Chou-k'ou-tien cave near Peking in China, German anthropologist Franz Weidenreich has reconstructed a complete skull of the extinct hominid species *Sinanthropus pekinensis*. Known popularly as "Peking man," the hominid was first identified as a new fossil human by Canadian anthropologist Davidson Black in 1927, who defined the type by studying a single tooth. Weidenreich's skull has confirmed Davidson's findings. It has a cranial capacity almost as large as modern man, despite the age of the fossils, which can be dated to the Middle Pleistocene period (900,000 to 130,000 years ago).

A reconstruction of the skull of "Peking man." ▶

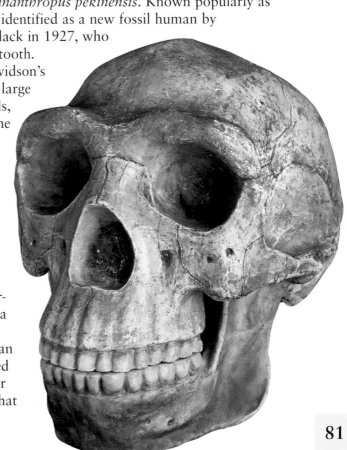

COMPUTERS

"The Turing machine"

A Cambridge mathematician has developed a revolutionary machine that can be taught to perform any logical task. At present, this machine is only a theory proposed in a mathematical paper by Alan Turing, but it could well have far-reaching implications. Turing's interest is focused on whether a process can exist by which all mathematical questions can be decided. In his paper, Turing describes how logical processes can be broken down into precise steps, which can, in principle, be carried out by a machine. Turing originally proposed a different machine for each task, but he has now developed this into a universal machine that can read a set of instructions and be taught to perform any task.

81

1826	1855	1861	1890	1906
The first photograph is taken by Nicéphore Niepce.	The theory of three-color photography is published by Maxwell.	Maxwell demonstrates the first color photograph.	F.E. Ives patents the first commercial color process.	A studio in London, England, offers the first color portraits.

COLOR PHOTOGRAPHY

Color photography is almost as old as photography itself. But early color techniques were cumbersome and difficult to use—for many years people simply painted over black-and-white photographs with colored ink. Over the years, many color processes were developed but none really took off. One company even resorted to touching up prints by hand in an attempt to improve the color accuracy but often only succeeded in making matters worse. Good quality color photography finally arrived in the 1940s.

▲ *The first color photograph.*

▲ *Godowsky (left) and Mannes.*

Filtered image

In 1861, British scientist James Maxwell made three separate images of a tartan ribbon. Each was photographed through a red, green, or blue filter. When the images were projected through the same filters, they combined to make the first color photo.

Three-layer film

Musicians Leopold Mannes and Leo Godowsky developed the first really successful color photographic process in the 1920s. Until their Kodachrome® film was introduced in 1935, the layers of film of a color photograph (each with a different part of the colored image) had to be processed individually. Mannes and Godowsky combined three layers of light-sensitive material onto the same film.

Cheap color processing

During the 1950s, color photography began to replace black-and-white as the most popular form of snapshot. The new color films—Kodachrome or Agfacolor® for slides and Kodacolor® for prints—could be used in ordinary cameras and, unlike earlier color processes, did not require special knowledge on the part of the photographer. The film still had to be sent away for processing, but the overall costs were no longer high. Color photography was now within the reach of ordinary people.

◀ *Kodachrome and Kodacolor film enabled ordinary people to take color photographs.*

1924
The three-layer color process is patented by Mannes and Godowsky.

1942
Agfa and Kodak introduce color paper.

1963
Polaroid introduces the first instant color film.

1973
A 35-mm camera with built-in microprocessor is made by Canon.

1980
Sony introduces the first camcorder for domestic use.

How film for color prints works

Color film is made up of three layers of a light-sensitive material (emulsion). The yellow layer is sensitive only to violet, blue, and cyan light (1), the magenta layer to yellow, green, and cyan light (2), and the cyan layer to red, orange, and yellow light (3). When light of the right color strikes each layer it causes a chemical change to tiny grains of a silver salt in the emulsion. When the film is developed, colored dyes are released within the vicinity of the altered grains, creating a negative, or reversed, image. The silver is then washed away. Light-sensitive color paper is exposed by shining light through the negative, reversing it to form a positive photographic print. The three layers, when combined, give a color image.

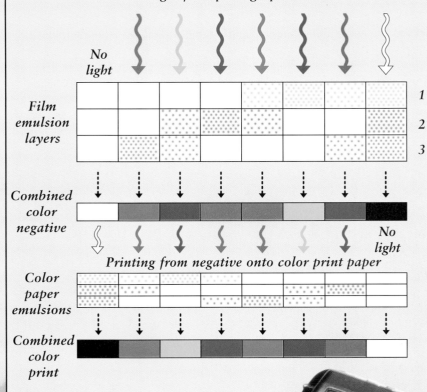

Light from photographed scene

No light

Film emulsion layers
1
2
3

Combined color negative

No light

Printing from negative onto color print paper

Color paper emulsions

Combined color print

Pull-out image ▶
As the exposed photograph leaves the camera, it passes between two rollers. These squash the photograph and spread the chemicals that develop the image.

Instant pictures

The photograph that emerges from a self-developing camera, such as a Polaroid® camera, contains layers of light-sensitive material and developing chemicals, which cause dye release. The developing chemicals and dyes move to the surface, where a separate layer of chemicals stops the development process. The surface is coated with plastic to protect the image and seal in the chemicals.

Digital revolution

Digital cameras take the hit-and-miss element out of photography. Light entering the camera lands on a light-sensitive screen. The image is then converted into digital information that can be stored in the camera's memory. Because there are no chemicals involved, an unwanted image can simply be deleted from the memory and replaced by another picture.

◀ *Digital camera*
Information stored in the camera's memory can be transferred to a computer and then printed out onto paper.

The first fountain pen

American insurance salesman and inventor, Lewis Edson Waterman, came up with the first practical fountain pen in 1884. Waterman's design used capillary action, whereby the ink is released when the nib is pressed against the page, to maintain a smooth flow of ink from the barrel to the nib. Although successful, people found Waterman's pen fussy to fill. So, in the early 20th century, pen makers modified Waterman's design, adding a rubber tube that could be squeezed to suck up the ink or, better still, a metal lever that you pulled to suck ink into the pen.

COMMUNICATIONS

Laszlo Biro is on the ball with his new pen

Have you ever blotted a line using a fountain pen or, even worse, a messy dip pen? If so, you will soon be thanking Hungarian journalist Laszlo Biro for his new variety of pen. Biro's pen uses a form of quick-drying ink that the inventor first saw in a printing company in his native Budapest. The ink flows out of the pen via a tiny rolling metal ball, which ensures that the new Biro® writes as smoothly as the best fountain pen. Biro, now working in Argentina, says that it will be possible to manufacture the pen cheaply, and that one day everyone will own at least one.

▲ *Cheap to make, soon everyone will own a Biro pen.*

TRANSPORTATION

World's largest liner

The world's largest oceangoing luxury liner was launched on September 27, named after George VI's queen, Elizabeth. The ship is one of two (the other being the *Queen Mary*) built for the Cunard Line to provide a two-ship weekly service across the Atlantic. No expense has been spared. There were over 7,000 tests made on models before the ship's final shape was designed. She is over 1,000 feet (300 meters) long and she is to be fitted out in extreme luxury at the Clyde shipyards.

The Queen Elizabeth, *the world's largest oceangoing liner.* ▼

ENGINEERING

More light, less voltage

Fluorescent lamps are now available in the United States, providing a low-voltage alternative to gas-discharge lights. They produce about four times as much light. A fluorescent lamp consists of a tube about 2 feet (60 centimeters) long that contains a filament. It is coated on the inside with phosphor and is filled with mercury vapor. This gives out invisible ultraviolet light in an electric discharge. The phosphor fluoresces, or turns the ultraviolet light into visible white light. The General Electric Company of the United States has been developing these lamps since about 1934.

▲ The coelacanth—more closely related to land animals than to fish—was thought to have died out about 80 million years ago.

Something fishy found in Africa

ZOOLOGY

Marjorie Courtenay-Latimer, the curator of a tiny museum in the port of East London, South Africa, has discovered an amazing "fossil fish" among the catch of some local fisherman who have been trawling near the mouth of the nearby Chalumna River. The fish, about 5 feet (1.5 meters) long and a dark blue color with white flecks, is called a coelacanth and belongs to a group of fish that was thought to have been extinct for millions of years. Its discovery has been described as the most important zoological find of the century. Coelacanths were common inhabitants of the earth's oceans from Devonian to Jurassic times (about 400 to 150 million years ago).

First domestic steam iron

HOME APPLIANCES

Ironing just got easier! Edmund Schreyer, of Ridgefield, Connecticut, has introduced a new steam iron, aimed directly at the home user. Schreyer's iron uses a jet of steam to dampen the fabric as you press it, making it quick and simple to smooth out every unwanted crease as you go. There have been steam irons before, but they have been modeled on industrial irons, and so have proved more popular in laundries than with home users. What makes the new iron better is that it is fitted with an adjustable thermostat. You set the required heat for the type of fabric you are ironing and the iron keeps to that temperature—it should never overheat and consequently ruin your clothes with scorch marks.

A thermostat means that the new steam iron should never overheat. ▼

Increase in carbon dioxide levels

ENVIRONMENT

Scientists have detected an increase in the levels of carbon dioxide in the atmosphere. They believe that this is the result of the increase in the burning of fossil fuels (coal, oil, and gas) in industry and transportation. When fossil fuels are burned, carbon dioxide is one of the waste gases that is produced, along with soot, smoke, carbon monoxide, and other pollutants. These fuels are used in factories, which have increased in number over the past 50 years. But scientists point to the automobile as the chief cause of the rising carbon dioxide levels: since 1915, autos have become more affordable, and they now rule the roads.

▲ The automobile is held responsible for the increase in carbon dioxide levels.

Science News 1938

- The first satisfactory instant coffee is produced by Swiss company Nestlé.

- American chemist Roy J. Plunkett accidentally discovers a new nonstick substance and calls it Teflon®.

- German engineer Ferdinand Porsche produces the prototype Volkswagen Beetle®.

Wallace Hume Carothers

Born in Iowa in 1896, Dr. Wallace Carothers (*above*) attained worldwide fame as the man who developed nylon. In 1928, he was hired to head a team at DuPont's research laboratory developing artificial materials. During the 1930s, silk was in short supply and DuPont wanted to develop a synthetic alternative. Pursuing the goal ultimately led Carothers' team to develop nylon, which was harder-wearing and less expensive than silk.

A TV set costs almost as much as an automobile. ▼

MATERIALS

DuPont begins to market nylon

Nylon mania looks set to sweep the nation with the unprecedented demand for clothes made from the world's first synthetic fiber. People caught their first glimpse of nylon at this year's World's Fair in New York. The chemical giant DuPont has also begun to manufacture nylon commercially. Initially developed five years ago by a research team led by Wallace Carothers, nylon is produced in a reaction between an acid and an amine. Through varying the reaction components, it is possible to change the properties of the fiber from hard and tough to soft and rubbery.

▲ *Stockings were one of the first items to be made from nylon.*

TRANSPORTATION

The first jet aircraft

The first plane powered by a jet engine took off in Germany on August 24, piloted by Captain Erich Warsitz. During another flight made three days later, the plane reached a speed of 400 miles (640 kilometers) per hour. The plane is the He 178, built by the German Heinkel company which used the HeS 3 gas turbine ("jet") engine, the brainchild of 25-year-old German scientist Dr. Hans von Ohain. It has short, stubby, wooden wings and a barrel-shaped metal fuselage. The German military have watched the plane, but can see no place for it in their air force.

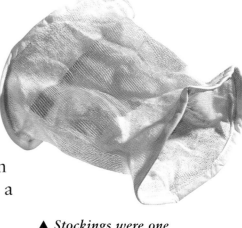

Science News 1939

- In Great Britain, John C. Duncan discovers that the Crab Nebula is expanding, and is about 800 years old.

- In the United States, the first handheld electrical knives for slicing food are introduced.

- American Edward Adelbert Doisy isolates vitamin K.

ENTERTAINMENT

TV at the World's Fair

After some years of experimental programs, regular television broadcasts have begun in the United States at last. It all started at the World's Fair, which was opened by President F.D. Roosevelt on April 30. NBC televised the opening ceremony and is now offering between 10 and 15 hours of broadcasting every week. People watch television sets with 5- or 9-inch (12.5- or 23-centimeter) screens in large, floor-standing cabinets—which you can also buy at the fair. Among the most popular programs to date are sports broadcasts, including live tennis, baseball, football, and hockey games. Few Americans are buying televisions, however, because the sets cost almost as much as new automobiles!

Full-scale production of polythene

Six years ago, two researchers were nearly killed when their high-pressure experiment exploded. Today chemical company I.C.I. launches polythene, the plastic that was formed during that explosion. The original experiments involved pressurizing ethylene gas to 20,000 atmospheres and heating it to 338°F (170°C). After the explosion, the project leader, Dr. Michael Perrin, had to continue these experiments in secret.

Fortunately, his team managed to recreate the experiment without the explosive climax. Opening the reactor door, the researchers were greeted by a flurry of plastic snow. Now out in the open, the researchers went on to study the properties of this new material, discovering it was an exceptional electrical insulator but rapidly melted if held against a flame. While polythene can be used in anything from packaging to communication cables, it is polythene's military applications that may well come to the fore soon.

Lise Meitner and Otto Hahn. Their discovery of nuclear fission raises the specter of the production of very powerful bombs based on chain reactions of disintegrating uranium atoms. ▶

Lise Meitner
b. 1878 d. 1968

Meitner was born in Vienna, Austria, and studied physics in Vienna and Berlin, where she worked as an assistant to the German physicist Max Planck. In 1917, Meitner and Dr. Otto Hahn discovered a new chemical element, protactinium. During the 1930s, she began studying (with Hahn) the effects of bombarding uranium with neutrons. In 1938, she fled Nazi Germany to Sweden. Following the announcement of uranium fission, Meitner refused to become involved in the development of atomic bombs.

Nuclear fission discovered

Lise Meitner has announced that atomic nuclei of the radioactive element uranium have been split, releasing energy and free neutrons. The discovery, which Meitner is calling "nuclear fission," is based on the work of the chemists Otto Hahn and Fritz Strassmann. A few months ago, Hahn sent Meitner the latest accounts of their experiments, which showed that one of the products from bombarding uranium was a radioactive form of a much lighter element, barium. Meitner realized that uranium atoms had been split, and, together with her nephew Otto Frisch, she described the physical characteristics of the division, calculating the huge amount of energy released in the process.

First helicopter designed for mass production

Russian-born aircraft designer Igor Sikorsky has developed the first practical single-rotor helicopter for United Aircraft, the VS-300. It has a steel body with an open cockpit, a single main three-bladed rotor, plus a small tail rotor to prevent torque (twisting), and is powered by a 65-horsepower Lycoming engine. After its maiden test flight on September 14, during which it was tethered to the ground by a long rope, Sikorsky realized that much more work has to be done to turn it into a practical machine, and set to work revising the design and controls.

The VS-300 helicopter, designed for mass production. ▶

SOUND AND MUSIC

Recording technology has revolutionized our experience of listening to sound and music. Over the century live music became a rarity as people began to listen to far more recorded sound.

In the first two decades of the twentieth century, simple mechanical gramophone record players brought recorded music into the home. Electrical advances in the decades that followed enabled recorded sound to increase in quality. They also enabled us to miniaturize the machines that were built to replay sound.

A gramophone player. ▶

Mechanical music

Gramophones were mechanical contraptions that did not need electricity to make sound. As a record spun on a record player, its grooves vibrated a thin metal pin, called the "stylus." The stylus, in turn, vibrated a lightweight sheet, called the "diaphragm." This was at the narrow end of a hollow tube. The moving diaphragm made the air inside the tube vibrate, generating sound.

Tape recorders

Reel-to-reel tape recorders used magnetic audio tape. Developed in the late 1930s, the tape is covered in a thin layer of rust granules. The recorder varies the magnetism of the granules to store sound. By 1950, tape recorders of this type were being used widely in the radio and recording industries. Manufacturers began to produce stereo tape recorders for use in the home during the mid-1950s. In the 1960s, the introduction of audio cassette tapes revolutionized the tape recorder market, which began to compete with record players.

Some earlier magnetic recorders didn't use tape at all. One designed by Valdemar Poulsen in 1893 stored sound on a magnetized steel wire. The wire moved through the machine at dangerously high speeds.

How a microphone works

A microphone turns sound into a varying electrical signal that flows through its wires. This microphone has a built-in battery, which makes a steady electrical signal, even when there is no sound. The electrical signal from a microphone can be boosted by an amplifier. This makes it possible to record quiet sounds.

Sound waves

Moving, charged diaphragm

Wire carrying signal

▲ **Signal production**
Sound waves entering the microphone cause the charged diaphragm to vibrate, altering its electrical properties. This varies the electrical signal.

Battery

Processing circuit

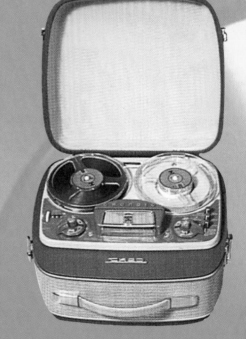

▲ *A reel-to-reel tape recorder.*

1958
The first stereo records are sold.

1964
Philips sells the first audio cassette tapes.

1979
The Sony Walkman® becomes the first personal stereo.

1983
Music is sold on compact disk for the first time.

1987
Consumers can buy and record digital audio tapes (DAT).

How a CD player works

When CDs first came onto the market in the early 1980s, people thought they were virtually indestructible. A CD has to be handled with care, but small scratches on its playing surface are unlikely to spoil playing quality. This is because a CD stores sound digitally in the form of billions of "pits" burned into a track that spirals from the center of the CD to its edge. In addition to sound, every music CD also holds a special type of data, called an "error correction code." This enables a CD player to convincingly fill in any gaps when small fragments of sound are missing. The error correction code helps to disguise the effects of minor wear and tear.

▶ *The CD spins around 500 times a minute when the laser is nearest the center. It spins around 200 times a minute when it reaches the outer edge.*

▼ *A laser beam is focused on the track and reflects back to a detector that turns the varying beam intensity (caused by the pattern of pits) into a sound signal.*

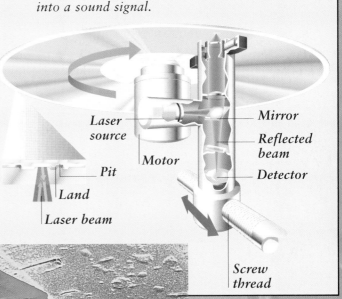

Laser source
Motor
Pit
Land
Laser beam
Mirror
Reflected beam
Detector
Screw thread

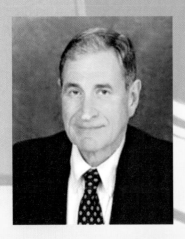

◀ *Ray Dolby.*

◀ *The pattern of pits (and intervening regions called "lands") on the track is a code. The CD player reads this code to make sound. Shown here is a single pit.*

Audio innovator

One of the most famous twentieth-century names associated with audio is that of Ray Dolby, the inventor of a noise-reduction system that bears his name. The founder and Chairman of Dolby Laboratories, Inc., was born in 1933 in Oregon. He devised a system in the 1960s for boosting the softer sounds during recording to block out any noise, reducing it again during playback. Since then millions of audio products have been sold worldwide that are licensed to use Dolby. Several thousand movies have been released with Dolby® soundtracks, and most big movie theaters use Dolby sound equipment.

▲ *This early version of the Minidisc came with a protective plastic cover.*

New formats

Today many new digital sound formats are battling for consumers' attention. One is the Minidisc, a small, CD-like disc that can be recorded on by users. A competitor, MP3, offers portable sound on a machine that has no moving parts. An MP3® player stores sound in microchips instead of a disk or tape. It enables users to listen to near CD-quality sound, without having to worry about moving parts that wear out.

Discovery of penicillin

A Scottish bacteriologist, Alexander Fleming (*above*), discovered penicillin in 1928, while working at St. Mary's Hospital medical school, London. One morning, he noticed that a mold had contaminated one of his bacterial cultures and was preventing the bacteria from growing. He identified the mold as *Penicillium notatum*, and called the antibacterial substance that it contained "penicillin." Isolating the mold, he grew a pure culture of it in a broth. After a few days, he confirmed that the broth had acquired a capacity to kill a range of disease-causing bacteria.

MEDICINE

Penicillin can be used to combat germs

Two Oxford University scientists, Howard Florey and Ernst Chain, have isolated and purified, from a species of mold, a substance that they hope will become an extremely useful drug. The drug, called penicillin, is able to kill infectious microorganisms (that is, "germs") inside the body. Florey's and Chain's development of penicillin results from an investigation that they started last year into naturally occurring antibacterial substances. They soon came across Alexander Fleming's work on penicillin and this led to the small-scale manufacture of the drug.

▲ *Plans are afoot to use penicillin to fight bacteria, such as those that can cause pneumonia.*

PHYSICS

Atomic bomb moves one step closer

Physicists in the United States are developing a more detailed understanding of the mechanics of "nuclear fission"—the splitting of uranium atoms to release energy in a chain reaction. Recently, John Ray Dunning of Columbia University has shown that, of the two main isotopes of uranium, the rare form (termed U235) is much more fissionable than the more common form, U238 (isotopes are different forms of a chemical element, having different numbers of neutrons in their nuclei). This followed up on theoretical work by the renowned atomic physicist, Niels Bohr. The next step toward development of atomic energy—or an atomic bomb—is to find a method of "enriching" natural uranium so as to increase its U235 content.

ARCHAEOLOGY

They painted in caves

A group of French youngsters have stumbled upon one of the most outstanding displays of prehistoric art ever found, in the Lascaux woods near Montignac in southwestern France. The limestone caves include a main cavern 66 feet (20 meters) wide and 16 feet (5 meters) high, containing many steep galleries, magnificently decorated with engraved and painted figures. Archaeologists date the site to the last Ice Age, between 15,000 and 13,000 B.C. Altogether, there are 600 painted animals and prehistoric symbols, and 1,500 engravings. The Ice Age artists painted mainly in shades of red, yellow, black, and brown, using charcoal and mineral pigments. The most remarkable pictures are of four 16-foot- (5-meter-) long aurochs (large oxen); other animals include red deer, horses, and stags, some of which appear to be swimming across a river. Anthropologists have suggested that the caves were used as a place for practicing magical rites.

▲ *One of the remarkable cave paintings in the Lascaux woods, in southwestern France.*

World's first automatic door

ENGINEERING

A restaurant in New York has installed the first automatic swing door. As a person approaches the door, their body is detected by a photoelectric cell. The cell's circuitry is connected to a motor that opens the door long enough for the person to pass through. Then the door closes once more. The device is catching public attention, with passersby stopping to watch it as it opens, as if by magic. But the automatic door is not just a clever gimmick. It is already a favorite with delivery drivers whose hands are full.

▲ *Doors now open as if by magic.*

Science News 1940

- The Pennsylvania turnpike becomes the first modern highway in the United States.

- In the United States, freeze-drying starts to be used for the preservation of food.

- Vincent Du Vigneaud, an American biochemist, identifies the sulfur-containing vitamin, biotin.

Artificial elements created

CHEMISTRY

Scientists in Italy and the United States have found they can create hitherto unknown chemical elements by bombarding the atoms of known elements with highly energetic subatomic particles. This year, physicists Philip Abelson and Edwin McMillan created the metal neptunium (atomic number 93) by bombarding uranium 238 with neutrons produced by a cyclotron (type of particle accelerator). This follows the synthesis in 1937 of another metal, technetium (atomic number 43), by Italian scientists Emilio Segrè and Carlo Perrier. They obtained technetium by bombarding a sample of molybdenum with deuterons (particles consisting of a combined proton and neutron). Technetium was the first new element created and is named after the Greek word *technikos*, "artificial." The "new" elements appear to exist only as short-lived, unstable, radioactive isotopes.

Autos go automatic

TRANSPORTATION

In America, Oldsmobile, now part of General Motors, has brought out the first car with automatic transmission. The system is called the Hydra-Matic® and provides true clutchless driving with four forward speeds. The fluid coupling between engine and transmission means that the clutch, and the footwork it entails, is now a thing of the past. It costs an extra $57 to fit the system onto any Olds model and so, for American drivers at least, the easy ride is within easy reach.

◀ *An Oldsmobile fitted with a Hydra-Matic system.*

The history of radar

Radio pioneer Guglielmo Marconi first had the idea of bouncing radio waves off invisible objects in 1922. In Great Britain, scientists working at the Signals Experimental Establishment, Woolwich, during the early 1930s, were conducting tests using radio waves to detect ships. By 1939, when World War II began, Great Britain already had a string of radio masts along the coast, set up to detect approaching aircraft more than 100 miles (161 kilometers) away and displaying their positions on cathode-ray tubes. Soon, radar was being used to find ships at sea and to detect enemy bombers and fighter planes in the air.

MILITARY TECHNOLOGY

Allies develop radar and take advantage

Great Britain and her Allies are benefiting from radar, a method of detecting invisible objects such as enemy aircraft in the night sky. Radar (the name derives from radio detection and ranging) works by sending out radio waves into the atmosphere. When an aircraft enters the area covered by the radio waves, some of the waves bounce back, telling the operator that there is something there. The time taken by the waves to bounce and return tells the operator how far away the object must be. Radar helped British pilots win the Battle of Britain in 1940.

▲ *Radar is helping the war effort.*

BIOLOGY

How genes work

At Stanford University, two biologists studying genes (the carriers of hereditary information in living organisms) have come up with an explanation of how they work. George Beadle and Ed Tatum say that every gene controls a specific chemical reaction in the cells of an organism. These reactions are usually steps in the manufacture of essential substances that the organism needs. Since chemical reactions in living things are caused by types of proteins called enzymes, they have concluded that each gene controls the production of one enzyme.

Science News 1941

- The first freeze-dried orange juice is supplied to the United States Army.

- A portable writing board, called a clipboard, goes into production in Germany.

- A fighter plane with a liquid-cooled engine makes its first flight in Japan.

COMMUNICATIONS

Kodak produces color negative film

There have been color photographic processes before, but these have produced glass-plate images or color transparencies. Color prints are what most photographers want, and they are about to get them with Kodacolor®, a new film from the Kodak laboratories in the United States. Whereas black-and-white film has a single layer of light-sensitive emulsion, the new film has three layers, each sensitive to one of the three primary colors of light (red, green, and blue). When the film is developed, three different-colored dyes are formed. This is a color negative. When it is printed, a similar process occurs on the paper to produce a positive print.

▲ *Color negative film will produce color prints.*

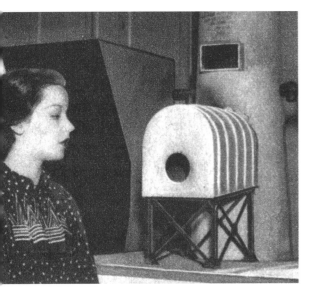

HOME APPLIANCES

Smoke alarm promises safer workplaces

From paint shops to explosives factories, fire is a hazard in many workplaces. In the United States, a new invention, Jaeger and Mell's smoke alarm, is likely to save lives. The alarm works best with fires that produce a lot of smoke. Inside the unit is a photoelectric cell. In normal conditions, when plenty of light enters the cell, an electric current flows through it. But if a plume of smoke gets into the cell, the light is cut down, reducing the current. When the current drops, a loud alarm sounds, alerting the workforce, who can escape from the building and call the fire department.

◀ *The smoke alarm could be a life saver.*

MILITARY TECHNOLOGY

Jet fighter with an ejector seat

It is rumored that in Germany, the Heinkel Company has devised a solution—an aircraft ejector seat—to help reduce the Luftwaffe's mounting pilot losses. If an aircraft becomes damaged and is about to crash, the pilot can make a quick exit by pressing a button to operate the ejector. The pilot is launched skyward by a sudden release of compressed air, and can then return to the ground by parachute. The ejector is fitted to the newly developed German fighter, the Heinkel He 280, a remarkable plane that is also the first combat aircraft to be powered by a gas turbine ("jet") engine. The plane is a single-seater with a 40-foot (12-meter) wingspan, an oval fuselage with a twin fin and rudder tail, and has a maximum speed of about 500 miles (800 kilometers) per hour. The fighter has already shown its mettle in mock dogfights, although whether the German military will give the plane its full backing is unclear at present.

ENERGY

Limitless electricity from wind

A new type of farm could soon appear across the countryside, consisting of windmills that produce electricity. For centuries, windmills have been used as a power source but the wind was transformed directly into mechanical energy, for example, to crush grain for flour. The idea that wind can be used as a "free" power source for electricity has been around for about 50 years. In the 1890s, P. LaCour in Denmark patented a system of sails that were placed on a steel tower and powered a generator. Today, experimenters have replaced the broad sails with propeller blades similar to those on airplanes. Smith and Putnam, two American engineers, have developed the first truly successful design. They have erected a twin-blade windmill near "Grandpa's Knob" in Vermont that is more efficient than any previous windmill. An era of environmentally friendly, renewable electricity could be upon us.

"Grandpa's Knob" in Vermont ▶ promises greater efficiency than any other windmill.

The history of the parachute

Leonardo da Vinci first recognized the principle of parachute descent in the 16th century, but Frenchman Louis-Sébastien Lenormand gave the first practical demonstration in 1783. His fellow countryman, André-Jacques Garnerin, made some exhibition jumps from 8,000 feet (2,400 meters) in England in 1802.

MILITARY TECHNOLOGY

Nylon is used for parachutes

The American military has adapted the synthetic fiber nylon to use for making parachutes. Parachutes have become an essential part of modern warfare, used by pilots for escaping from damaged aircraft, dropping spies behind enemy lines, and landing supplies and troops. Until now all parachutes have been made from silk spun by silk worms. Silk production is slow and costly. Nylon parachutes can be manufactured cheaply and on a massive scale to aid the Allied war effort.

A parachute canopy is made of many separate panels, which makes it extraordinarily strong, and confines any tears to only one part of the parachute. ▼

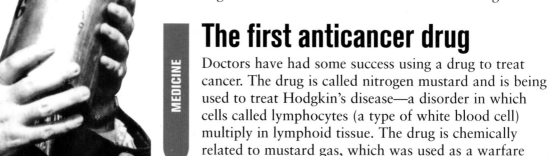

Enrico Fermi's discovery is another step toward the development of an atomic bomb, but it also has an application in the production of a new, inexpensive form of energy for the world. ▼

PHYSICS

Atomic power controlled

A team led by the Italian-American physicist Enrico Fermi has created the first sustained and controlled generation of "atomic power" by means of a nuclear chain reaction—one based on uranium atoms fissioning (splitting) and releasing neutrons that cause splitting of further uranium atoms. The reaction was made to take place in a pile of uranium and graphite bricks, interspersed with cadmium control rods. As the control rods were gradually withdrawn, the number of free neutrons (a type of subatomic particle) shooting around the pile were monitored. At a precise point predicted by Fermi, the neutron activity took off on an exponential (constant) curve, indicating that the reaction had become self-sustaining.

MEDICINE

The first anticancer drug

Doctors have had some success using a drug to treat cancer. The drug is called nitrogen mustard and is being used to treat Hodgkin's disease—a disorder in which cells called lymphocytes (a type of white blood cell) multiply in lymphoid tissue. The drug is chemically related to mustard gas, which was used as a warfare agent in World War I. When doctors examined WWI soldiers who had been exposed to mustard gas, they discovered the soldiers had reduced numbers of white blood cells, especially lymphocytes. Now nitrogen mustard has been found to have a similar effect.

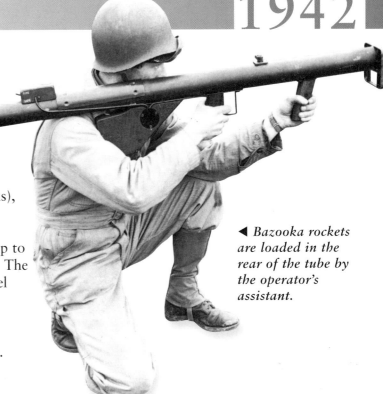

Tank-buster launched

MILITARY TECHNOLOGY

In North Africa this year, American infantry gave German tanks an unpleasant surprise by using the new M9A1 Rocket Launcher against them. Popularly nicknamed the "bazooka" by American soldiers (after a crude horn used by radio comedian Bob Burns), the handheld antitank weapon gives the ordinary foot soldier the power to fight back against the previously indestructible tank. The bazooka can be used at ranges of up to a few hundred yards to attack tanks and fortified positions. The weapon consists of a five-foot- (1.5-meter-) long hollow steel tube, equipped with a hand grip, shoulder rest, sights, and trigger mechanism. It fires a 3.5 pound (1.5 kilogram), 20-inch (50-centimeter) long rocket, which contains an explosive powerful enough to penetrate most armor plating.

◀ *Bazooka rockets are loaded in the rear of the tube by the operator's assistant.*

Science News 1942

- Napalm (a substance designed to start fires) is developed by U.S. military scientists at Harvard University.

- Italian microbiologist Salvador Luria takes the first good electron photomicrograph images of bacteriophage.

- T-shirts are made for U.S. Navy sailors.

Alaska Highway completed

TRANSPORTATION

The only major land route from Alaska to Canada and the rest of the United States has been completed after eight months' work. The federal government has built the road to transport military supplies. The Alaska Highway connects Fairbanks in central Alaska to Dawson Creek on the western edge of British Columbia, Canada. It is 1,523 miles (2,451 kilometers) long, of which 600 miles (970 kilometers) are in British Columbia, and it connects with all other major highways in the state.

T-34 turns the tide

MILITARY TECHNOLOGY

Following the success of German tank tactics in France and Russia, the Red Army has responded this year by rearming its T-34 tank with a new, long-barreled 75 millimeter gun. First sent into action on the Eastern Front last year, many experts consider the T-34 the most versatile tank ever devised. It is good in rough terrain and can maintain high speeds across country. The T-34 is driven by a 500 horsepower engine that can reach speeds of 32 miles (55 kilometers) per hour, and has a simple construction that is easy for the four-man crew to repair. Armed with the new 75 millimeter gun and two machine guns, and protected by thick armor plating, the T-34 is capable of taking on the German panzers (tanks) and winning.

◀ *Hundreds of T-34s are being used in the desperate fighting at Stalingrad, where the Russians hope to stem the German advance.*

Enigma codes

Enigma was the code name for the coding machine designed and patented by Dutchman H.A. Koch in 1919. In 1929, the German army bought what they thought was an unbreakable coding system. After the outbreak of war in 1939, hundreds of Allied mathematicians were given the task of attempting to break the code. To help them figure out the trillions of possible combinations, they used electromechanical devices, which were the forerunners of electronic computers. After the code had been broken, the Allies used the decrypted messages to outmaneuver the Germans.

COMPUTERS

New machine breaks German super code

Every day, the German armed forces send thousands of coded communications across Europe using a device known as Enigma. To decipher the encrypted messages, British scientists at Bletchley Park have developed an electronic decoder named "Colossus." Colossus contains 2,400 vacuum tubes and fills four tall electronic racks. The coded communications are fed into Colossus using punched tape; Colossus then reads through each message many times, comparing the message to known Enigma codes, until it comes up with a match and prints out the decoded information.

▲ *Colossus is no genius; it deciphers each code using sheer speed—it can process 25,000 letters a second.*

MEDICINE

Streptomycin, the new antibiotic

Following the success of penicillin, American biochemist Selman Waksman has discovered another promising agent for combating infectious diseases. The new "antibiotic," as Waksman calls it, has been given the name streptomycin. Like penicillin, it's a natural substance made by a microbe—*Streptomyces griseus*. All bacteria fall into two groups: gram positive and gram negative. Penicillin is excellent for killing gram-positive bacteria, but it seems to have no effect on the gram-negative ones, which include the germs responsible for tuberculosis and typhoid fever. Happily, streptomycin kills these gram-negative bacteria so it complements penicillin perfectly.

MILITARY TECHNOLOGY

Dams busted

On May 17, British Royal Airforce Lancaster heavy bombers from 617 Squadron breached the dams at Moehne, Eder, and Sorpe in the Ruhr valley, causing extensive flooding to this vital industrial area of Nazi Germany. Flying in under cover of darkness, the bombers were able to destroy the dams using a revolutionary new type of explosive device, the "bouncing bomb." Dropped from a low altitude, the barrel-shaped bombs were designed to rotate while falling through the air so that when they hit the water, they skipped across the surface in a bouncing motion until impacting against the dam wall.

The bouncing bombs were developed by Neville Barnes Wallis, a British aeronautical engineer. ▶

The first answering machine

As telephone usage spreads throughout the world, more and more people are worried about what will happen if they do not get an important call. Businesses are especially concerned that they will miss a vital deal or a new order. The solution is a new machine invented in Switzerland, which can answer the telephone automatically when you are out. At the heart of the machine is steel tape-recording technology. The user records a message on the tape and connects it to the phone. From then on, anyone who calls will hear this announcement. After a prompt, the caller can leave his or her own message, which may be played back when the recipient arrives home.

◄ *The miniature Minox camera is small enough to hide in the palm of the hand.*

Science News 1943

- In Great Britain, the first prestamped aerograms are introduced.

- A volcano appears suddenly in a field close to the town of Parícutan in Mexico, growing to a height of 500 feet (150 meters) within a few days.

- The Thornycroft *Terrapin 1*, an amphibious tank, is tested in Great Britain.

I spy, with my little eye …

Miniature cameras are proving to be a valuable asset for both the Allies and Germans in this fourth year of the war. Used by spies and intelligence agents on all sides, the Latvian-made Minox® camera is small enough to hide in the palm of the hand. The Ur-Minox was first produced in 1938 by Walter Zapp, as a pocket-size camera for the general user. However, intelligence services were quick to realize its suitability for espionage, and now agents of all nationalities and affiliations carry this essential piece of equipment. The only real problem with the Minox is the tiny size of its negatives, which have to be enlarged 25 times to be read. Even the smallest speck of dust on the film might obscure a vital word.

Cousteau introduces "Aqua-Lung"

French naval captain Jacques-Yves Cousteau has created a device that allows divers to swim and breathe underwater without any need for a line to the surface. The device is called an "Aqua-Lung." The first working model of the device has already been built and tested by Cousteau and Emile Gagnan, a Parisian expert on industrial gas equipment. It consists of a cylinder of compressed air, which the diver wears strapped to the back, a special valve that controls the flow of air from the cylinder, and two rubber air hoses that run from the valve to a mouthpiece, which the diver clenches between his or her teeth. The valve delivers air only when the diver breathes in, and it supplies the air to the diver's lungs at exactly the same pressure as the external water pressure.

Captain Cousteau demonstrates his "Aqua-Lung." ▶

A GLANCE AT THE PAST

The history of the rocket

In 1232, the Chinese first fired gunpowder encased in paper tubes at invading Mongols. In 1792, Indian prince Tippu Sultan fired rockets at the British Army. This led Englishman William Congreve to develop a rocket with a metal body (*above*) that was used to bombard French ports in the Napoleonic Wars. Later, British engineer William Hale improved the accuracy of rockets. They were used by the U.S. Army in the Mexican War and the Civil War.

Titan appears orange through a telescope. ▼

MILITARY TECHNOLOGY

Rocket bomb launched

The Nazis have launched the first rocket-propelled missile, the A-4 V2 "vengeance weapon," against Allied cities. After years of trials led by German scientist Werner von Braun, the gasoline-fueled rocket follows the V1 flying bomb. Nicknamed "the doodlebug," the V1 was used earlier this year, but because of its slow speed and poor guidance system, it was easily shot down and often missed its target. The Germans are now bombing London and Allied-occupied Antwerp with the much faster and more accurate V2.

▲ *The V2 dives toward its target at a rate faster than the speed of sound—the screaming descent is heard only after the explosion.*

ASTRONOMY

Titan has atmosphere

Dutch-American astronomer Gerard Kuiper has proved that Titan, the largest moon of Saturn, has an atmosphere—unlike any other moon in the solar system—and that it consists at least partly of the simple hydrocarbon gas, methane. Kuiper's findings come from spectroscopic analysis of sunlight reflected from Titan. This shows a band of light absorption strongly indicating the presence of methane, and another suggesting the presence of ammonia. Other gases, such as nitrogen, may also be present.

Science News 1944

- The first plastic artifical eyes are manufactured in the United States.

- In Great Britain, chemists develop chromatography, a technique used to separate mixtures of liquids or gases.

- Germany introduces postal codes to help make mail delivery more efficient.

BIOLOGY

DNA is life's "super-molecule"

For years, scientists have been searching for the substance that encodes genes—a "super-molecule" that controls the biological characteristics of all living organisms. Now an American bacteriologist, Oswald T. Avery, of the Rockefeller Institute Hospital in New York, has shown that the molecule responsible is a substance called deoxyribonucleic acid, or DNA. So far, little is known about the structure of DNA or how it encodes the information that determines biological characteristics.

TRANSPORTATION

First mass-produced helicopter

Igor Sikorsky has improved the VS 300, which was first test-flown in 1939, with the launch of the new VS 316 (R-4). An enclosed cockpit to protect the pilot and adjustable pitch for the rotor blades make it much easier to maneuver than earlier machines. United States naval chiefs and the Coast Guard see the potential of the new helicopter for rescuing people, reconnaissance, and the delivery of supplies to otherwise inaccessible places. Mass production was set up for military requirements in 1942 and the first large batches have been delivered this year.

▲ *The VS 316 (R-4) is the world's first mass-produced helicopter.*

Igor Sikorsky
b. 1889 d. 1972

Born in Kiev in Tsarist Ukraine, Igor Sikorsky was interested in flying machines from an early age. Sikorsky trained in the Russian Naval Academy, before resigning to pursue his own research. He designed a number of fixed-wing airplanes, and his S-1 biplane was tested in 1910. He emigrated to the United States in 1919. By the late 1930s, Sikorsky was producing aircraft at his factory in Connecticut for the United Aircraft Corporation. With a well-trained engineering team behind him, he returned to his first love, the helicopter, and in 1939, the VS-300 successfully completed its first test flight.

ZOOLOGY

Desert reptiles stay cool

In their book, *Thermal Requirements of Desert Reptiles*, U.S. zoologists Raymond Cowles and Charles Bogert have revolutionized scientific understanding of so-called "cold-blooded" animals, such as reptiles. Previously, it was thought that a lack of "warm blood" (the ability to generate heat internally) made reptiles assume the body temperature of their environment. However, Cowles and Bogert have discovered that desert reptiles actually regulate their body temperatures through their behavior. For example, during cool periods, they increase their heat absorption by maximizing the surface areas of their bodies exposed to the Sun's rays. Once the air heats up, they stay cool by seeking out the shade, panting, and even by changing their color.

◀ *In the desert, reptiles such as this Sahara sand viper can regulate their own body temperature.*

ASTRONOMY

Solar system formed from clouds of gas

German physicist Carl von Weizsacker has proposed a new model of how the solar system was formed. This has been a puzzle for centuries, as none of the numerous theories previously put forward has convinced a majority of scientists. Weizsacker's theory looks like it may be more acceptable. It proposes that the solar system started from a large, slowly swirling cloud of gas and dust within our galaxy that gradually contracted, as a result of gravitational forces, into a spinning disk. A central region, being more dense, contracted more rapidly and formed the Sun. Around this, a thin dust disk and a thicker gas disk rotated. Within these disks, particles of dust and gas built up to form the rocky inner planets, like Earth and Mars, and gaseous outer planets, like Jupiter. Once the Sun started to produce its own energy, the radiation blew away the remaining dust and gas, resulting in the solar system as it is today.

A GLANCE AT THE PAST

Cells are life's building blocks

The recognition that cells are the building blocks of animals and plants dates from the 1830s. In 1835, the Czech physiologist Jan Purkinje, looking through a microscope, noted that animal tissues are, like plant tissues, made from cells. Two German scientists investigated further. In 1838, the botanist Matthias Schleiden recognized that cells are the fundamental components of plants, and in 1839 the biologist Theodor Schwann extended this cellular theory to animal cells. The Schleiden–Schwann theory was the name given to cellular theory for many years. (The image above shows cells in the skin of an onion.)

BIOLOGY

Living cells have a complex internal structure

The electron microscope is revolutionizing our understanding of how living organisms are organized at the subcellular level. The Belgian-American scientist Albert Claude, working at the Rockefeller Institute for Medical Research in New York City, has recently completed electron microscope studies of many different types of animal and plant cells, and announced not only that cells contain a variety of substructures (called organelles) but that these substructures themselves often have a complex internal organization as well.

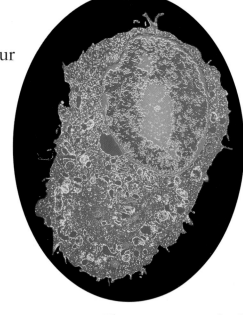

▲ *Electron micrograph of a single mammalian cell.*

COMMUNICATIONS

Arthur C. Clarke proposes telecommunication satellites

In an article published in *Wireless World*, the science fiction writer Arthur C. Clarke has come up with a proposal for a global radio and telecommunications service. It involves using rockets to place artificial satellite stations in "geosynchronous orbit." This means the satellites would be positioned about 26,250 miles (42,250 kilometers) above the equator, where they would orbit Earth once every 24 hours—exactly the time it takes for Earth to rotate once on its own axis. As a result, each satellite would appear fixed in the sky from half of Earth's surface. Clarke realizes many people will consider his proposals far-fetched, but says they are just a "logical extension of developments in the last 10 years."

COMPUTERS

"Computer bug" discovered

Mathematician Grace Murray Hopper has discovered the "computer bug." A lieutenant in the U.S. Navy, she has been working at Harvard University on the IBM Mark I, the first large-scale automatic calculator. Recently the Mark I unexpectedly broke down after several weeks of running smoothly. After opening up the machine, Hopper attempted to track down the source of the problem—she discovered that a moth had infiltrated into the heart of the machine and caused a short circuit.

◀ *Grace Murray Hopper has coined the term "bug" to refer to all unexplained computer failures.*

The atomic bomb dropped on Hiroshima decimated two-thirds of the city. ▶

ENIAC computer

COMPUTERS

Engineers at the Moore School of Electrical Engineering at the University of Pennsylvania have developed the first all-purpose digital electronic computer. The machine is called ENIAC (standing for electronic numerical integrator and computer,) and it is a monster, filling an entire room. It weighs 30 tons (27 metric tonnes,) consumes 200 kilowatts of power, and generates vast quantities of heat. The computer has been built for the U.S. War department to perform complex calculations in ballistics—the science of firing missiles in the right direction so that they will hit their targets. ENIAC has been designed and built by Dr. Presper Eckert and Dr. John Mauchly. Vacuum tubes, over 19,000 of them, are the principal elements in the computer's circuitry.

Japanese cities devastated

MILITARY TECHNOLOGY

The most powerful weapon known to humanity—the nuclear bomb—has just been used by the Americans to end the war in the Pacific. Allied scientists, led by Edward Teller, Enrico Fermi, and J.R. Oppenheimer, have been working since 1941 to develop a nuclear explosive device ahead of the Germans. After billions of dollars was spent on research, a small plutonium bomb was successfully exploded on July 17 in the desert in New Mexico. Following calls for the Japanese to surrender, on August 6, a single uranium bomb, "Little Boy," was air-burst 900 feet (275 meters) above the city of Hiroshima. Analysts estimate that half of Hiroshima's 350,000 inhabitants will be dead by the end of the year from exposure to radiation. Three days later, an American B-52 bomber air-burst a plutonium bomb, nicknamed "Fat Man," 1,650 feet (500 meters) above the city of Nagasaki, causing terrible devastation and killing an estimated 70,000 people.

Science News 1945

- Airline passengers are offered precooked frozen meals for the first time, courtesy of Maxson, a company in the United States.

- The first influenza vaccine is tested on U.S. army soldiers.

- The sunflower is developed as an oil-producing crop in Great Britain.

Fluoridation of water

MEDICINE

The citizens of Grand Rapids, Michigan, are to be subjected to an experiment sponsored by the U.S. Surgeon General: A chemical, fluoride, has been added to the city's water supply to see if it reduces the incidence of dental caries (tooth decay) in the town's children. In 1936, Dr. H. Trendley Dean, head of the dental hygiene unit at the National Institute of Health (NIH), speculated that adding fluoride to drinking water at safe levels might help fight tooth decay. Now, his ideas are to be tested.

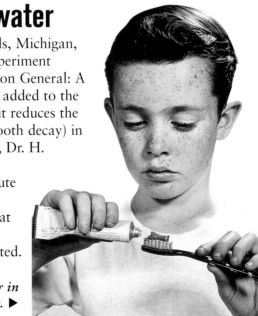

Fluoride is to be added to water in an attempt to fight tooth decay. ▶

A.D. 690	1792	1806	1903	1926
A Chinese book on warfare gives details of the use of rockets.	*Troops armed with rockets fight the British in India.*	*The British use a powerful rocket against the French.*	*Tsiolkovsky describes how a rocket could take humans into space.*	*The first successful liquid-fueled rocket is launched by Goddard.*

ROCKETRY

Although rockets have been with us for thousands of years, it was the introduction of liquid fuels in the twentieth century that led to space travel. The explosive combination of liquid oxygen and liquid hydrogen or kerosene gave humans the power to break free of Earth's gravity for the first time.

Driven on by the rivalry between the United States and the Soviet Union, rocket development soared in the 1960s. By the end of the century, rocketry had become big business and former rivals were working together to build better, cheaper launch vehicles.

One of Goddard's L-series rockets. ▲

First in space

On April 12, 1961, Yuri Gagarin became the first person in space. After traveling once around Earth, he reentered the atmosphere and ejected from his *Vostok* spacecraft to land by parachute. The whole flight took just 108 minutes. One month later, the United States was able to put a human into space when Alan Shepard was sent on a 15-minute flight in his *Mercury* spacecraft. By the following year, the United States, too, had put an astronaut into orbit.

Goddard's rockets

In March 1926, Dr. Robert Goddard launched the first successful liquid-fueled rocket at Auburn, Massachusetts. The first step toward outer space was a small one. The rocket flew for just 2.5 seconds, reached a height of 41 feet (12.5 meters) and landed 184 feet (56.1 meters) away. Goddard went on to solve many of the problems of rocket flight with a series of increasingly sophisticated devices like the L-series of the late 1930s.

◄ Vostok 1 *blasts into space on top of its Korolev-designed* A2 *rocket.*

Brilliant engineer

While Yuri Gagarin shot to fame as the first human in space, the engineer behind the achievement was known to most of the world simply as the "Chief Designer." Sergei Korolev dreamed of space flight from an early age and along with fellow enthusiasts started to build rockets in the 1930s. Thirty years later, he had become the Soviet Union's leading rocket expert.

◄ *Gagarin* (far left) *and Korolev.*

1944	1957	1961	1969	1998
A German V2 rocket launched from Holland explodes in London.	The Soviet Union launches the first artificial satellite, Sputnik 1.	Yuri Gagarin becomes the first person in space.	Neil Armstrong is the first person on the Moon.	The U.S. Halo rocket, built by amateurs, almost reaches outer space.

◄ *Von Braun.*

Rocket man

Werner von Braun was a visionary of space exploration. His career began when he helped other enthusiasts to build rockets in the 1930s. Experience gained in building Germany's war rockets took him to the United States where he became the driving force behind the U.S. space program in the 1950s and 1960s.

How a liquid-fueled rocket works

A rocket is a straightforward means of propulsion. Hot gas is thrown out in one direction and the rocket moves in the opposite direction—a perfect example of Newton's third law of motion: "To every action there is always an opposed and equal reaction." Unlike a jet engine that uses oxygen from the air to burn with its fuel, a rocket engine needs to carry its own supply of oxygen. Fuel and oxygen are carried in separate tanks then pumped to a combustion chamber where they are mixed together and burned.

▶ **Fuel**
Hydrogen (fuel) and oxygen (oxidizer) are stored in liquid form by keeping them very cold. If stored as gas, they would need much bigger tanks.

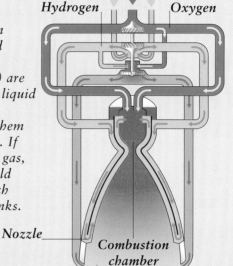

From fuel tanks

Hydrogen   *Oxygen*

Nozzle

Combustion chamber

Hot gas

◄ **Turbopumps**
These draw the hydrogen and oxygen from the fuel tanks.

◄ **Combustion chamber**
Liquid oxygen is mixed with liquid hydrogen.

◄ **Nozzle**
This is shaped to smooth the flow of hot gas. Liquid hydrogen is pumped round the nozzle to keep it cool.

Shuttle to space

The space shuttle was the world's first reusable space craft. Designed to cut the cost of space flight, it proved even more expensive than disposable rockets. The cost of reconditioning the shuttles between flights was much higher than predicted. But the shuttle can do things that disposable rockets cannot do—flying repair missions and even returning satellites to Earth. The shuttle continues to play an important role in the building of the International Space Station.

◄ *The space shuttle takes off.*

Early particle accelerators

The first workable particle accelerator was developed by the American physicist Ernest Lawrence (*above*) in 1931. His machine accelerated particles along a spiral path and was called a cyclotron. In 1932, Cambridge physicists made the first major scientific breakthrough with an accelerator when they used high-speed protons to "split" the nuclei of lithium atoms. Their machine accelerated the protons along a straight line and was called a linear accelerator. The particles produced by these early accelerators were much less energetic than those produced by the 1946 synchrocyclotron.

PHYSICS

New atom smasher in California

A new type of particle accelerator, called a synchrocyclotron, has been built at the University of California at Berkeley. Like all particle accelerators, it is a machine that produces a beam of fast-moving, electrically charged, subatomic particles using electric and magnetic fields. The particles are smashed into target atoms, or made to interact with other particle beams, for purposes of atomic research or to create new particles.

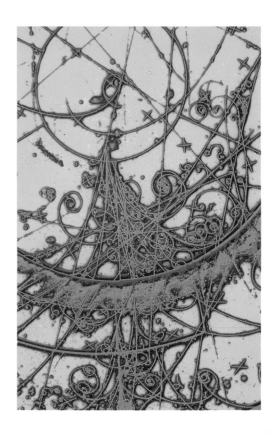

Particle paths in a bubble chamber ▶ following collisions of accelerated particles.

ARCHAEOLOGY

Carbon-14 dating developed

A new method of determining the age of fossils and archaeological specimens has been developed by American chemist Willard F. Libby. Known as "carbon-14 dating," the method depends on measuring the decay to nitrogen of radiocarbon in carbon-containing materials. Radiocarbon (carbon 14) is a radioactive form of carbon that forms a small part of the carbon in Earth's atmosphere. It is produced by the effects of cosmic radiation on the atmosphere, and so is continuously forming and decaying. All life-forms are carbon-based, and take in fresh carbon until their death. Libby discovered that when things die, the radiocarbon they contain decays at a given rate. By measuring the amount of radiocarbon in organic materials—such as bones, shells, charcoal, and wood—scientists can now determine when death occurred.

EARTH SCIENCE

The first artificial snowstorm

American chemist Vincent Schaefer has created an artificial snowstorm—the first time someone has manipulated the weather. Schaefer was researching the problem of ice forming on aircraft wings. He found that this occurs when aircraft fly through "supercooled" clouds—air, heavy with water vapor, that has cooled below the freezing point. Under these conditions, ice crystals form rapidly. In his laboratory, Schaefer discovered that pellets of dry ice also cause ice crystals to form. In an experiment, he scattered dry-ice pellets from a plane flying through clouds over Massachusetts. A snowstorm resulted.

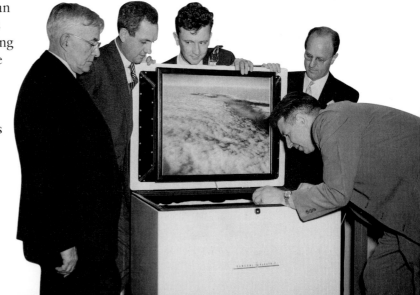

Dr. Schaefer (far right) *demonstrates how to make snow in a home freezer.* ▶

How enzymes work

BIOLOGY

The renowned American chemist Linus Pauling has come up with a theory for how enzymes—special proteins that cause chemical reactions within living organisms—actually work. According to Pauling, it's got to do with enzyme shapes. Like most proteins, enzyme molecules are large and have complex but precise three-dimensional shapes. Pauling believes that these shapes are complementary to the shapes of "activated complexes" that form momentarily during chemical reactions as the reacting substances transform into products. In other words, during the course of a reaction, the reacting substances take up a molecular configuration that fits the shape of an enzyme like a hand fits a glove. Pauling says that by providing a stable environment for activated complexes to form, enzymes lower the energy required for a reaction to proceed, and this speeds up the reaction.

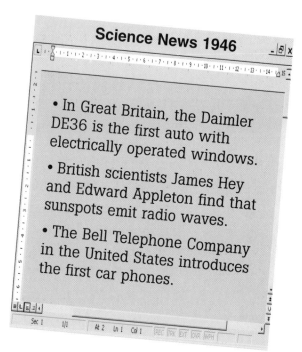

Science News 1946

- In Great Britain, the Daimler DE36 is the first auto with electrically operated windows.

- British scientists James Hey and Edward Appleton find that sunspots emit radio waves.

- The Bell Telephone Company in the United States introduces the first car phones.

Fossil ▲ of a soft-bodied animal found in the Ediacaran hills.

Ancient fossils found in South Australia

PALEONTOLOGY

An Australian geologist, Reg Sprigg, has made a remarkable discovery of some extremely ancient fossils in the Ediacaran hills of South Australia. The fossils consist of variously shaped blobs, ribbed fronds, and ribbons impressed in some sandstone rocks. They range from about half an inch to 3.3 feet (13 millimeters to one meter) in length and are believed to be the remains of soft-bodied animals, such as jellyfish, worms, and frondlike corals, that lived in shallow-water seas some 550 million years ago. This discovery has changed scientists' views of ancient life dramatically, providing the first convincing evidence that multicellular animals existed as far back as the Precambrian era (prior to 545 million years ago).

Espresso machine helps keep you awake

HOME APPLIANCES

Italian inventor Achille Gaggia has perfected a so-called espresso machine for making coffee. The machine uses lever action to force highly heated or boiling water through finely ground, roasted coffee beans, which are compressed in a special compartment. The water passes through the packed grains to produce an intensely strong cup of black coffee, ideal for digestion after a heavy meal or for keeping you awake. This method of making coffee dates back to the early nineteenth century. One of the first steam-powered espresso machines was demonstrated at the Paris Exhibition in 1855. It was said to produce 1,000 cups an hour but tended to blow up from time to time. Being steamless, Gaggia's machine avoids this problem.

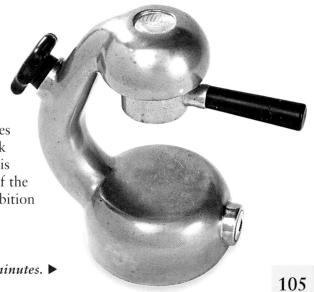

An espresso maker produces strong, high-quality coffee in just a few minutes. ▶

A GLANCE AT
THE PAST

Sperry's autopilot

American inventor Elmer Ambrose Sperry (*above*) first came up with the idea of a gyrostabilizer for airplanes in 1914. The earliest successful device was a row of small gyroscopes, each connected to one of the plane's controls. He demonstrated his invention at Bezons, near Paris. Sperry's son, Lawrence, took off over the Seine, stood up in the cockpit, and held his hands in the air to show he was not controlling the plane. His mechanic walked out over the wing, and the plane stayed level with the horizon.

TRANSPORTATION

Plane crosses Atlantic on autopilot

A United States Air Force C-54 Skymaster transport has flown itself across the Atlantic, guided by its autopilot—a gyrostabilizing system built from a series of gyroscopes that automatically adjust the plane's instruments to follow a preprogramed flight path. The autopilot was first used in 1929, but this is the first time such a huge plane—the C-54 has a 117-foot 6-inch (35.9-meter) wingspan—has used the system for a journey of this length.

▲ *Pilots refer to their autopilots as "George."*

ARCHAEOLOGY

Dead Sea scrolls found in cave

A Bedouin shepherd searching for his lost sheep has found jars containing seven ancient scrolls in a cave near Qumran, by the Dead Sea in Palestine. Scholars have been astonished to discover that the scrolls include the oldest copy of the biblical scripture of Isaiah ever found. The sacred texts were written on leather or papyrus and wrapped in linen cloth thousands of years ago. Experts estimate the manuscripts were written sometime between the third century B.C. and 68 A.D. by a Jewish monastic group, the Essene sect.

◀ *The Great Isaiah Scroll.*

COMMUNICATIONS

Photos in 10 seconds!

American inventor Edwin Land has produced a camera that develops its own pictures—instantly! Land's work is based on research begun by the Agfa photographic company in the 1920s. The camera uses a special film with two thin layers of chemicals, one sensitive to light, the other a developer. When you take a picture, the light-sensitive chemicals are exposed in the normal way. The film is pushed through a pair of rollers, releasing the second layer of chemicals, which develop the film.

Edwin Land's camera produces mono images in around 10 seconds. ▶

▲ *The rocket-powered Bell X-1 is painted bright orange for easier visibility from the ground.*

Plane breaks sound barrier

United States Air Force Captain Charles E. (Chuck) Yeager has broken the sound barrier by taking his Bell X-1 airplane to Mach 1.06 (700 miles per hour; 1,120 kilometers per hour) at Muroc Dry Lake, California. The specially built plane is shaped like a bullet, with wings sharpened to a razor edge. Its four-chamber rocket XLR-11 engine, nicknamed "Black Betsy," is fueled by a mixture of liquid oxygen and dilute ethyl alcohol. The little plane, with the pilot in the cockpit, is carried up in a B-59 bomber, then released at 20,000 feet (6,096 meters), when the pilot ignites the rockets one at a time.

Science News 1947

- In the United States, the first tubeless tires are introduced by Goodyear.

- The first microwave ovens go on sale in the United States, but they fail to make any impact on the public.

- In China, a typewriter is produced that has 5,400 characters.

Bacterial mating discovered

Life-forms as simple as bacteria can mate with each other and exchange genetic material, according to biologists at Yale University. Ed Tatum and Joshua Lederberg made the discovery from studying the bacterium *E. coli*. They cultured two strains of the bacteria that differed in their nutritional needs. When the two strains were mixed and raised together, new strains emerged that had acquired properties of both of the originals—the only possible explanation is that genes must have passed between individual bacteria in the mixture. Pairs of bacterial cells must have literally "cuddled up" to each other so that deoxyribonucleic acid, or DNA (a genetic material), could be injected from one of the pair into the other. The scientists are calling the process "bacterial conjugation."

Dinosaur graveyard found in New Mexico

Paleontologists from the American Museum of Natural History have discovered dozens of fossilized dinosaur skeletons at a place called Ghost Ranch in northern New Mexico. It is one of the largest collections of dinosaur deposits ever discovered. The dinosaurs are all of the same species named *Coelophysis*—a long-legged, fast-moving predatory carnivore, believed to have lived 220 million years ago. The deposit includes well-preserved specimens of various sizes, from hatchlings less than three feet (91 centimeters) long to fully grown adults up to 10 feet (3.05 meters) long. One academic, Dr. Edwin H. Colbert, believes the dinosaurs must have died together.

◀ *Two of the fossilized* Coelophysis *skeletons.*

A GLANCE AT THE PAST

The original contact lenses

The first artificial lens worn on the surface of the eye was developed by Adolf Fick in 1887. Made of glass, it was developed to correct irregular astigmatism—defects in the lens of the eye. These early lenses were uncomfortable and could not be worn for long. The lens covered the whole of the eye and the discomfort was caused by the fact that oxygen could not reach the surface of the eye. The original contact lens had only limited use.

With larger screens, the whole family can gather around the television. ▼

MEDICINE

New easier-to-wear contact lens developed

To date there has been little alternative for anyone suffering from defects of vision than to wear eyeglasses. But a practical contact lens has been developed by U.S. optician Kevin Tuohy; its practicality stems from the fact that it is made of plastic rather than glass. Tuohy's new lens allows more oxygen to reach the eye as it only covers the iris and pupil rather than the whole of the eye. While the wear time has been extended, the lens still causes irritation and requires a period of adaptation when first worn.

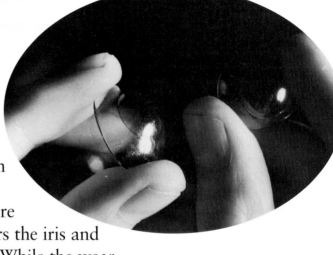

▲ *This new plastic contact lens covers only the iris and pupil.*

PALEONTOLOGY

Fossil ape skull discovered

The fossilized skull of an 18-million-year-old extinct ape has been found on Rusinga Island in Lake Victoria, Kenya. It is the only ape skull of such an age ever found, although other parts of the skeleton of the same ape, called *Proconsul*, have been found within the same area of Africa. Intriguingly, the skull displays some hominoid (humanlike) features. This suggests that *Proconsul* may have been closely related to the ancestors of humans—in other words, it is close to being a "missing link" between apes and humans. The find was made by the British-Kenyan anthropologists Mary and Louis Leakey. Mrs. Leakey was the first to see some small fragments of the skull, where they had been washed out on the slope of a gully that she was exploring. She directed the attention of her husband to the fragment. Cutting back into the slope, he brought this unique fossil to light.

ENTERTAINMENT

TV explodes in popularity

Television, the great entertainment invention of the 1920s and 1930s, suffered a severe setback during World War II—but now it is alive and kicking again. Most European countries stopped TV broadcasts during the war, while production of TV sets ceased in the United States due to the war effort. Now the first post-war Olympics are being held in London and the games are being broadcast. Suddenly, everyone who can afford it wants a television set, and sales are booming. Many people are upgrading their TV receivers, going for bigger screens so that the whole family can gather around the set. There are today almost one million TV receivers in the United States and there are 46 commercial TV stations, with a further 78 under construction.

Computers to have magnetic memories

Computers can now perform thousands of calculations every second. Many of these complex calculations require the machine to store numbers to be used later. Until recently the most successful form of memory has used cathode ray tubes or CRTs; these tubes are similar to those found in the new television sets. The numbers are stored as spots on the screen but this method is rather fickle, with bits of information frequently being dropped. A new form of fast, reliable magnetic drum memory looks set to replace CRTs. This technology has the potential to provide inexpensive large-capacity memories. A magnetic drum is simply a cylinder whose surface is coated with a material that can be magnetized.

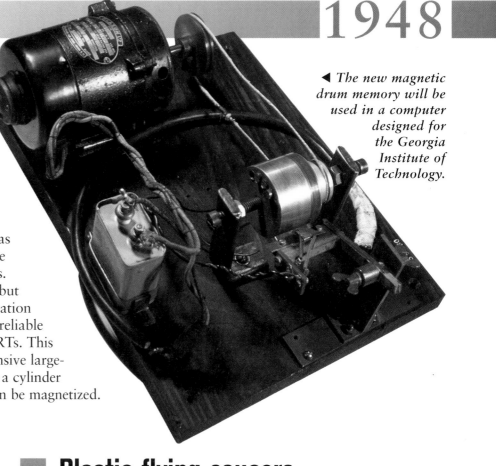

◄ *The new magnetic drum memory will be used in a computer designed for the Georgia Institute of Technology.*

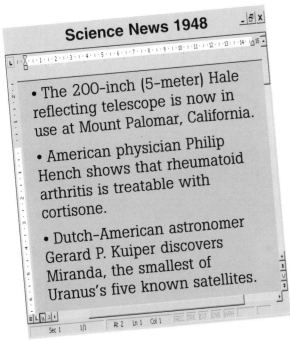

Science News 1948

- The 200-inch (5-meter) Hale reflecting telescope is now in use at Mount Palomar, California.

- American physician Philip Hench shows that rheumatoid arthritis is treatable with cortisone.

- Dutch–American astronomer Gerard P. Kuiper discovers Miranda, the smallest of Uranus's five known satellites.

Plastic flying saucers

"Flying saucers" have been hitting the headlines recently, but now a Utah-born carpenter, Fred Morrison, has invented a plastic version—as a recreational toy for tossing from one person to another. Morrison started by taking a pie tin and welding a steel ring inside the rim to improve its aerodynamic stability. The result didn't fly too well, so Morrison and a friend, Warren Francioni, turned to using plastic, butyl stearate. The resulting plastic flying disk flies farther and straighter than the metal prototype but so far sales haven't taken off—perhaps a catchier name is needed. For years, students at Yale University have been throwing empty pie tins and cookie tin lids to each other on campus, yelling "Frisbie!"—after the Frisbie Pie Company—to warn bystanders. Hmmm?

Paintings safely restored

American scientists Rachel Brown and Elizabeth Hazen, who work for the New York State Department of Health, have isolated the chemical nystatin, which promises to be the first safe fungicide (an agent that kills fungi). The chemical they have isolated seems destined to be used in many different ways, most obviously to treat human diseases such as athlete's foot, which are caused by fungi. But the surprise benefit of their discovery is in the field of art restoration. Many old paintings are damaged by the growth of molds.

◄ *Nystatin can be used to kill the molds on old paintings.*

The invention of DDT

During the 18th and 19th centuries, farmers were desperate to find a means of killing crop pests. They used various methods, including nicotine and arsenic. In 1874, an Austrian student developed DDT but did not realize it could be used as a pesticide. In 1939, Swiss chemist Paul Herman Muller tested the chemical and discovered its pesticide properties. During World War II, DDT was used to kill fleas and head lice. After the war, it was sprayed on crops worldwide.

AGRICULTURE

DDT reduces pest insect population

A powerful new pesticide (a substance used to kill insect pests) is dramatically reducing the population of insects, such as the Colorado potato beetle, that destroy and damage farm crops. It was first used in Switzerland in 1939, and since 1942 has been used to spray crops in the United States as well. The pesticide is a synthetic chemical called dichloro-diphenyl-trichloroethane, called DDT for short. More effective than any pesticide known before, DDT kills in two ways—if it makes contact with any part of an insect's body, or if the insect swallows the poison.

▲ *Because it kills in two ways, DDT can destroy not only leaf-eating, crop-damaging pests but also disease-carrying insects such as mosquitoes.*

Ready-made cake mixes provide homemade cakes without the work. ▼

FOOD

Have your cake and eat it

Beating eggs, flour, butter, sugar, and flavorings by hand to make a cake is now a thing of the past. United States flour companies General Mills and Pillsbury have both introduced ready-made cake mixes with all the necessary dry ingredients already mixed together and available in a box. Both companies offer three kinds—chocolate, yellow, and white fudge cakes. You only add water, eggs, and sometimes butter, to the dry ingredients to produce a perfect cake. Earlier, in 1945, Pillsbury introduced its first convenience baking product—a ready-mixed pie crust.

MATERIALS

New diapers developed

The days of washing cloth diapers could be over! The British Robinson Company has launched the world's first disposable diaper. Called Paddi Pads, the diapers are designed to be used once and thrown away when soiled, saving time, work, and unpleasant smells. The company claims that there is another advantage. Made of highly absorbent paper, the Paddi Pads are said to soak up waste products better than normal fabric diapers, so that babies using them are less likely to get rashes.

Childproof fiber developed

Parents are going to love polyester, a new, cheap, hard-wearing synthetic fiber that may prove to be the most childproof fiber yet developed by chemists. Realizing its potential market, chemical giants are lining up to develop this new fiber and are already creating trade names such as Dacron® and Terylene®. The polyester family of fibers is made from the reaction between ethylene glycol and terephthalic acid. These fibers have many inbuilt defenses against children, in that they quickly return to their original shape even after the most vigorous of stretching and are resistant to most chemicals. An unexpected bonus for parents is that they will be able to hear their children removing their polyester clothes from many feet away. These fibers are excellent accumulators of static charge, and produce a characteristic crackling sound when clothes are taken off and dumped on the floor.

Science News 1949

- Sneakers with molded rubber soles are introduced by Adidas in Germany.
- Australian physician Frank Burnet shows that immune responses to tissue transplants are acquired during life rather than inborn.
- The first landing pad made for helicopters (the Heliport) opens in New York.

Structure of penicillin

Using the technique of X-ray analysis, and with the help of an IBM computer, English chemist Dorothy Hodgkin has determined the chemical structure of the antibiotic penicillin. Antibiotics are substances that kill disease-carrying bacteria, and penicillin was the first one to be discovered. In 1928, Alexander Fleming noticed that mold growing on a dish had killed staphylococci bacteria around it. He called the mold penicillin, but did little further research into it. In 1940, Howard Florey and Ernst Chain managed to isolate the drug, tested it on humans, and began mass production. Since then, penicillin has revolutionized medicine, providing treatment for many life-threatening infections such as pneumonia. Hodgkin's discovery now makes it possible to produce penicillin in the laboratory.

◀ *Dorothy Hodgkin took seven years to work out the chemical structure of penicillin.*

Meteoroid theory of lunar surface

In his book, *The Face of the Moon*, American astrophysicist Ralph Belknap Baldwin has put forward a convincing explanation for how the Moon acquired its distinctive surface. Baldwin believes the lunar craters were produced through bombardment by meteoroids (asteroids and comets). The Moon, he says, was formed about the same time as Earth, and not long after its formation, tremendous meteoroid impacts produced thousands of craters in its outer crust. For several hundred million years, there was widespread volcanic activity, with lava pouring out from below the crust and flooding the largest craters to produce the dark-colored basins or "maria," visible today.

Prior to Baldwin, scientists thought the Moon's craters were volcanic. ▶

1860s	1880s	1890s	1904	1906
Maxwell develops the theory of electromagnetism.	Hertz is the first person to detect and produce radio waves.	Marconi develops wireless telegraphy.	Fleming develops the first thermionic valve (diode).	Fessenden makes the first voice transmissio by AM radio.

THE RADIO STORY

Today there are more than 200,000 radio stations across the globe, transmitting news and entertainment to the world's population. It's a far cry from 1900, when radio was called "wireless telegraphy" and was restricted to sending Morse code.

The invention of an electronic component called the thermionic valve in 1904 made it possible for radio waves to carry voices and music. By the 1920s, there were radio stations in many countries, broadcasting news, music, important events, and advertisements.

▲ *Prewar radio*
This is a classic 1930s valve receiver.

How radio works

Every radio station broadcasts at a particular frequency. To understand what this means, imagine a piano keyboard. Each key produces sound at a different frequency from all the others. In a similar way (but with radio waves instead of sound) each radio station transmits its carrier signal at a different frequency. Turning the tuning dial of a radio selects just one frequency, so the listener hears just one station. In the earliest days of radio, transmitters simply produced energetic bursts of radio waves at a range of frequencies. This is like pressing down on all the keys of a piano at once. It was the invention of the thermionic valve that made it possible to produce individual carrier signals at precise frequencies and to modulate (change) the signals to carry sound.

▲ *Transistor radio*
During the 1950s an 1960s, pocket-sized s became popular.

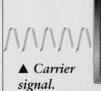

◀ **Radio station**
When a disc jockey in a radio studio talks into the microphone, his voice is turned into electric sound signals. These signals go to the transmitter via the modulator and amplifier.

Transmission tower. ▶

Modulated signal ▼
The modulator varies the carrier signal's strength (for AM or amplitude modulation) or its frequency (FM or frequency modulation).

Electric sound signal. ▶

▲ *Carrier signal.*

◀ *Modulator.*

▼ *Amplifier.*

Amplified radio signal. ▼

1907
De Forrest invents the amplifier vacuum tube (triode).

1920
First regular licensed commercial radio broadcast.

1940s
First FM radio station goes on the air.

1950s
Pocket-sized transistor radios become popular.

1990s
Digital radio is introduced.

Radio shrinkage

During the 1920s and 1930s, most households acquired radio receivers, which could be as large as a suitcase. A diode valve in the receiver demodulated the AM signals (extracted the sound information from the carrier wave) and a triode amplified the signals. After the invention of the transistor in 1948, radios shrank to briefcase-sized and then to pocket-sized. Transistors function in the same way as triodes but are smaller, use less power, and are cheaper and more reliable. Some modern radios contain silicon chips, which produce high-quality sound and help with tuning.

This tiny radio ▶ set can clip onto a jacket.

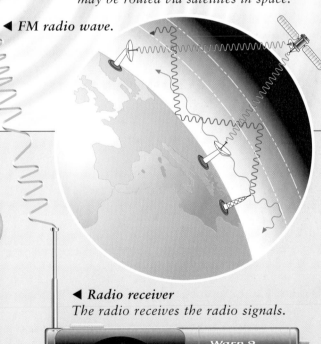

Transmitting across the world ▼
Short-wave and some medium-wave radio transmissions are reflected by layers in the atmosphere. Ultra-high frequency waves may be routed via satellites in space.

◀ FM radio wave.

◀ Radio receiver
The radio receives the radio signals.

How radio waves work

Just like light and X rays, radio waves are a form of electromagnetic radiation. They are produced by high-frequency, alternating electric currents in an antenna, and consist of oscillating electric and magnetic fields, traveling out in all directions from the antenna at the speed of light.

▲ Long wave
Low-frequency radio waves that carry AM broadcasts; also used for military communications.

▲ Medium wave
Medium-frequency radio waves. Many music radio stations broadcast using AM in the medium-wave band.

▲ Short wave
High-frequency waves used by international radio stations and amateur enthusiasts.

▲ VHF (very high frequency)
Used by popular radio stations to broadcast FM signals; also used to carry TV signals.

▲ UHF (ultra-high frequency)
Used by cellular phones and digital radio.

Invention of Silly Putty

During World War II, a shortage of rubber in the United States led to the government asking industry to research synthetic substitutes. In 1943, while working on this task at General Electric, Scottish engineer James Wright mixed some silicone oil and boric acid in a test tube. He noticed that the chemicals reacted to produce a semisolid, stretchy goo. While trying to remove this from the test tube, he accidentally dropped some on the floor and observed that it bounced. Further testing showed that while the compound didn't have a future as a synthetic rubber, it did make a great toy!

ENTERTAINMENT

Silly Putty® leaves its mark on the world

A new material has been launched across the United States. It's called Silly Putty—and, at first glance, it seems just like a type of soft, pink gooey dough. However, it has special properties—it can be stretched without breaking but can be snapped off cleanly; it bounces higher than a rubber ball; if you smash it with a hammer it keeps its shape, but gentle pressure flattens it easily.

◀ *Silly Putty is a silicone-based polymer. It is nontoxic and nonirritating to the skin.*

COMPUTERS

Credit where it's due

A small plastic card can now be used to purchase anything, with the bill simply being charged to your account. The idea has been around for decades—in the United States individual companies such as hotel chains began issuing cards that could be used at any of their outlets. However, every company had its own card and no other company would accept it. But now Diners' Club has come up with a universal credit card. Under this system, Diners' Club International charges its cardholders an annual fee and bills them on a monthly basis. All those shopkeepers who accept the card as payment also pay a service charge of about five percent of total sales. With other financial institutions soon to follow, a credit boom could send us on a huge shopping spree—unfortunately, a monthly bill will surely follow.

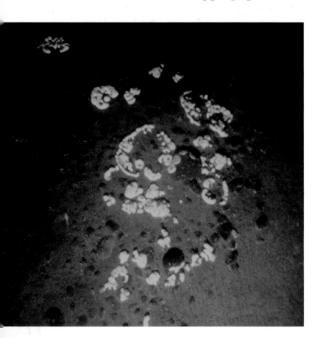

BIOLOGY

Living organisms found on the Pacific bed

Scientists aboard the Danish research vessel the *Galathea* have discovered organisms living in some of the very deepest areas of the world's oceans—more than 34,000 feet (10,360 meters) down in the Philippines trench in the Pacific. Previously, it was not thought possible that life could exist at such depths, due to the high pressure and lack of sunlight. The scientists were very surprised, therefore, when dredges that had been dropped down into the trench were hauled up and found to contain swarms of invertebrates (small animals without backbones, like worms, mollusks, and crustaceans). The *Galathea* is on a two-year voyage around the world in search of unusual organisms living in extreme conditions. It carries more than 50 scientists and is administered by the Zoological Museum of Copenhagen, Denmark.

◀ *Colony of bacteria on the floor of the Pacific Ocean.*

A GLANCE AT THE PAST

The basic chemical nature of proteins

Thomas Burr Osborne, an American chemist, carried out some early work on protein structure around the turn of the 20th century. His work demonstrated that proteins come in many different forms and that they are a source of nutrients called amino acids, some of which are essential to body functioning. Polypeptides (protein subunits) are now known to be formed from the joining together of amino acids in various combinations.

BIOLOGY

New ideas on the structure of proteins

American chemist Linus Pauling has taken an important new step toward understanding the structure of proteins—the molecules that play many roles in living organisms. Previously, Pauling established that proteins consist of "polypeptide" chains (formed from smaller units called peptides). These chains contain a backbone of carbon and nitrogen atoms, to which other chemical units, including atoms of hydrogen and oxygen, are attached. Pauling has shown how a polypeptide chain can coil up into a helix (3-D spiral)—weak bonds between the hydrogen and oxygen atoms in successive "turns" of the spiral provide stability.

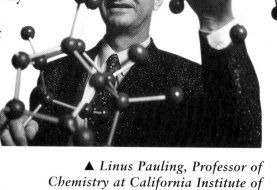

▲ *Linus Pauling, Professor of Chemistry at California Institute of Technology.*

ENTERTAINMENT

Cinerama® movies

A new kind of movie is about to stun the public. Called Cinerama, it projects films onto a semicircular surface six times bigger than a normal cinema screen. The Cinerama process involves three cameras that film the left, right, and center portions of each shot. Three matching projectors are used in the movie theater and a jagged edge where the three pictures meet obscures the joints.

In Great Britain, the "zebra" crossing aids road safety. ▼

Science News 1951

- The Chrysler automobile company introduces power steering in the United States.
- American chemist Robert Woodward synthesizes the steroid hormones cortisone and cholesterol.
- In Germany, the Tetra Pak® milk carton is introduced by Ruben Rausing.

TRANSPORTATION

Stripes and crosses

In 1934, Lord Hore Belisha, then Minister of Transport, introduced the pedestrian crossing to Great Britain. He gave his name to the bright orange beacons that stood guard on each side of the road to warn motorists of the crossing. But traffic has increased since then, and now new high-visibility, black-and-white striped crossings are being installed on the nation's major roads. Naturally, they have soon become known as "zebra" crossings. Drivers are meant to stop when they see a pedestrian set foot on one of the zebra's stripes.

A GLANCE AT
THE PAST

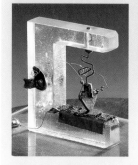

The history of the transistor

The transistor was invented In 1947 by three American physicists, John Bardeen, Walter Brittain, and William Shockley, at the Bell Telephone laboratories. It immediately proved to be a viable alternative to the vacuum tube. Transistors work by controlling electrons; they are made up of layers of silicon containing certain impurities. The impurities give the transistor its electrical properties. Transistors have played a pivotal role in the advancement of electronics due to their small size, low power consumption, and reliability. They can also be miniaturized until thousands fit onto a single computer chip.

COMMUNICATIONS

Hearing aids incorporate the new transistor

Bardeen, Brittain, and Shockley, the physicists who invented the transistor, have developed one of its first applications—a miniaturized hearing aid. For years, most hearing aids used the same basic technology as the telephone. Vacuum tubes brought electronic amplification of sound, but early models were large, expensive, and unreliable. By the 1930s, newer hearing aids were more reliable, but the problems of high power usage and large size remained. Transistors have removed these obstacles.

▲ *Hearing aids are becoming more compact. This model has the additional advantage that it can be plugged into a telephone.*

ARCHAEOLOGY

Diving gear improves

The development of improved diving gear is revolutionizing the exploration of underwater wrecks and other archaeological sites. Jacques Cousteau, the inventor of the Aqua-Lung, has introduced further innovations such as the airlift—an underwater vacuum cleaner that can be used to suck up sand and silt covering underwater sites. Already Cousteau and his diving team have unearthed the hull of an ancient Greek wine freighter, buried deep in fossil mud 60 feet (18 meters) under water off the French coast near Marseilles. The 2,000-year-old wine was intact, but undrinkable. Cousteau has now bought and equipped a research vessel, *Calypso*, a former minesweeper.

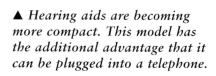

Science News 1952

- Archaeologists in Cyprus discover a 2,000-year-old mosaic depicting Homer's epic poem *The Iliad*.

- Swedish Airways flies the first passenger airliner over the North Pole.

- The United States tests a hydrogen bomb in the southern Pacific Ocean.

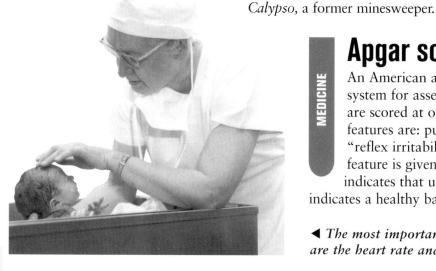

MEDICINE

Apgar score for new babies

An American anesthesiologist, Virginia Apgar, has introduced a system for assessing the health of newborn babies. Five features are scored at one minute and at five minutes after birth. The features are: pulse, muscle tone, color, respiratory effort, and "reflex irritability" (crying when pinched or poked). Each feature is given a score of 0, 1, or 2. A total score of 0 to 3 indicates that urgent resuscitation is required. A score of 7 to 10 indicates a healthy baby.

◀ *The most important features of Apgar's baby-health system are the heart rate and the infant's attempts to breathe.*

COMPUTERS

Eisenhower landslide predicted by computer

A machine has correctly predicted that Dwight Eisenhower would win the U.S. presidential election by a landslide, but no one believed it. The UNIVAC® I computer made the astonishing prediction with only seven percent of the vote counted. This high-profile role is only one of many taken up by the world's first computer designed for business use. UNIVAC I was the brainchild of John Mauchy and John Eckert, two men who share a vision of the commercial success of computers. The computer weighs more than 16,000 pounds (7,260 kilograms), uses 5,000 vacuum tubes, and can perform 1,000 calculations per second.

BIOLOGY

The brain never sleeps

Even when we're fast asleep, the brain is active. This new understanding of sleep patterns is the result of work by American Eugene Aserinsky who, together with Nathanial Kleitman, has been researching sleep. Aserinsky hooked his eight-year-old son up to an old electroencephalogram (EEG), a machine that measures brain activity. He noticed that his son's sleep patterns varied between calm periods, and active ones when his son's eyes moved rapidly under his eyelids, even though the boy was deeply asleep. Aserinsky called the active periods rapid eye movement (REM) sleep. Each REM period lasted about 20 minutes.

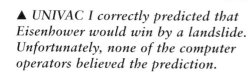

▲ *UNIVAC I correctly predicted that Eisenhower would win by a landslide. Unfortunately, none of the computer operators believed the prediction.*

ENERGY

New reactor makes more fuel than it uses

An experimental nuclear reactor that promises to produce more fuel than it uses to generate energy is up and running. This new "fast breeder" reactor has been designed and built by American scientists at the National Reactor Testing Center in Idaho. The first generation of nuclear reactors relied on the scarce uranium-235 isotope for fuel; fast breeder reactors can use uranium-238, which accounts for nearly all the uranium on Earth. In the reactor's heart, the uranium-238 fuel is converted to plutonium through neutron bombardment. When plutonium itself absorbs neutrons, it splits in two and releases energy and more neutrons. These keep the energy-producing reaction going and convert more uranium-238 to plutonium. The energy released, in the form of heat, goes on to produce steam for generators.

Decaying atoms go ▶ on to power massive steam turbines.

1953

Discovery of cosmic rays

In the 1900s, it was noticed that an unknown form of radiation was causing the formation of charged particles in the atmosphere. Initially, the radiation was thought to come from Earth. But in 1911, using a variety of instruments, Austrian physicist Victor Hess (*above*) found that the radiation's intensity increased with altitude—indicating it must come from space. In 1925, U.S. physicist Robert Millikan, who gave the radiation the name "cosmic rays," confirmed Hess's theory. The radiation is now known to consist mostly of highly energetic subatomic particles traveling through space at close to the speed of light.

PHYSICS

First pictures from a bubble chamber

The first images of cosmic ray tracks have recently been published by the American scientist Donald Glaser following his invention of the "bubble chamber"—a device capable of imaging such phenomena and also other types of subatomic interaction. The bubble chamber is a pressurized chamber filled with liquid—usually liquid hydrogen. When the pressure is released, for a few critical milliseconds the liquid hydrogen turns into an unstable "super-heated" state. During this time, tiny vapor bubbles form around the tracks of any subatomic particles speeding through the chamber.

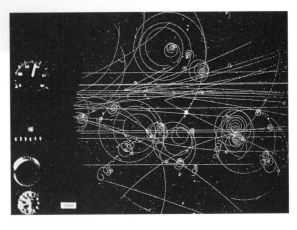

▲ *In a bubble chamber the tiny bubbles form trails, which can be photographed.*

BIOLOGY

First full chemical analysis of a protein

English biochemist Frederick Sanger has completed the first full chemical analysis of a protein—insulin—and discovered its structure. Proteins control cell activities and play an essential part in the way the body breaks down foods. Protein molecules consist of chains of important chemicals called amino acids. Sanger discovered the structure by painstakingly breaking down molecules of insulin, which is a fairly simple protein, into smaller and smaller fragments until he was able to work out the entire sequence of amino acids and the way they fit together to form chains.

ENTERTAINMENT

Color TV—yippee!

Engineers in the United States have triumphed with a fully electronic color television system—and it really works! Trial broadcasts two years ago using a "spinning disk" system were a failure. There were problems with the color sets and millions of unhappy black-and-white viewers were deprived of their old-style programs. So engineers at RCA have taken another look at color TV and have come up with a completely new camera. The invention works by adding low-definition color to a black-and-white picture.

◀ *A program being made with one of the new color TV camera systems.*

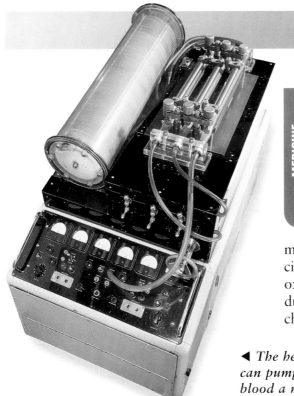

Machine keeps patient alive

MEDICINE

A previously inoperable condition has been successfully treated thanks to a revolutionary pump that can take over the function of the heart for several hours. On May 6, at the Jefferson Medical College in Philadelphia, Cecelia Bavolek's heart was stopped and a mechanical pump circulated her blood for half an hour while a team led by John Gibbon corrected a defect in the right-hand side of her heart. Developed by Gibbon, the device known as the "heart-lung" machine is a mechanical pump that maintains the patient's blood circulation during heart surgery. It diverts blood away from the heart, oxygenates it, and finally returns it to the patient. The heart, relieved of its duties, can be drained of blood and opened up, allowing defects inside the chambers to be corrected.

◀ *The heart-lung machine can pump up to five liters of blood a minute.*

Is this how life started?

BIOLOGY

Stanley Miller, an American biochemistry student, has demonstrated that a number of different biological molecules can be formed when an electric current, simulating lightning, is passed through a mixture of simple substances that would have been present in Earth's early oceans and atmosphere. Miller stirred a mixture of sterilized water, hydrogen, methane, and ammonia for a week, and subjected it to the occasional electrical discharge. Afterwards, Miller analyzed his "primordial soup" and found that it contained three different amino acids—organic substances that join up to make proteins. If Miller can create three amino acids in a week, it is argued that whole proteins could have arisen in Earth's ancient oceans over millions of years.

Science News 1953

- Radial tires are introduced by Michelin of France and Pirelli of Italy.

- American physicist Charles H. Townes invents the maser, a forerunner of the laser.

- South African James Smith acquires the second specimen of the thought-to-be extinct coelacanth fish in the Comoros Islands.

Structure of DNA discovered

BIOLOGY

Two Cambridge University scientists have discovered the 3-D structure of DNA (deoxyribonucleic acid), the "supermolecule" that carries hereditary information in living organisms. American James Watson and Englishman Francis Crick have found that DNA has a "double-helical" structure, consisting of two intertwined spiral strands of linked chemical units called nucleotide bases. The discovery occurred as a result of two breakthroughs. First, by examining some X-ray diffraction images of DNA, Crick worked out that the molecule must have a spiral structure. Second, Watson was experimenting with models of the four different types of nucleotide bases in DNA when he realized how they link to each other in specific pairs. The 3-D structure is convincing because it is sufficiently complex to store large amounts of information but is also straightforward enough to copy when living cells divide.

▲ *Watson and Crick with their 3-D structure of DNA.*

A GLANCE AT THE PAST

Stars produce energy by nuclear fusion

In 1939, the German-born American physicist Hans Bethe proposed that the energy produced by the Sun and stars is created by a fusion of hydrogen nuclei into helium—exactly the same process as used in thermonuclear bombs (H-bombs.) During the fusion process, some of the mass of the hydrogen is transformed into huge quantities of energy. The process worked out by Bethe involved a complex chain of six nuclear reactions in which carbon atoms acted as catalysts.

MILITARY TECHNOLOGY

H-bomb tested in the Pacific

After a series of tests, the world's first thermonuclear bomb or "H-bomb" has been successfully exploded in the Pacific Ocean by the American military. A hydrogen device, named "Bravo," it was detonated on March 1, producing an explosion that was a thousand times more powerful than the one created by the bomb dropped on Hiroshima nine years earlier. A thermonuclear reaction was created from a fusion of deuterium (a stable isotope of hydrogen) and tritium (a radioactive isotope of hydrogen).

▲ *The explosion caused by the "Bravo" device was equivalent to 15 million tons (13.5 metric tonnes) of TNT.*

BIOLOGY

Humans have 46 chromosomes

Scientists Jo Hin Tjio and Albert Levan, working in Sweden, have discovered that human cells contain 46 chromosomes, which are arranged in 23 pairs. This is a shock because scientists had believed that the number was 48. Chromosomes are found in the nucleus of living cells. They store DNA and carry the genes, the basic units of inheritance that determine each person's characteristics. Until recently it has been almost impossible to study them because they are so squashed inside cells. However, a laboratory accident showed that dilute salt solution causes cells to swell and chromosomes to scatter. Tjio and Levan therefore immersed cells in a dilute salt solution and used a drug to freeze the cells at the moment when the chromosomes were most visible. The chromosomes could then be accurately counted for the first time.

MATERIALS

Polypropylene developed

A new synthetic fiber, polypropylene, has been developed by Italian chemist Giulio Natta. It is strong, with a high melting point, and has potential uses in carpets, ropes, and clothing. Last year, Natta began a study of large molecules often made up of thousands of atoms, known as macromolecules. He found that under the right conditions thousands of propylene molecules would join together to form one huge polypropylene molecule. Natta also discovered that if a catalyst originally developed by Karl Zeiger was placed in the reaction chamber, then the reaction would take place at low temperatures and pressures.

◄ *Factories can produce polypropylene goods cheaply.*

Cook dinner in no time!

Pressure cookers hit the shops

Pressure cookers have been around for years, impressing people because they can cook quickly by using high-pressure steam. It is the cooker's airtight lid that allows the pressure to increase, enabling the water to boil at a higher temperature than normal and so dramatically decreasing cooking time. Pressure cookers have been especially popular since Alfred Vischer brought out a model with an improved seal and interlocking lid. Now Vischer's patent has run out and many manufacturers in the United States are cashing in by producing Vischer-type pressure cookers.

◀ *The pressure cooker makes homemade fast food possible.*

PALEONTOLOGY

1.9 billion-year-old microfossils discovered

Two American paleontologists have made a remarkable find among some chert rocks on the northern shores of Lake Superior near Schreiber, Ontario. Elso Barghoorn and Stanley Tyler have proposed that some unusual shapes visible in the rocks are fossilized microorganisms, primarily bacteria. They are the first fossils of microorganisms ever found and are thought to be the same age as the chert itself—1.9 billion years old. Furthermore, their proposed age makes them the world's oldest known fossils. The discovery pushes back the estimated period during which life has been present on Earth by at least 1.5 billion years. The actual fossils are visible only under a microscope and appear as various sphere- and chain-like threads, unlike anything ever seen before in rocks. Many have a striking similarity to modern-day species of microorganism known as cyanobacteria or blue-green algae.

Science News 1954

- In the United States, researchers at the Bell Laboratories develop the photovoltaic cell.

- The first nuclear power plant for peacetime use is built in the Soviet Union.

- In France, Vincent du Vigneaud produces the first synthetic hormone—oxytocin.

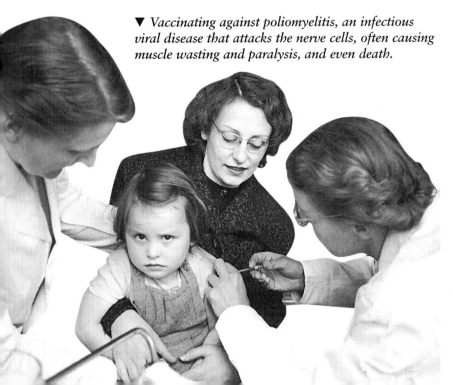

▼ *Vaccinating against poliomyelitis, an infectious viral disease that attacks the nerve cells, often causing muscle wasting and paralysis, and even death.*

MEDICINE

Mass inoculations of antipolio vaccine

A nationwide child immunization program has begun in the United States this year with a vaccine against the debilitating infectious disease, poliomyelitis.

Developed by Jonas Salk, head of the virus research laboratory at the University of Pittsburgh, the vaccine is of the "killed" variety, which means it contains chemically inactivated polio virus particles. Initial results from the vaccination program are encouraging, with a sharp reduction in incidence of the disease. Unfortunately, there has been one severe setback, with 200 people caused to develop polio as a result of an error in the production of one batch of vaccine.

NUCLEAR ENERGY

At the beginning of the twentieth century, no one knew that atoms have central nuclei—scientists had only just realized that atoms have any internal structure. Yet within 40 years this structure was known, and it was realized that within certain atomic nuclei a huge amount of energy was waiting to be released.

In 1939, scientists found that by bombarding uranium atoms with high-speed particles, they could split the uranium nuclei and obtain energy through a chain reaction. The discovery came at the start of World War II, and initial research focused on the creation of bombs. But work on how to use fission for peaceful purposes began soon after, and by the 1950s electricity-producing nuclear plants had started up in the United States, Great Britain, and elsewhere.

▲ *Niels Bohr.*

Atomic pioneer

The development of nuclear energy grew from the work of hundreds of pioneering scientists in the first half of the twentieth century. One of the most important was the Danish physicist Niels Bohr, who played a major part both in establishing the structure of atoms and working out the detailed mechanism for obtaining energy from atomic fission.

How nuclear fission works

Most nuclear reactors generate energy by a process called fission. In this process the nuclei (central cores) of unstable atoms are "split" by fast-moving subatomic particles called neutrons in chain reactions that release huge quantities of energy. In most reactors the substance whose atomic nuclei are split is an isotope (form) of the metallic element uranium, called uranium-235 (U235). A substance called a moderator is used to increase the chances of neutrons hitting uranium nuclei.

▼ *Neutron impact*
The fission process starts with a neutron hitting the nucleus of a U235 atom.

▼ *Chain reaction*
Some of the released neutrons collide with other U235 nuclei, starting a chain reaction.

Neutron

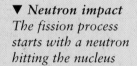

Neutron

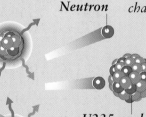

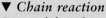

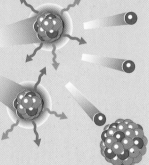

U235 nucleus

U235 nucleus

▲ *Fission*
The U235 nucleus, which contains protons (blue) and neutrons (black), splits in two, releasing nuclei of the elements barium and krypton, as well as two or three fast-moving neutrons.

▲ *Energy release*
As each U235 nucleus splits, a tiny amount of mass is converted into energy. This is released in the form of heat (red arrows) and gamma radiation (blue arrows).

Handling ▶
nuclear material
Because it is radioactive and a potential hazard to health, any type of nuclear fuel or the products of fission have to be handled with great care.

How a reactor works

The most common type of nuclear reactor is a pressurized water reactor, of which the core (where the fission reaction actually takes place) is shown here. The fuel consists of uranium rods. These are interspersed with control rods, which adjust how fast the reaction proceeds. Water acts both as a moderator for the reaction and as a coolant, carrying away the energy produced in the form of heat.

▶ **Coolant**
Pressurized water enters the chamber at a temperature of about 530°F (275°C) (blue arrows), absorbs energy from the reaction, and exits at a temperature of about 590°F (310°C) (red arrows).

▶ **Rod assemblage**
This includes hundreds of rods of the uranium fuel, interspersed with control rods.

▶ **Welded-steel jacket**
The jacket resists the pressure of the water inside the reactor.

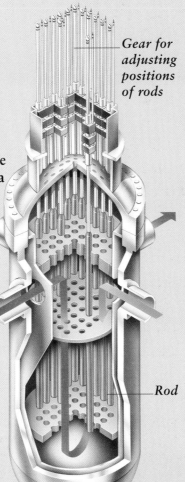

Gear for adjusting positions of rods

Rod

Steel jacket

Spent fuel
The amount of fissionable material in the fuel rods diminishes until it can no longer sustain a reaction. Here, spent fuel rods are being removed from a reactor core. ▼

Pros and cons

Today, over 400 nuclear plants operate globally (providing about 17 percent of the world's electricity). Overall, nuclear energy is cleaner than most other major sources of energy. But nuclear plants are expensive to build and dismantle. The products of fission are often radioactive, and there have been worries about reactor safety. In the future, nuclear fission may be abandoned in favor of a yet more powerful source of energy—nuclear fusion (the bringing together of small atomic nuclei to make larger ones).

123

A GLANCE AT THE PAST

DU PONT HARD BASE QUALITY
TEFLON
SCRATCH-RESISTANT *finish*
No stick cooking with no scour cleaning

The history of PTFE

Delaware scientist Roy J. Plunkett was working on refrigerant chemicals for the DuPont Company in 1938. During his experiments he came across a chemical called polytetrafluoroethylene (PTFE for short). Because it was no good for refrigeration, Plunkett was not really interested in PTFE. But the chemical had some qualities that were to prove useful in other fields. It was resistant to high temperatures, could withstand attacks from corrosive substances, and could be used to reduce friction. PTFE was first used as a container for dangerous chemicals, before Marc Grégoire realized that its qualities were ideal for nonstick pans.

MATERIALS

Nonstick (Teflon®-coated) pans introduced

French engineer Marc Grégoire has come up with a winner for the kitchen. Aware that the chemical PTFE could be used to reduce friction, Grégoire used it to stop his fishing line from sticking. He came up with a PTFE coating for pans when his wife asked if he could stop food from sticking to her saucepans. The couple believe that cooks everywhere will want to use nonstick saucepans, and so they have founded a company, called Tefal®, to manufacture them.

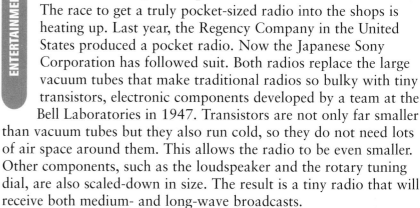

▲ *Grégoire is already selling millions of his Teflon-coated pans.*

ENTERTAINMENT

A tune in your pocket

The race to get a truly pocket-sized radio into the shops is heating up. Last year, the Regency Company in the United States produced a pocket radio. Now the Japanese Sony Corporation has followed suit. Both radios replace the large vacuum tubes that make traditional radios so bulky with tiny transistors, electronic components developed by a team at the Bell Laboratories in 1947. Transistors are not only far smaller than vacuum tubes but they also run cold, so they do not need lots of air space around them. This allows the radio to be even smaller. Other components, such as the loudspeaker and the rotary tuning dial, are also scaled-down in size. The result is a tiny radio that will receive both medium- and long-wave broadcasts.

◄ *Tiny transistor radios allow listeners to enjoy sound on the go.*

HOME APPLIANCES

New Velcro® fastener patented

A Swiss engineer, George deMestral, has patented a new fastening method he's calling "Velcro." The system consists of two pads, the surfaces of which are covered in microscopic hooks and loops made of a synthetic material. When pressed together, the hooks and loops entangle, producing a strong adhesion. DeMestral got the idea after going for a stroll in the countryside. Returning home, he noticed that his jacket was covered with cockleburs. He found that the cockleburs were covered with hooks, and the hooks had become embedded in the fabric of his cloth jacket. He applied this principle to his invention.

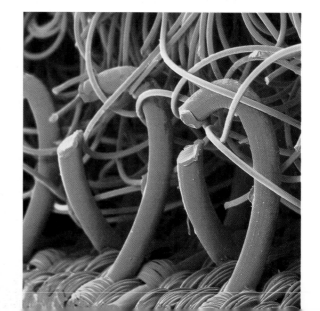

An electron micrograph of the nylon hooks and loops in Velcro. ▶

- The first successful kidney transplant is performed by a team of American surgeons.

- Briton Christopher Cockerell builds a test rig hovercraft out of a can of cat food inside a coffee can connected to a vacuum cleaner.

- In the United States, deep freezers capable of freezing fresh food go on sale.

Structure of viruses explained

BIOLOGY

In some pioneering work on the structure of viruses—the simple infective agents that cause illnesses such as influenza and measles—the German-American biochemist Heinz Fraenkel-Conrat has shown that one type, at least, consists of just two main parts. Fraenkel-Conrat's experiments have concentrated on a type of plant virus, tobacco mosaic virus.

At the center of each virus particle is some nucleic acid (a molecule of the same type as DNA, the "supermolecule" that carries the genetic information in animals and plants). Around this nucleic acid core is a capsule made of protein. Fraenkel-Conrat has disassembled the virus into its protein and nucleic acid components, and then, by recombining them, succeeded in reconstituting the fully infective virus. He's also shown that viral infectivity resides only within the nucleic acid portion—the protein capsule appears to function mainly to protect the nucleic acid core.

LEGO® is launched

ENTERTAINMENT

The Danish LEGO company is introducing a revolutionary new construction system based on colorful bricks that can snap together in an astronomical number of different combinations. Ole Kirk Christiansen, a carpenter, formed the toy company in the 1930s, adopting the name LEGO by forming together the Danish words "leg" (play) and "godt" (well). Later, Christiansen realized that by coincidence the Latin word lego means "I put together." For its first 15 years, LEGO made only wooden toys but branched out into plastic ones after World War II. Automatic Binding Bricks, a forerunner of LEGO bricks, were introduced in Denmark in 1949 and proved to be a hit. Now the European "roll-out" is taking place and doubtless we'll soon see the new construction system in the United States.

This year, 28 LEGO sets and eight LEGO vehicles are launching in Europe. ▶

The first nuclear-powered sub

MILITARY TECHNOLOGY

The world's first nuclear-powered submarine has been tested in sea trials by the U.S. Navy. Launched last year, the USS *Nautilus* is powered by propulsion turbines that are driven by steam produced by a nuclear reactor carried on board the submarine. The new vessel is considered a revolution in sea warfare. The nuclear reactor allows the sub to stay submerged for prolonged periods, while it can maintain high speeds of up to 20 knots almost indefinitely. At 319 feet (97 meters) long and displacing 3,180 tons (2,862 metric tonnes) the *Nautilus* is also much larger than the diesel-electric submarines used in World War II. With the development of this new type of vessel, the U.S. Navy has the advantage on its Soviet rivals, and gained a serious strategic advantage in the cat-and-mouse maneuvers of the Cold War.

The USS Nautilus is armed with six torpedo tubes and carries a crew of 105. ▼

Discovery of the mid-Atlantic ridge

The mid-Atlantic ridge is an underwater mountain chain that runs down the middle of the Atlantic Ocean. It is formed by the lava that seeps up from the seabed to form the mountains, some of which break the surface as volcanic islands, such as Iceland (*above*.) The ridge was discovered in 1925 when a German oceanographic expedition, conducted from the *Meteor*, mapped the seafloor using echo sounding, or sonar (called asdic at that time.)

OCEANOGRAPHY

Worldwide extent of mid-ocean ridges

Working with two assistants, Bruce Heezen and Marie Tharp, American marine geologist Maurice William Ewing has established that the mid-Atlantic ridge, an underwater mountain range that runs down the middle of the Atlantic Ocean, is just part of a world system of mountains—known as seamounts—and rifts that runs along the floor of all oceans of the world. Known as mid-ocean ridges, they extend worldwide for some 37,000 miles (60,000 kilometers) below the surface of the oceans.

▲ *Dr. Maurice Ewing, a professor of geology, aboard the research vessel* Atlantis.

MEDICINE

Cardiac catheterization

Imagine having a flexible tube inserted into your arm and pushed into you until it reaches your heart. This was the nightmarish experiment that a German physician, Werner Forssmann, performed on himself. Forssmann carried out this procedure in 1929 and watched the progress of the tube, known as a catheter, on a fluorescent scope. This experiment was condemned as dangerous until he later refined it into a practical procedure, assisted by two other doctors in the United States, André Cournand and Dickinson Richards. This year, the trio's efforts have been rewarded with the Nobel Prize in Medicine. Forssmann's method of cardiac catheterization permits doctors to measure blood pressure inside the heart.

COMPUTERS

Transistors set to bring down size of computers

Computers look like they could be getting much smaller with the introduction of transistors as their primary components. These fingernail-sized electronic devices, commonly used in radios, are increasingly being used in computers to replace clumsy fist-sized vacuum tubes as the main logic elements. Transistors generate less heat than vacuum tubes, which means that computers based on transistors should be more reliable. U.S. manufacturer Sperry-Rand, makers of the Universal Automatic Computer (UNIVAC®) has introduced UNIVAC II, which has been based partially on transistors.

◀ *The entire Bible has been recorded using a UNIVAC system like this.*

COMMUNICATIONS

Video tape recorder marketed

Before now, there was no method of recording television pictures. This meant that a broadcast that went out in New York at, say, 6 P.M. was seen on the West coast at 3 P.M. The Ampex Corporation of California has come up with the answer to this problem. The Ampex® video recorder records television programs in the same way that a tape recorder records sound—by magnetizing fragments of iron oxide on a continuously running plastic tape. Because television programs are much more complex than audio tracks, the tape has to be much bigger (2 inches or 5 centimeters wide) and whizzes past the recording head at some 15 inches (38 centimeters) per second. Now it is possible to record programs and then edit them, so that the broadcast version is word- and picture-perfect.

▲ *The video recorder looks set to transform television program-making.*

Science News 1956

- The first large-scale nuclear plant opens in Great Britain.

- The first transatlantic telephone cable is set up by the Canadian Overseas Telecommunications company, AT&T of France, and the GPO in Great Britain.

- Birth-control pills are tested on a large scale in Puerto Rico.

MEDICINE

Artificial kidney cleans up blood

Life for your kidneys is not an easy one, having to clear out all the poisons in your blood. Without kidneys, poisons like urea can build up to life-threatening highs. A Dutch physician, Willem Kolff, has developed an artificial kidney which is to be used for the first time in the United States. Blood from a patient's artery is diverted into the dialysis machine, which looks like a large rotating drum. The blood enters a cellulose membrane, which is wrapped around the drum. As the drum rotates, the cellulose is immersed in a salt solution. The membrane allows all the poisons to pass out of the blood. The blood cells are too large to pass through and stay within the membrane. The newly cleaned blood can then be pumped back into the patient. Kidneys can fail for many reasons but at least now it is no longer an automatic death sentence.

ENTERTAINMENT

"Go-karts" get on track

Parking lots around the Pasadena area of California have this year been witness to a strange new phenomenon—"go-karting." It involves grown men, and sometimes kids, charging around a track marked by gas cans on crude little vehicles powered by surplus lawn mower engines. The "father" of karting is believed to be Art Ingels, a race car builder at Kurtis Craft, who was finding his hobby of "hot-rodding" too expensive. He fashioned a rugged tubular chassis, added suspension, then connected four wheels with semi-pneumatic tires, a seat, and a 2.5-horsepower, two-cylinder engine.

▼ *The first go-kart could reach 30 miles (50 kilometers) per hour.*

The history of radio astronomy

Radio signals from space were first detected in 1931 by the American radio engineer Karl Jansky (*above*)—he was trying to establish the source of interference in radiotelephone links. The signals appeared to be coming from the center of the Milky Way galaxy. The first intentional radio telescope was built in 1937, by U.S. engineer Grote Reber. Reber mapped the distribution of galactic radio emissions and also detected radio signals from the Sun. During the 1940s, sources of radio emission were cataloged in increasing numbers.

ASTRONOMY

New radio telescope tunes in to the universe

A new steerable radio telescope, the world's largest, has been installed at the Jodrell Bank radio astronomy observatory in Cheshire, England. Radio astronomy is a branch of astronomy in which celestial objects are studied by examining their emission of signals in the radio portion of the electromagnetic spectrum. A radio telescope is a huge curved dish that points toward the sky and collects radio waves just as a mirror focuses light in a reflecting telescope. The new telescope will study medium-wavelength radio signals from the Milky Way and galaxies beyond.

▲ *Jodrell Bank's new radio telescope.*

COMPUTERS

Typewriter threatened by new computer printer

Computers can perform calculations in a fraction of a second, but until now, if you wanted the result printed out you had to wait a lot longer. Researchers at IBM have now developed the dot-matrix printer that can print up to 500 characters per minute. The dot-matrix printer can achieve these high speeds by having—instead of separate keys—24 tiny pins arranged in a rectangle. Any of these pins can be pushed up to create the shape of the desired character. The shapes are then pressed against an ink ribbon to produce the character on paper. With high-quality printouts from computers, is this the end of the humble typewriter?

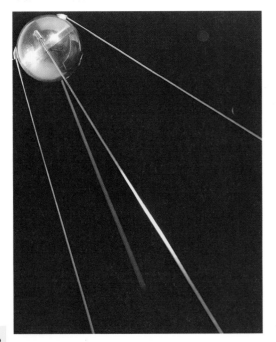

SPACE EXPLORATION

First artificial satellite, *Sputnik I*

The Soviet Union has put the world's first artificial satellite, *Sputnik I*, into orbit. It was launched by a converted intercontinental ballistic missile, designated R-7 8K71 (also known as a Sapwood missile) from Baikonur cosmodrome in Kazakhstan. The satellite is a 0.08-inch (2 millimeter) thick aluminum sphere about 23 inches (58 centimeters) in diameter with four antennae to send radio signals back to Earth. To announce that it is in space, *Sputnik* emits a beeping sound. Inside the sphere there is a variety of instruments that are intended to measure the density and temperature of the top of the atmosphere and gather information about cosmic rays and meteoroids. The satellite will send results down to Earth for a few weeks until its batteries run out. After that it is expected to reenter Earth's atmosphere and burn up. *Sputnik I* weighs 184 pounds (83 kilograms) and has an elliptical orbit between 141 and 588 miles (225 and 950 kilometers) above Earth's surface.

◀ *The name* Sputnik *is Russian for "fellow traveler."*

John Bardeen
b. 1908 d. 1991

Bardeen won two Nobel prizes, both shared. The first was for his work on semiconductors, the second for the BCS theory of superconductivity. He was born in Madison, Wisconsin, and graduated in electrical engineering from the University of Wisconsin in 1930. After research in solid-state physics and war service as a physicist, he joined Bell Telephone Laboratories in 1945. In the 1950s, at the University of Illinois, he resumed his superconductivity research.

HOME APPLIANCES

Electric watches introduced

A new era in timekeeping has begun with the Model 500 electric watch from Hamilton Watches. Unlike traditional watches, the Hamilton watch is powered by a tiny battery—which means that you never have to wind it. Inside the watch, tiny contact points make and break an electric circuit exactly five times a second, enabling the watch to keep perfect time. It is the easiest of watches to use, although, like any ordinary mechanical watch, it needs servicing once every two to three years. During servicing, the technician will replace any worn parts, adjust the delicate contact wires, and replace the battery if necessary. The watch should then give more years of accurate timekeeping.

▲ *The electric watch never needs winding.*

PHYSICS

"Superconductivity" explained

Three U.S. physicists, John Bardeen, Leon Cooper, and John Schrieffer, have developed a comprehensive theory to explain the phenomenon of "superconductivity." Superconductors are peculiar materials that suddenly lose all resistance to the flow of electrical current when they are cooled to extremely low temperatures. This makes them very fast and efficient electrical conductors. The BCS theory (the initial letters of the scientists' surnames) proposes that in a cooled superconductor electrons form into pairs called Cooper pairs, and the movements of the pairs become linked or coordinated. When an electrical voltage is applied, all the Cooper pairs move in unison. When the voltage is removed, the current cannot stop, because, to do so, all the Cooper pairs would have to halt at the same time—a highly unlikely occurrence. Instead, the current continues to flow indefinitely.

ENTERTAINMENT

Records go to great lengths

Long-playing records (LPs) are getting more popular. The generous playing time of around 25 minutes per side (as opposed to about four minutes for a 78 revolutions per minute record) has made people rush out to buy LPs—and a new development may make them even more attractive. LPs are set to appear with stereo sound. Manufacturers and scientists have been arguing for years about the best recording system for stereo. Now the Record Industry Association of America has come to a decision. At a demonstration, the U.S. Westrex® and British Decca® systems were both tried, and the Association voted for Westrex.

◄ *The way is now open for stereo sound using LPs.*

A GLANCE AT THE PAST

A GLANCE AT THE PAST

The first passenger jet airline

The jet age for commercial passengers started in 1952, when BOAC flew the De Havilland 106, the *Comet I* (*above*), between London, Great Britain, and Johannesburg, South Africa. Unfortunately, after two years the planes began to explode in mid-air. Investigation showed that the *Comet's* body was not strong enough to stand up to the difference in pressure between the interior pressurized cabin and the thin air outside. A valuable lesson was learned by all jet plane designers. De Havilland withdrew the *Comet 1* and developed new, strong-bodied replacement planes.

TRANSPORTATION

First transatlantic jet service

On October 4, BOAC (British Overseas Airways Corporation) inaugurated the first transatlantic jet airline service between London and New York. Eighty-four passengers made the first flight in a De Havilland *Comet 4*, which is 111 feet (34 meters) long with a wingspan of 115 feet (35 meters), and cruises at a

▲ *BOAC's De Havilland* Comet 4.

speed of 535 miles (856 kilometers) per hour, using four Rolls Royce Avon Engines. Only three weeks later, U.S. jets took to the skies when Pan American flew 150 passengers in a Boeing 707, powered by four Pratt & Whitney engines, from New York to Paris.

ASTRONOMY

Solar wind demonstrated

American astrophysicist Eugene Parker has demonstrated that the Sun throws off a "wind" of charged particles that blows across the solar system, bathing Earth and all the other planets. The first indication that such a wind might exist came from the examination of comet tails, which always stream away from the Sun. Some comets have two tails. One is caused by dust being blown from a comet by the pressure of photons (particles of light) emitted by the Sun. The second is thought to consist of ions (charged particles) blown from the comet by the solar wind. Parker has calculated that the wind originates from the Sun's outer layer, or corona. As the Sun spins, some particles in the corona are energetic enough to escape the Sun's gravity and spiral away from it at an average speed of about 250 miles (400 kilometers) per second.

MEDICINE

Ultrasound used to "see" inside the body

Doctors now have a new diagnostic tool that can examine the inside of patients without any of the risks of X rays. Ian Donald, professor of gynecology at the University of Glasgow, has developed a novel method of diagnosis using sonar, a technique developed by the military for the underwater detection of objects. Pulses of ultrasound (high frequency sound waves) are transmitted and are reflected back if they hit an object. When the waves travel through the body, they are reflected back at any point where there is a change in density. Such a change occurs on the border between two different organs. The usefulness of ultrasound has already been demonstrated when a patient originally diagnosed as having inoperable cancer was shown to have an easy-to-remove ovarian cyst.

Images of an unborn child may be obtained by means of ultrasound. ▶

Stereo records go on sale in the United States

Practical stereo records are available at last! Music lovers have been hearing about the concept of stereo for more than 20 years. The idea behind stereo is that there are two loudspeakers to match our two ears, giving a much greater feeling of space and depth to the sound. To achieve this, companies such as Audio Fidelity in the United States and Pye in Great Britain are producing records that have two signals (one for the right-hand channel and one for the left) in every groove. You play these back using a special pickup, which sends the two signals, via the separate channels of a stereo amplifier, to the two speakers. Listeners who have invested in the new equipment say that the improvement in the realism of the sound is stunning.

▲ *Two speakers give depth to sound.*

Science News 1958

- The United States launches its first satellite, *Explorer I*, from Cape Canaveral in Florida.

- Michael Roberts and Alex Bernstein develop a computer chess program that performs to a fair amateur standard.

- Ilya Darevsky finds an all-female lizard species in Soviet Armenia, which reproduces without male fertilization.

The first aluminum cans

The German beer company Kaiser has introduced the first aluminum cans, which will replace the steel-plated tin cans that have been used until now for beer and other products. Aluminum is a lightweight metal that can be formed into almost any shape. It is produced commercially from an ore known as bauxite. The first aluminum was produced in 1825, but the first successful technique of separating aluminum from its ore was developed in 1888 by the Austrian chemist Karl Joseph Bayer.

"Superglue" can be used to bond a wide range of materials. ▼

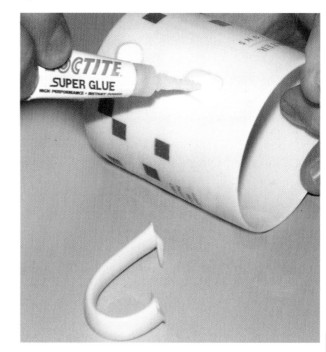

Superglue sold as a quick fix

A new adhesive has arrived in the stores that promises to be a "superglue." Virtually all manufactured and many natural adhesives are made up of polymers—giant molecules formed by linking together thousands of simpler ones. The molecule that makes up superglue is cyanoacrylate, which has a special property— that it turns itself into a polymer upon exposure to water in the atmosphere. As a consequence of this, cyanoacrylate is being sold as an adhesive that can bond two materials in seconds. Once bonded, superglue is very strong, exhibits long-term durability, and is resistant to heat and solvents. It is being sold as an instant fix for all those household breakages.

1840
Parkes develops Parkesine as a replacement for ivory.

1870
Hyatt brothers patent celluloid, a hornlike substance.

1908
Brandenberger develops cellophane.

1909
Baekeland patents his tough, durable plastic Bakelite.

1910
The first rayon stockings go on sale, in Germany.

PLASTICS

Daylight could destroy the fragile plastics, such as celluloid, that were available at the beginning of the twentieth century. But by the end of the 1930s, a great variety of durable plastics, including Bakelite®, offered usable alternatives to horn, ivory, wood, and other natural materials. Since then, many different plastics have been developed, each with its own distinctive properties.

Plastics all share a very useful characteristic. In certain conditions, for example, when they are warm, plastics can be stretched, distorted, or otherwise reshaped without breaking. Once a plastic material has been changed in this way, it will not return to its original shape. Manufacturers use this property to make plastic objects in many different shapes.

Plastic homes

Made from plastic and other synthetic materials, the House of the Future was a star attraction at Disney's Tomorrowland® in the early 1960s. Opened in 1957, it was built to show how new technologies could reshape our homes. Its architects exploited the properties of fiberglass to give the home a sleek, curving outer shell. According to some reports, this shell was so strong that it had to be cut away with hacksaws when the house was demolished.

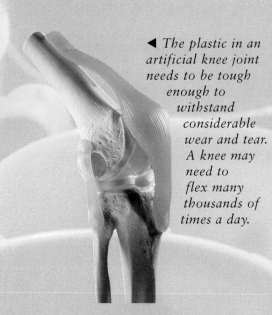

◀ *The plastic in an artificial knee joint needs to be tough enough to withstand considerable wear and tear. A knee may need to flex many thousands of times a day.*

Replacement knees

Some plastics are tough enough to replace hard-wearing parts of the body. Millions of people, for example, have artificial knees made of plastic and metal alloy. The plastic replaces the body's cartilage—the tough material that stops bones from scraping together and wearing away.

Early plastic ▼
Many of the plastics developed in the early part of the twentieth century, such as celluloid, were highly flammable.

Pliable plastic ▼
Bakelite could be molded into any shape and was particularly popular for the casing of clocks and radios.

The plastic House of the Future. ▲

How plastics are made

The atoms that make up a plastic are bonded in small units called "monomers." These link together to form long chains, called "polymers." The polymers, which can be twisted and bent in various ways, give plastics their characteristic properties. Some link more rigidly than others so the form of the plastic produced can vary.

Teflon plastic
In a polymerization reaction (2), the monomers are linked to form a polymer (3), in this case polytetra-fluoroethene (PTFE), or Teflon. ▼

Bonded atoms
To make the plastic Teflon®, carbon and fluorine are first combined into monomers (1), each containing two carbon and four fluorine atoms.▼

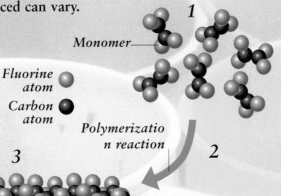

Monomer

Fluorine atom
Carbon atom

Polymerization reaction

Polymer

Plastics that glow

A recent development in plastic technology is the light-emitting polymer, or LEP—a material that emits a bright glow when subjected to an electrical voltage. An LEP has a physical structure similar to a semiconductor (like silicon), allowing some movement of both electrons (negative charge carriers) and "holes" (positive charge carriers) through it. When the electrons and holes meet, energy is given off as a fluorescent glow, which can vary from green to orange-red. Various different applications have been thought of for LEPs, including warning signs and illuminated advertising. Initially, however, LEPs are likely to be used in products where compactness and low-supply voltage are crucial, such as in Personal Digital Assistants (PDAs) and cellular phones.

Household material

Many early plastic objects, such as the "tortoiseshell" hairbrush (far left), tried to mimic natural materials. However, as the twentieth century progressed, designers became increasingly interested in exploiting the synthetic appearance of plastic. By the 1950s molded-plastic objects in bright, synthetic colors were the height of fashion.

Unbreakable bottles ▼
Plastic replaced many glass items.

▼ Safe and sturdy toys
Children's toys are often made of plastic because it is resilient and safe.

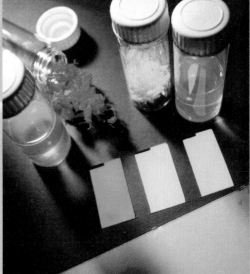

▲ Some solid and liquid samples of LEPs, a piece of glass coated with a thin layer of the polymer, and three small LEP display panels (center).

◀ An array of plastic objects made throughout the twentieth century.

The first xerographic copy

American physicist Chester Carlson made the first xerographic copy during the 1930s. He worked for a patent company and did all his experiments in a cramped room in his own apartment in Astoria, New York. He did not have much money and was always at risk from the materials (which included sulfur). But he carried on, producing his first copy on October 22, 1938 (*above*). It contained the date and the word "ASTORIA." Carlson called his invention xerography, from two Greek words meaning "dry" (because there is no messy ink) and "to write." Eventually, the invention was taken up by the Haloid Company, which later changed its name to Xerox.

OFFICE TECHNOLOGY

First commercial Xerox® copier

Offices everywhere are clamoring for a simple, fast way of copying documents. The photocopier is the answer. First developed back in the 1930s, photocopying works by using electrical charges to make a powdered black toner stick to a sheet of paper. Applying heat to the paper fixes the toner in place, making a clear, cheap, long-lasting image of the original document. The Xerox Company is now set to make the first commercial copier.

▲ *Photocopying is now a reality for offices all over America.*

▲ *The pacemaker produces continuous impulses at regular intervals, creating a fixed heartbeat.*

MEDICINE

Pacemaker implanted

A healthy heart has its own electrical system that controls both the rate and order of cardiac contractions. Heart diseases can interrupt this electrical system; thus an external source of electricity is required to keep the heart functioning. Doctors have been developing such a device, known as a pacemaker, for over 20 years. And now a team led by Ake Senning at the Karolinska Institute in Stockholm has successfully implanted a small pacemaker into a patient.

BIOLOGY

Bacteria develop antibiotic resistance

Less than 20 years after the introduction of antibiotics, scientists are concerned that some bacteria have already developed resistance to the drugs—the antibiotics no longer kill the bacteria. Recently, an outbreak of dysentery occurred in Japan, caused by resistance of the bacterium *Shigella dysenteriae* to several antibiotics, including streptomycin and sulfonamide drugs. Now Japanese scientists have discovered that some *Shigella dysenteriae* organisms carry genes that protect them against antibiotics—and these genes can be spread by a process called bacterial conjugation. The scientists have found that small circular pieces of DNA, called plasmids, exist in the bacteria, separate from other bacterial chromosomes. These plasmids are responsible for carrying the resistance genes—they can replicate themselves and pass between bacteria when the bacterial cells come into contact.

Science News 1959

- Volvo, the Swedish car manufacturer, invents the seat belt.

- The St. Lawrence Seaway, linking the St. Lawrence River and the Great Lakes, is opened in North America.

- The South African company De Beers synthesizes the first artificial diamond.

TRANSPORTATION

Ski-Doo® snowmobile

Joseph-Armand Bombardier of Valcourt, Quebec, has introduced his snowmobile to the public. It was christened the Ski-Dog, but a typographical error, which Bombardier decided not to correct, changed its name forever. Bombardier's company, L'Auto-Neige Bombardier Limitée, has been manufacturing tracked vehicles, large snowmobiles, and tractors since 1942, but the Ski-Doo is smaller and faster than previous snowmobile models, and is the first snow vehicle designed for recreation and personal transport.

SPACE EXPLORATION

Pictures of the far side of the Moon

A Soviet space probe, *Luna 3*, has passed around the Moon and returned photographs to Earth—providing humankind with views of the Moon's far side for the first time. Launched on October 4, *Luna 3* traveled on a long figure-eight trajectory around both Earth and the Moon, passing over the Moon's far side, which was sunlit, on October 7. The television system obtained a series of 29 photographs over 40 minutes, covering 70 percent of the surface. The photographs were developed and scanned on board the spacecraft, and 17 were then radio-transmitted to Earth ground stations in facsimile form on October 18. The images are indistinct but do show a number of features. The surface of the far side appears to be heavily cratered, mountainous, and rugged, but has fewer dark areas or "seas" than the familiar near side.

◄ *Luna 3, here being launched on an 8K72 rocket from Baikonur cosmodrome, is the third space probe launched toward the Moon by the Soviet Union this year. Luna 1 missed the Moon. Luna 2 crash-landed onto the Moon on September 14.*

ANTHROPOLOGY

Africa, the birthplace of mankind

English-born archaeologist Mary Leakey has discovered the well-preserved, fossilized skull of an early hominid in the Olduvai Gorge, Tanzania. Her husband, the British-educated Kenyan anthropologist Louis Leakey, has christened the remains *Zinjanthropus boisei*. He believes the fossil is a previously unknown species of hominid who walked on Earth 1.5 to 2 million years ago. This early ancestor of humankind is thought to be closely related to *Australopithecus africanus,* a hominid first discovered by Raymond Dart at Taung, South Africa, in 1925. In the centennial year of Darwin's theory of evolution, the find conclusively shows that the origins of mankind are to be found in Africa, and not in Asia as was previously thought.

The early hominid's skull confirms that man's origins are in Africa.►

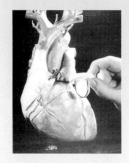

Heart surgery developments

During World War II, surgeons began operating to remove fragments of bullets lodged inside combatants' hearts. To do so, they cut a small hole in the still-beating heart muscle, inserted a finger, and removed the foreign object. By around 1950, surgeons had extended this technique to widening narrowed heart valves. But more complex procedures were not possible until the invention of the heart-lung machine.

MEDICINE

First successful artificial heart valve

Surgeons in Oregon have saved a man's life and restored him to health by implanting a plastic and metal valve in his heart. The man has survived for three months since the operation—the longest anyone has ever lived with an artificial heart valve. A team of 23 surgeons and assistants, led by Dr. Albert Starr of the University of Oregon Medical School, implanted the new valve. Dr. Starr also designed the new valve, in collaboration with engineer Lowell Edwards.

▲ *The valve consists of a silicone ball that moves freely within a metal cage.*

Consisting of 800 ▶ symbols, Mayan inscriptions were used from the third to the seventeenth century A.D.

ARCHAEOLOGY

Sign language

After years of detailed study, Russian linguist Tatiana Prouskouriakoff has convincingly argued that the ancient writing system of the Mayan people of Mexico is primarily historical, recording the events and lives of the Mayan rulers. Prouskouriakoff has followed up the work of Yuri Knorozov, who established that the writing system contains both logograms (symbols representing entire words or phrases) and phonetic signs representing syllables. Although the writing has been known to Western scholars since the Spanish conquest of Mexico, the symbols were previously assumed to represent simple objects and activities or religious expressions.

COMPUTERS

A more compact computer

Computers are complex machines that can fill whole rooms and require plenty of staff. However, a group of engineers led by Kenneth Olsen believe it is possible to produce simpler, smaller, office computers. Three years ago, in Massachusetts, they founded the Digital Equipment Corporation (DEC) to make their vision a reality. The majority of business users require computers to carry out mundane tasks like calculating a payroll; Olsen realized that these users would be better off with small, more reliable, inexpensive machines. This year, DEC launched its first computer, the Programmed Data Processor model 1, or PDP-1, at an initial price of only $120,000. Although the main part of the computer is cabinet-sized, it features a control panel and typewriter (for inputting data) that sit on a desk. While giants like IBM think bigger, the PDP-1 proves that small can also be beautiful.

▲ *The PDP-1, which the user or programmer can control from the comfort of an office chair.*

The first dog in space

The first space traveler was a dog named Laika (*above*) who was launched into orbit aboard the Soviet satellite *Sputnik II* on November 3, 1957. Signals from her monitoring equipment indicated that Laika suffered no ill effects from space flight. But there were no arrangements for bringing Laika back to Earth, and she died after a few days in space when her capsule overheated. In 1960, the Soviet Union put two more dogs into orbit and returned them safely to Earth.

SPACE EXPLORATION

First manned space flight

Yuri Gagarin of the Soviet Union became the first person to travel in space when he was blasted into orbit in the spacecraft *Vostok I* on April 12. Scientists were uncertain what effect weightlessness might have on Gagarin, so his flight was controlled from the ground. After completing a single orbit, during which he traveled 25,000 miles (40,200 kilometers) in 108 minutes, his space capsule returned him to the ground.

▲ *Former test pilot, Yuri Alekseyevich Gagarin, just before his historic flight.*

ANTHROPOLOGY

Man's African ancestor

After examining fossil remains in the Olduvai Gorge, Tanzania, anthropologist Louis Leakey has proposed the existence of a new type of hominid, *Homo habilis* ("handy man"), named after the simple work tools found with the remains. The find is estimated to be between one and a half and two million years old. The new hominid has a larger cranial capacity and smaller teeth than the *Australopithecus boisei* (previously called *Zinjanthropus boisei*) uncovered two years earlier. Leakey's find is quite extraordinary, since it suggests there were two distinct groups of hominids that coexisted for several hundred thousand years.

"Acid rain" takes its toll on the environment. ▼

Science News 1961

- The Soviet Union launches a space probe to Venus, but contact with it is lost.

- In America, Frank L. Horsfall Jr. announces that all forms of cancer are a result of changes in the DNA of cells.

- U.S. physicist R. Hofstadter discovers that protons and neutrons have a structure.

ENVIRONMENT

Acid rain kills fish

Fish are dying in lakes in Sweden and the Adirondack Mountains in the United States. Scientists have confirmed that the lakes are becoming more acidic, which is having a devastating effect on wildlife. They believe that the acidity is caused by air pollution, which is created by nitrous oxide fumes produced by car exhausts and sulfur dioxide generated by the burning of fossil fuels. When these poisonous substances mix with water in the atmosphere they fall as a kind of "acid rain," damaging the environment.

1926
Baird demonstrates a working TV system.

1929
Zworykin unveils an electronic TV scanner, the iconoscope.

1932
Baird sells 10,000 of the first commercial TV sets, "televisors."

1936
The BBC adopts an electronic TV system and starts broadcasts.

1939
Regular TV broadcasting starts in the U.S.A.

THE TV AGE

A family ▶ watches TV in the 1950s.

With the development of radio and electronic amplification in the early twentieth century, television quickly became a possibility. During the 1920s, two rival systems existed for scanning images. One, championed by John Logie Baird, was a part-mechanical system. Using this system, Baird demonstrated a working television in 1926. But it was an all-electronic system, originally devised by Vladimir Zworykin, that eventually triumphed.

TV takes off

TV entered an age of explosive growth in the late 1940s and 1950s. At the start of 1946, there were an estimated 7,000 television sets in the U.S.A. By 1962, this number had grown to 70 million. At first TV sets were small and the pictures were in black and white. The system deployed in the U.S.A. displayed 525 lines, each changing 30 times per second (a standard established in 1941).

Worldwide TV

A color broadcasting system that was also compatible with black-and-white sets was introduced in the United States in 1953. By the 1960s, color television had become the norm in the U.S.A. and it soon spread worldwide, though with changes to the American standard. For example, the SECAM system adopted in France had up to 819 screen lines. A wider range of TV programming became accessible with the arrival of local cable TV networks, which grew rapidly through the 1960s.

◀ *Typical TV set of the 1960s.*

How a TV screen works

A color-TV screen contains millions of tiny phosphor strips, colored red, green, and blue (the three primary colors of light that when mixed in different combinations form all possible colors). Three electron beams, carrying image data, pass through an aperture grille, which ensures that each beam hits phosphor strips of the correct color. As they do this, the phosphor strips glow either red, green, or blue in proportion to the intensity of the electron beams. The electron beams pass over the whole screen many times a second, creating three separate primary-color images with each pass. The eye and brain combine the images to produce a full-color picture and interpret the rapid changes in the picture as movement.

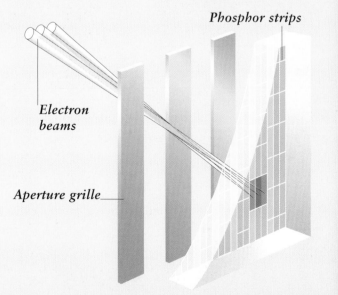

Phosphor strips

Electron beams

Aperture grille

138

1948
First community access TV (forerunner of cable TV).

1950s
Commercial color TV begins in the U.S.A; videotape is introduced.

1962
Telstar relays the first intercontinental TV pictures.

1980s
High-definition TV debuts in Japan.

1990s
Flat screens based on plasma display panels are introduced.

The antenna ▶
This receives the video, synchronization, and audio data.

Tuner

Audio decoder

The color decoder ▶ converts the video data into red, green, and blue signals and sends these to the electron guns. The synchronization unit splits the synchronization signal into two parts that are routed (yellow and blue lines) to the deflection coils.

Synchronization unit

Color decoder

Electron guns

The audio decoder amplifies audio signals and sends them to the speaker. ▶

Speaker

Deflection coils

Phosphor screen

How a television receiver works

At the center of a color TV is a tube, containing no air, that opens up at one end into a viewing screen (*see opposite page*). At the base of the tube are three electron guns, one for each primary color of light (red, green, and blue). Different electronic components decode the TV signals received by the antenna. One of these analyzes the video data and sends signals to the electron guns, which emit beams of electrons toward the screen. The three beams are made to scan across the screen at the same time by the deflection coils, which are controlled by a separate set of signals.

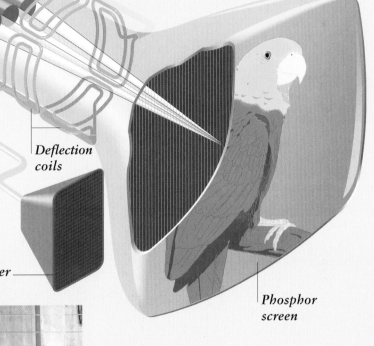

TV of tomorrow—today

Today, most people own VCRs and are no longer tied to TV schedules. Cable and satellite TV have added to the range of programming available, while interactive TV services, such as video-on-demand, are being tested. Another innovation is the flat-screen TV, or plasma display panel (PDP), which consists of thousands of tiny gas-filled cells. PDPs could be ideal for viewing high-definition television (HDTV). This new system has a wide-screen, cinema-style format with 1,125 screen lines.

◀ *A plasma display panel TV.*

Studying Earth's surface

The "plate" theory of Earth's crust, which explains how the Himalayas (*above*) were formed, brings together many historical threads. In 1912, Alfred Wegener proposed that some continents had drifted apart. In 1929, English geologist Arthur Holmes suggested that heat-flows within Earth might cause movements of the continents. Over the next 35 years, discoveries of geological features such as mid-ocean ridges confirmed this theory.

EARTH SCIENCE

Earth's crust may consist of slow-moving "plates"

A large body of evidence is accumulating that Earth's topmost "crust" consists of several irregularly shaped rigid chunks or "plates." These plates are very slowly pushed around on Earth's surface by heat flows within the mantle (the layer of rock underneath the crust). Plate motions make some continents move apart and others collide, causing mountain chains to form. Plate movements may also be responsible for earthquakes and volcanic activity. Recent work by American geologist Harry Hess supports the plate theory.

▲ *Earth's plates now (top),* and how they *may look in 50 million years' time* (bottom).

HOME APPLIANCES

Electric toothbrush

The idea of the electric toothbrush has been around for years, but now the first electric toothbrush, made by Squibb and Company, has appeared in stores. Sales records show that it is not only people who like gadgets who are buying the new toothbrushes. The brush that vibrates at the touch of a button also appeals to those who want to give their teeth a really thorough cleaning—you get more strokes per second than any manual toothbrush can give.

An electric toothbrush takes the ▶ *hard work out of brushing teeth!*

ENVIRONMENT

Silent Spring

American scientist and writer Rachel Carson has pricked the world's environmental conscience with the publication of her book, *Silent Spring*. Carson has spent many years researching the effects of DDT, the most effective insecticide ever produced. From her research, she has concluded that DDT is dangerous to the environment because it not only kills insect pests, but enters the food chain, causing the death of millions of birds that feed on the poisoned insects.

◀ *Rachel Carson, author of* Silent Spring, *the first major book to raise public awareness of the damage caused by pesticides.*

Industrial robots used on automobile assembly line

ENGINEERING

Forty-one years after the Czech playwright Karel Capek introduced the term "robot" to the world (it is from the Czech word meaning "to drudge"), the first machine that does human work has come into service. It is not the humanoid automaton imagined in Capek's play, but an electronically driven giant arm designed by George C. Devol to work an automobile assembly line. General Motors is the first manufacturer to install industrial robots, and many car workers fear that their jobs are threatened by the new invention.

◄ *Automobiles being constructed by robots.*

American orbits Earth

SPACE EXPLORATION

Astronaut John Glenn has become the first American to go into orbit. His flight in the Mercury spacecraft, *Friendship 7*, on February 20, took him around Earth three times and lasted almost five hours. Even though he was traveling at 17,500 miles (28,160 kilometers) per hour, Glenn reported seeing what he thought looked like fireflies floating outside his cabin window! (These have never been explained.) During reentry, there was some concern that *Friendship 7*'s heat shield might disintegrate in a fireball. However, Glenn emerged unharmed after his Mercury craft splashed down in the Atlantic.

John Glenn is a ► *former test pilot in the U.S. Marine Corps.*

Science News 1962

• American space probe *Mariner II* sends back the first close-up images of the planet Venus.

• The launch of *Telstar*, the first active communications satellite, takes place in the United States.

• The tunnel linking France and Italy under Mt. Blanc in the Alps is completed.

Lasers used in eye surgery

MEDICINE

To date, surgeons have operated on patients using a variety of manual tools; this year, another tool has become part of the surgeon's tool kit—the laser. Light produced by lasers is far more directional and powerful than ordinary light and can be focused to a small spot with great intensity. Once focused, the beam can produce great heat on the tiny area it hits. Conventional surgery is difficult to perform on the eye and especially the retina, the part of the eyeball sensitive to light. The retina is inaccessible using conventional surgery and patients can lose their sight if it becomes detached. The intense heat of a laser can literally weld a detached retina back in place.

History of FM

Radio signals have to vary, so that the receiver can translate these variations into the speech or music that make up a broadcast. Until 1935, transmitters always sent signals that varied in strength or amplitude via amplitude modulation, or AM. However, these signals were often affected by interference. In 1935, Edwin Armstrong, a major in the U.S. Army, devised a way of sending signals that varied with their frequency instead. These signals were much less sensitive to interference.

ENTERTAINMENT

"Stereo" for all as FM radio makes waves

Stereophonic radio broadcasts are now being received in many parts of the United States. It all began with pioneering work by the Zenith and General Electric Corporations in 1961. These companies have developed a way of sending two channels as a single, combined radio signal. To hear the broadcast in "stereo," listeners need a radio receiver with a decoder to unscramble the signal and route it through a two-channel amplifier to two separate speakers. By broadcasting their stereo material on FM to reduce interference, radio stations are producing programs with better sound than ever before.

▲ *Rock and roll with new FM sound.*

MATHEMATICS

Chaos looms

An American meteorologist, Edward Lorenz, has discovered that many physical phenomena —from the dripping of a tap to weather in the North Atlantic—are characterized by a kind of predictable unpredictability that can be described as "chaotic." Lorenz has found it impossible to predict how most natural phenomena will evolve long-term, no matter how much information is known about them. There's talk of a new branch of math being devoted to the study of "chaotic" behavior.

Science News 1963

- The first crossing of the English Channel by hydrofoil is made, between Belgium and the United Kingdom.

- A Russian cosmonaut, Valentina Tereshkova, is the first woman to be launched into space.

- The lava lamp is invented by Edward Craven Walker in Great Britain.

◀ *The Polacolor instant camera.*

COMMUNICATIONS

Full-color images in a minute

When instant-picture cameras first appeared in 1947, many people were disappointed with the results. The pictures were in black and white, and were not very clear. Now, Polaroid® photography has taken a leap forward, with the first instant-picture color system, Polacolor®. The new film works in a similar way to the black-and-white Polaroid system, with two types of chemicals—light-sensitive material and developer. But with the color film, there are three kinds of light-sensitive chemicals, sensitive to the primary colors of light: red, blue, and green. The new film is already being greeted with enthusiasm, especially by the police, who may use it to take rapid pictures for identification purposes.

Carbon fiber used to strengthen composites

MATERIALS

A revolution in materials that started 10 years ago has now filtered through to household objects. The main driving force for this revolution has been the U.S. space program, which needs incredibly strong and lightweight materials. In order to meet these twin demands, scientists came up with new materials made from a number of component parts. These parts are combined to produce "composite" materials with characteristics far superior to those of the individual parts.

Carbon fibers are now used in many such materials. By themselves, such fibers are strong only in one direction. If they are trapped in a second material, then the fibers are held in place, giving the material strength in all directions. Composite materials also have useful thermal and electrical properties. In sports equipment, composites can be used to make new lightweight rackets for tennis and badminton, and golf clubs.

New carbon-fiber golf clubs are the lightest and strongest ever. ▶

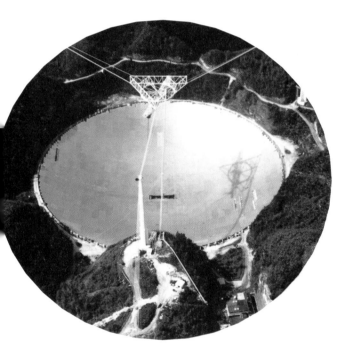

World's largest radio telescope

ASTRONOMY

The largest stationary radio telescope in the world, the Arecibo telescope, has been completed in a northern area of Puerto Rico. The telescope, which is part of Cornell University's National Astronomy and Ionosphere Center, features a 1000 foot- (304 meter-) wide receiving dish consisting of nearly 40,000 individual reflecting panels attached to a network of steel cables. The panels focus radio waves from outer space onto detectors fixed on a platform suspended above the dish. The position of the platform can be adjusted to enable the telescope to observe well over half of the heavens. The telescope may be used to search for signs of extraterrestrial life.

◀ *The Arecibo radio telescope dish is set into a natural hollow.*

Seat belts fitted to automobiles

TRANSPORTATION

Since the 1950s, American automobile manufacturers have been providing bulky seat belts based on the harness and lap belt model. They were considered an accessory rather than a standard feature. However, this year, the Swedish automobile manufacturer Volvo has introduced the single belt fixed to three anchor points, which is much easier to put on. All their mass-produced autos are now equipped with them. Based on a safety belt used in aeronautics, Volvo has been working on the design since 1959. Seat belts were considered important way back in 1903, when motor cars were in their infancy and Gustave Desiré Liebau took out a patent for "protective braces for use in automobiles and other vehicles."

Volvo has introduced the seat belt as a standard feature. ▶

1964

A GLANCE AT THE PAST

Early space probes

Space probes are unmanned, instrumented, spacecraft sent beyond Earth to investigate other parts of the solar system. Before the U.S. *Ranger 7* (*above*), some 20 probes had been launched, but many were failures. Two of the earliest successes were the U.S. *Pioneer 4*, which flew by the Moon in March 1959, and the Soviet *Luna 2*. *Luna 2* successfully crash-landed on the Moon on September 14 in the same year, confirming the Moon had no appreciable magnetic field. In 1962 a U.S. craft, *Mariner 2*, was the first successful probe to visit the planet Venus.

The first good close-ups of the Moon

A U.S. space probe, *Ranger 7*, has crashed into the Moon, but in doing so it has captured the first high-resolution images of the lunar surface. The series of over 4,000 images were taken from altitudes of between 1,500 miles (2,400 kilometers) and 1,700 feet (518 meters) above the lunar surface during the final 17 minutes of its flight. A moment after transmitting the last image, the craft smashed into the Moon at 6,000 miles (9,660 kilometers) per hour.

▲ Ranger 7 *was on a mission to discover if the Moon's surface is firm enough for spacecraft to land.*

Science News 1964

- Verrazano Bridge, the world's longest suspension bridge, opens, connecting Staten Island and Brooklyn in New York.

- American Baruch S. Blumberg discovers the "Australian antigen," the key to developing a vaccine for hepatitis B.

- Britain and France agree to build a tunnel under the English Channel.

Do quarks exist?

Many years ago, it was thought that atoms were indivisible—then it was shown that they consist of smaller particles, called protons, neutrons, and electrons, and that atoms can in fact be split. But now, a U.S. physicist, Murray Gell-Mann, has suggested that protons and neutrons may consist of even smaller components, which he's calling "quarks." Gell-Mann says that a number of different types (or "flavors") of quarks exist. These include "up," "down," and "strange" quarks. Of these, the "up" quark carries a two-thirds unit of positive charge, while the "down" and "strange" quarks carry a one-third unit of negative charge. A proton consists of two "up" quarks and one "down" quark, whereas a neutron contains one "up" and two "down" quarks.

Milton Bobbit, a composer ▶ *and director of the Columbia Princeton Electronic Music Center, with a Moog synthesizer.*

Moog synthesizer

The first synthesizer, a device that produces musical sounds electronically, is now on sale in stores. It is the brainchild of American professor Robert Moog, who has been working with two composers, Walter Carlos and Herbert Deutsch. The synthesizer works by generating "white noise" (a combination of all sound frequencies) and filtering out the unwanted frequencies to produce the sound required. People have said that the synthesizer is like having a whole orchestra in one box.

Dialysis machines enter the home

MEDICINE

For many years now, patients with kidney failure have been treated with artificial dialysis in hospitals. Soon, these patients will be able to forego their hospital appointments. Patients have needed to go to the hospital at least three times a week for treatment, which lasts up to four hours for each visit. Their blood is circulated through machines that filter out the poisons their kidneys can no longer remove. Cellulose tubing is used to filter out the poisons. However, new manufacturing techniques have produced hollow, cellulose filaments. These filaments provide a large area for filtration in a very small volume, which drastically reduces the size of the dialysis machine. Consequently, dialysis machines are now small enough to be placed in the patient's home, allowing daily treatment. Home dialysis is not without risk but the increased quality of life will probably make it a popular choice with patients.

▲ *Dialysis machines like this are now small enough to be placed discreetly in the home.*

New strain of "miracle" rice is developed

AGRICULTURE

The International Rice Research Institute at Los Banos in the Philippines has produced a new, experimental rice, which is being described as "miracle" rice. The rice is a dwarf variety, which has been created by crossing ordinary *indica* rice with a high-yielding *japonica* variety. The new strain, which is to be grown in tropical regions, produces double the yield of ordinary rice. It can therefore produce bumper harvests that may begin to solve problems of starvation in the world's poorer countries. However, for the rice to produce high yields, huge amounts of fertilizer, pesticides, and other additives, as well as plenty of water, must be used.

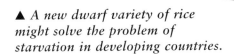

▲ *A new dwarf variety of rice might solve the problem of starvation in developing countries.*

Container ships introduced

TRANSPORTATION

International trading has become more efficient with the introduction of the container ship. From now on, cargo ships will carry or contain their cargo in sealed standard-sized containers. Guide rails and racks on the ships hold the containers securely in place. Once on land, the containers can be loaded onto specially adapted trucks or railway cars. The practice of using containers to transport cargo dates back to 1954, when American Malcolm MacLean began using them to transport goods between New York and Houston.

▲ *Container ships will make international trading much more efficient.*

The "Big Bang" theory

The "Big Bang" theory had its origins in the 1930s, when a Belgian astrophysicist, Georges Lemaître, proposed that the universe must have had a beginning ("a day without a yesterday") and was created by the explosion of a sphere of concentrated energy and matter, which he called the "cosmic egg." Lemaître's ideas were influenced by the discovery in 1929 that the universe is expanding. In 1948, a Ukrainian–born American physicist, George Gamow (*above*), further developed the theory, calculating in detail how matter and energy evolved during and after the explosion. He predicted that the Big Bang should have left a faint, lingering background radiation.

COSMOLOGY

Discovery of microwave "Big Bang" remnants

Two American radio astronomers, Arno Penzias and Robert Wilson, have announced the discovery of a faint but pervasive form of radiation in the microwave (short radio wave) region of the electromagnetic spectrum that seems to emanate from every direction in space. Astronomers are excited about the discovery, which they are calling the "cosmic microwave background radiation," or CMBR, because it provides strong evidence for the "Big Bang" theory of the Universe.

▲ *Maps showing the cosmic microwave background radiation.*

COMPUTERS

New "minicomputer" is marketed

U.S. computer manufacturer Digital Equipment Corporation has achieved several "firsts" with its new model, the PDP-8. The machine is already being called a "minicomputer" because it's so tiny compared with the normal room-sized "mainframes." In fact, the PDP-8 is no bigger than a large filing cabinet and is amazingly inexpensive—a "no-frills" version can be bought for less than $25,000! The machine has a whopping 4 kilobytes of core memory and is fast enough to be useful for a wide range of applications from scientific research to typesetting. It's also easier to operate than most of its predecessors.

COMMUNICATIONS

First home video recorder

The Japanese Sony Corporation has produced a new domestic appliance that many believe will change home entertainment forever. It is the video recorder, a device that allows the user to record television programs as they are broadcast, so that they can be viewed later. Professional video recorders have been used in television studios for years, but they have been large, unwieldy, expensive devices. The Sony, by contrast, is compact enough to sit on a small shelf or table, and is simple to operate. Sony predicts that one day, people will be able to buy movies on videotape and watch them in their own homes.

Changing the way we view—the video recorder. ▶

Mariner IV flies by Mars

The U.S. space probe *Mariner IV* has successfully flown by Mars—the first spacecraft ever to do so. As it passed some 6,120 miles (9,850 kilometers) above the surface of the red planet, the probe took 22 close-up photographs and transmitted these as a stream of signals back to Earth. Mars seems to be covered in craters and has a much thinner atmosphere than expected. For people hoping there may be life on Mars, the photographs may be a disappointment—there are no obvious signs of Martians, or indeed of any form of life, although natural waterways were evident in some regions of the planet. Launched last year, *Mariner IV* has taken seven and a half months to reach Mars. It carries a television camera and six other scientific instruments for studying interplanetary space and the region around Mars itself. The probe will now speed on to the far side of the Sun.

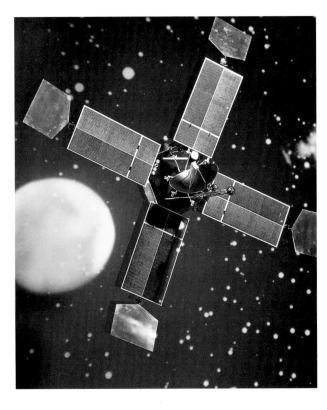

Mariner IV ▶ approaching Mars. The spacecraft's instruments are powered by sunlight.

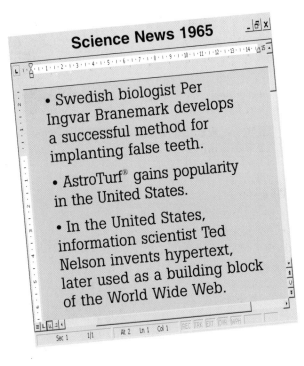

Science News 1965

- Swedish biologist Per Ingvar Branemark develops a successful method for implanting false teeth.

- AstroTurf® gains popularity in the United States.

- In the United States, information scientist Ted Nelson invents hypertext, later used as a building block of the World Wide Web.

Is Stonehenge a computer?

American archaeologist Gerald Hawkins has suggested that Stonehenge, the Stone Age monument in Wiltshire, England, may have been a combined astronomical observatory and computer. It has always been thought that the site was used for religious and magical rites. Stonehenge consists of three circular formations of holes, stones, and archways, with the outermost ring of holes having 56 marked positions, and the inner ones 30 and 29, respectively. Earlier, in the nineteenth century, British astronomer Joseph N. Lockyer demonstrated that the stones were arranged so as to align with the sunrise at the summer solstice, leading many to speculate that the builders were sun worshipers. Hawkins argues that the arrangement is a device for calculating months and predicting lunar and solar eclipses.

▼ Are the 4,000-year-old standing stones of Stonehenge a huge observatory?

The history of optical fibers

In 1955, Narinder Kapany, a scientist working at Imperial College, London, made the first optical fiber. It consisted of a narrow "thread" made of two kinds of glass—an inner core and an outer covering. When light was shone inside, it bounced along the core from side to side until it had traveled from one end to the other. Even if the optical fiber was bent, light still traveled through it, enabling light to be guided around curves for the first time. Optical fibers were soon being used to make endoscopes—instruments that allow doctors to see inside the human body.

A huge dam across the Rance River will force the rising and falling tides to flow through 24 10,000-kilowatt generators. ▼

COMMUNICATIONS

Making light work of communication

Scientists at the British Standard Telecommunication laboratory have discovered how to send telephone conversations along fiber-optic cables. First, speech is changed into a code made up of electrical impulses, which is in turn translated into pulses of light. The pulses are sent along fiber-optic cables and are decoded back into speech at the other end. Fiber optics have several advantages over ordinary cable, the main one being that they are very narrow, so that dozens can be bundled together to carry a huge number of messages at once.

▲ *Because messages travel as light, there is no electrical interference when fiber-optic cables are used.*

EARTH SCIENCE

The first weather satellite

The National Aeronautics and Space Administration (NASA) has launched the first Earth observation satellite that, in theory at least, provides coverage of the whole Earth. The satellite has been named *ESSA-1* (*Environmental Science Services Administration Satellite-1*). It's been put into a polar orbit, which means it passes over both of Earth's poles on each revolution. *ESSA-1* collects information about Earth's cloud cover, and relays the data to a number of ground receiving stations.

◀ *An ESSA satellite prepares to launch into space.*

ENERGY

Tidal power harnessed

There have been many attempts to harness some of the power stored in the rise and fall of the tides to generate electricity. Opening this year, the Rance tidal power plant in Brittany, France, will use this resource to generate power on an unprecedented scale. In order to generate power, a dam will be placed across the Rance River. When the tide enters, water flows through the turbines to generate electricity. A gate is then lowered from the dam, capturing all the water above it. When the tide goes out, the gate is raised and water flows out again through the generators, producing additional electricity.

SPACE EXPLORATION

Soviet craft soft-lands on the Moon

In January, the Soviet spacecraft *Luna 9* made the first soft landing on the Moon and sent television images of the Moon's surface back to Earth. The spacecraft featured a specially weighted egg-shaped capsule containing TV and transmission equipment that separated from the main lander on touchdown. It returned TV pictures to Earth for three days. The Soviets then put two more Luna probes into orbit around the Moon and a further one on the surface—these have all sent back photographs (the surface one has also tested the lunar soil's density and level of radioactivity). Meanwhile, the United States has soft-landed its own craft, *Surveyor 1*, on the Moon in June and sent a spacecraft, *Lunar Orbiter 1*, into orbit around the Moon in August.

▲ *Luna 9's egg-shaped capsule opened up* (bottom left).

▶ *The Harrier's versatility makes it an ideal fighter-bomber.*

MILITARY TECHNOLOGY

Harrier jet jumps to it

After many years of research and trials by British aircraft makers Hawker Siddeley, the Hawker Harrier jet made the world's first vertical takeoff on August 31. Powered by a single vectored-thrust turbofan engine, the plane is able to divert its engine thrust downward for vertical takeoffs using rotatable engine exhaust ports. The Harrier "jumpjet" is the world's first aircraft with a Vertical Take-Off and Landing (VTOL) capability, and so does not need a conventional runway. This makes the Harrier ideal for landing on aircraft carriers, or in small, confined spaces. With a length of 44 feet (14 meters), and a wingspan of 22 feet (7 meters), the Harrier is small and highly maneuverable.

Science News 1966

- Great Britain launches a performance-enhancing fuel injection system for automobile engines.

- The pocket television is unveiled by Clive Sinclair in Great Britain.

- Dynamic random access memory (D-ram) is invented by IBM in the United States.

COMMUNICATIONS

Modems used to send messages

Computers can now talk to each other more easily than ever before! People are beginning to connect computers together using a device called a modem (modulator–demodulator). A modem works by converting the digital-electrical signals produced by a computer into a series of tones that can be sent down an ordinary telephone line. This means that a computer equipped with a modem and connected to the telephone network can communicate with another, similarly equipped machine anywhere on the globe. Governments are already excited at the prospect of being able to send messages and documents all over the world, making data more widely available than ever before, and they are encouraging the development of a standard method for sending and receiving data. This could be the start of an information revolution.

1946	**1957**	**1959**	**1962**	**1969**
The U.S.A. and U.S.S.R. use V2 rockets for high-altitude research.	The U.S.S.R. launches Sputnik 1, the first artificial satellite.	Luna 1 is the first spacecraft to visit interplanetary space.	Telstar is the world's first communications satellite.	U.S. astronauts land on the surface of the Moon.

SPACE EXPLORATION

▲ Saturn IB *rocket*.

In October 1957, the world was astounded to hear that the space age had begun. *Sputnik 1* was a metal ball that took measurements of the upper atmosphere and broadcast a beeping signal that could be picked up on ordinary radios. It was the world's first artificial satellite.

Space exploration developed quickly and by 1959 *Luna 1* became the first probe to escape Earth's gravity. Animals soon followed the satellites into space, and in their turn, so did humans. In a little over a decade, humankind had reached the Moon. Although progress since then has been less spectacular, the development of space stations and deep-space probes has continued to push the frontiers of space exploration.

Testing times

Developed at incredible speed, the first manned *Apollo* spacecraft, *Apollo 7*, was launched in 1968, powered by a *Saturn IB* rocket. For 11 days the three-man crew tested the systems that would take humans to the Moon. Three more test missions were flown before *Apollo 11* carried Neil Armstrong, Buzz Aldrin, and Michael Collins on their historic mission to land on the surface of the Moon in 1969.

The Moon is the only celestial body other than Earth that humans have visited so far. ▼

Touch down

Taking manual control of the lunar module, *Eagle*, astronaut Neil Armstrong managed to avoid a field of large boulders before touching down on the Moon's surface on July 20, 1969. *Eagle*'s fuel tanks were almost dry. Over the next three years, 12 astronauts explored the lunar surface, bringing back rock samples for analysis and leaving behind equipment that beamed back information long after they had returned.

◀ *Sally Ride*.

Women in space

The first woman in space was the Russian Valentina Tereshkova in 1963. It was 1983 before the U.S. followed suit—the first American woman in space was Sally Ride, a physicist, who served as a mission specialist on a six-day flight of the Space Shuttle *Challenger*. Ride started a new trend. By 2000, over 30 women had flown in space.

1971
Salyut 1, *the world's first space station, is launched.*

1976
Vikings 1 and 2 land on the surface of Mars.

1977
Voyagers 1 and 2 set off on their long tour of the solar system.

1996
The French satellite Cerise is the first to be destroyed by space junk.

1999
The first units of the International Space Station are launched.

Ringed giant

Deep-space probes have hugely increased our knowledge of the planets of the solar system. The largest planet, Jupiter, was the subject of close scrutiny from the two *Voyager* probes, launched in 1977. They discovered that, like its neighbor Saturn, Jupiter is circled by rings. The probes also sent back valuable information about Jupiter's moons including Io, with its eight active volcanoes.

◀ *The* Voyager *probes found many small storms and eddies throughout Jupiter's banded clouds.*

Nuclear energy ▶
Too far from the Sun to rely on solar panels, Cassini uses three radioisotope generators (which use heat from the radioactive decay of plutonium) to power its instruments.

Huygens probe

Distant traveler

The American spacecraft *Cassini*, launched in 1997 on a mission to the planet Saturn, is one of the largest space probes ever built. It carries 1,515 pounds (687 kilograms) of science instruments connected by 8.7 miles (14 kilometers) of wiring and cables. *Cassini* will start orbiting Saturn in 2004, and will study the planet's rings and atmosphere. It carries a smaller probe, *Huygens*, which will investigate Saturn's largest moon, Titan.

Hubble space telescope

Most of the vast expanses of space have so far been explored only with telescopes. The Hubble Space Telescope (HST), placed in orbit around Earth in 1990, was designed to escape the problem of Earth's atmosphere distorting light from space. Most of the body of Hubble is a tube that funnels light onto a large mirror. This collects as much light as possible from distant objects and reflects it onto an electronic sensor. The information can then be beamed directly to Earth.

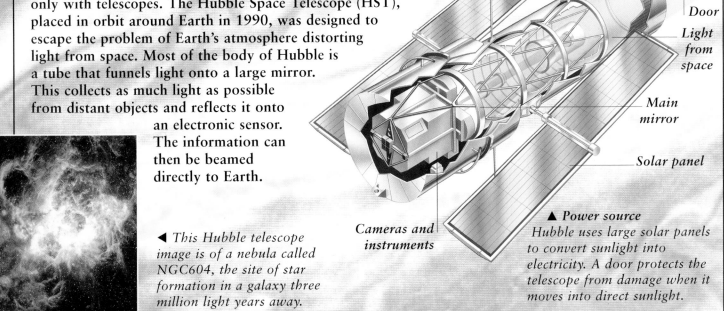

Antenna

Secondary mirror

Door

Light from space

Main mirror

Solar panel

Cameras and instruments

◀ *This Hubble telescope image is of a nebula called NGC604, the site of star formation in a galaxy three million light years away.*

▲ **Power source**
Hubble uses large solar panels to convert sunlight into electricity. A door protects the telescope from damage when it moves into direct sunlight.

The original microwave

The first microwave oven was produced in 1945 by the Raytheon Manufacturing Company of Newton, Massachusetts, in the United States. At its heart was a device called a magnetron, which produced ultra-short waves called microwaves, and which had been used previously with radars during World War II. The Raytheon® oven was large and expensive. Only big kitchens could accommodate one, and for many years, only professional caterers cooked with microwaves.

HOME APPLIANCES

First microwave oven for home use

Fast food has come to the kitchen as the first home microwave ovens go on sale. The ovens work by bombarding food with ultra-short microwaves. When the microwaves hit the food, they make the water molecules inside move millions of times a second. This movement generates friction, which in turn produces heat, cooking the food "from the inside."

▲ *Microwave ovens cook food 10 times faster than conventional ovens.*

Science News 1967

- China detonates its first hydrogen bomb (H-bomb).

- In Greece, Angelos Galanopoulos suggests that the volcano that destroyed the island of Thera was the basis of the Atlantis myth.

- In Cleveland, the first coronary artery bypass graft is performed by René Favaloro.

ENVIRONMENT

Warming warning

Scientists Syukior Manabe and Richard Wetherald are warning that human activity that increases the amount of carbon dioxide in the atmosphere, such as increased burning of coal and other fuels, causes a "greenhouse effect" that may eventually lead to global warming. The greenhouse effect occurs when fuels such as oil, coal, and wood are burned, releasing carbon dioxide and other gases into the atmosphere. These create a "blanket" around Earth, which traps heat from the Sun, preventing it from escaping and forcing it back down to Earth. As a result, temperatures rise. Scientists have long known that carbon dioxide in the atmosphere acts as a heat trap, but this is the first time its effects have been highlighted.

MEDICINE

Human heart successfully transplanted

A 59-year-old South African man, Louis Washkansky, has become the first recipient of a healthy human heart, taken from a dead body, to replace his own failing organ. A five-surgeon team performed the transplant operation on December 3 at Groote Schuur hospital in Cape Town. Without the new heart, which came from a 25-year-old auto accident victim, Washkansky would have died within a few days—his own heart had been severely weakened by a series of heart attacks. So far, Washkansky is making good progress, although there are some worries about a lung infection.

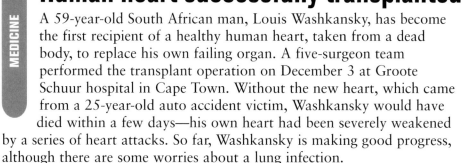

◄ *Dr. Christian Barnard, who led the transplant team.*

SPACE EXPLORATION

Test flight of *Saturn V* rocket

The National Aeronautics and Space Administration (NASA) has tested its new giant rocket, the *Saturn V*. NASA is planning to use this rocket to send astronauts to the Moon. *Saturn V* is 363 feet (110 meters) high—taller than the Statue of Liberty—and its total weight at launch is 2,950 tons (2,676 metric tonnes). The rocket has three stages. The five first-stage engines burn 12.6 tons (11.4 metric tonnes) of propellant (liquid oxygen and kerosene) every second during lift-off, providing a total thrust of about 7.7 million pounds (34.5 million newtons) of force. This is equivalent to several hundred large jet engines—of the type that power transatlantic airliners—all firing at once. The "payload" for the test flight was an unmanned Apollo spacecraft, called *Apollo 4*. A craft of this type will be the main "home" for astronauts for the forthcoming Moon missions.

◀ Saturn V *rocket on its launchpad.*

Dolby® sound is music to the ears

For years now, listeners to tape-recorded sound have noticed that there is an annoying background hiss. American engineer and physicist Ray Dolby has come up with a way of removing the hiss. The Dolby noise-reduction system works by breaking up each sound into its separate acoustic elements. Next, the system takes away the element that causes the hiss, then it reassembles the sound, which plays back loud, clear, and apparently undistorted. Dolby, who worked with the Ampex Corporation on early video recorders before setting up his own Dolby Laboratories in 1965, predicts that the system will be used in movie theaters and home tape recorders.

New fertility treatment

A new drug, clomiphene, has been introduced to help couples who have been having difficulties conceiving a child. The drug is taken by the would-be mother and acts on brain centers that control the release of female sex hormones. These hormones act on the woman's ovaries to stimulate the release of eggs, which may then be fertilized by sperm from the father. The drug is proving successful—many couples who have been trying to conceive for years, but without success, are now expecting a child. However, taking the drug also seems to increase the chances of conceiving not just once but several times over. So far, most of the multiple pregnancies have been twins, but there has also been an increase in triplets and even higher-number multiple births.

▶ *Only about one in 8,000 pregnancies unassisted by fertility treatments result in triplets. In women taking clomiphene, the chance of triplets is slightly higher than this.*

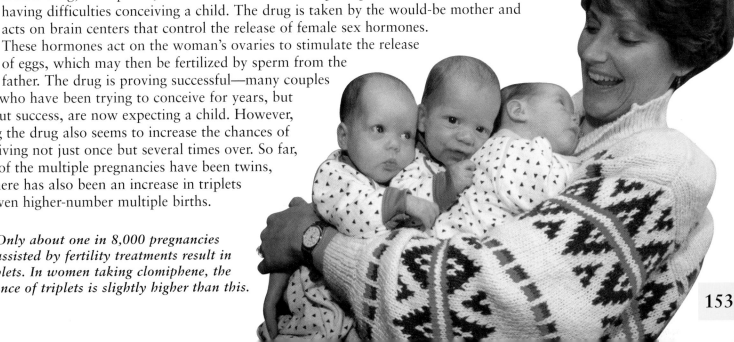

A GLANCE AT THE PAST

TRANSPORTATION

Regular hovercraft service crosses the English Channel

The first practical hovercraft

As early as the mid-nineteenth century, engineers had grasped the concept of the hovercraft, but they lacked the technology to build one. In 1916, the Austrian Navy tested a prototype, but it was not until 1955 that a way was found to reduce friction between the craft and the surface of the water. Christopher Cockerell, a British engineer, modified and improved the basic design and made it workable. (*A replica of Cockerell's 1955 hovercraft is shown above.*)

A new kind of ferry has come into use as British shipping lines introduce hovercraft service between England and France. The hovercraft, technically known as an Air-Cushion Vehicle, or ACV, is steered across water or land floating on a cushion of air generated by a powerful fan. The air is

▲ *A hovercraft crossing cannot be attempted in high winds.*

trapped underneath the vehicle by a flexible rubber skirt. The cross-channel hovercrafts can carry 175 passengers and 35 vehicles at a time. The crossing is much quicker than by conventional ship, but is extremely noisy and bumpy.

SPACE EXPLORATION

First view of earthrise from Moon

For the first time, three American astronauts—Frank Borman, James Lovell, and Bill Anders—have escaped Earth's gravity and made the 240,000-mile (386,000-kilometer) journey to the Moon. Their spacecraft, *Apollo 8*, was launched using a *Saturn V* rocket on December 21. By the morning of December 24, they were in lunar orbit, witnessing the extraordinary sight of Earth rising above the lunar horizon. Their mission was to prepare for a lunar landing mission next year. *Apollo 8* did not carry lunar landing craft; instead, the astronauts observed the lunar surface for possible future landing sites. To return home, *Apollo 8*'s engines were fired while the craft was behind the Moon and out of contact with Earth. The astronauts splashed down safely in the Pacific on December 27.

From 170 miles (273 kilometers) above the Moon's surface, the astronauts saw their first earthrise. ▼

Only half of Earth was illuminated due to the Sun's position almost directly above in the lunar sky. ▼

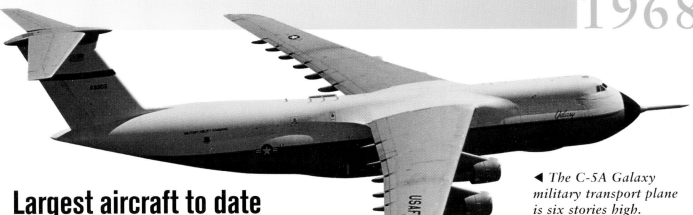

◀ *The C-5A Galaxy military transport plane is six stories high.*

TRANSPORTATION

Largest aircraft to date

Lockheed has introduced the world's largest aircraft, the C-5A Galaxy military transport plane. It is six stories high, as long as a football field, and can carry 100 tons (91 metric tonnes) nonstop for 4,000 miles (6,400 kilometers). Orville and Wilbur Wright could have comfortably made their historic first flight within its cargo bay! The Galaxy opens up at both ends to load and unload, and can easily carry six helicopters, or two battle tanks, or a 74-ton (67-metric tonne) mobile bridge, or 15 mobile hospitals. Its 28-wheel landing gear is designed so that it can take off and land on unpaved runways, and so can be used to land supplies in difficult terrain or bring relief to disaster-struck areas.

OCEANOGRAPHY

Glomar Challenger digs deep

The *Glomar Challenger*, a specialist drilling ship built by Global Marine Inc., has set out on a voyage of discovery. Commissioned by JOIDES (Joint Oceanographic Institutions for Deep Earth Sampling) as part of the ongoing deep sea drilling project, it is staffed by technicians from the Scripps Institution of Oceanography at San Diego, California. The ship has been designed to drill continuously in water 1,312 feet (400 meters) deep, so that scientists can test current theories of plate tectonics and the spread of the seafloor. Scientists also hope to find evidence for climate changes over the last few million years. The *Glomar Challenger* will make a number of eight-week trips, beginning in the Gulf of Mexico, then going on to the North and South Atlantic, the Caribbean, and the Pacific. The first trip will be led by Maurice Ewing.

Science News 1968

- The world's first supersonic airliner, the Tupolev TU–144, is demonstrated in the Soviet Union.

- In the United States, the first whirlpool bath, the Jacuzzi®, is marketed.

- Great Britain's first successful heart transplant is performed in London.

Earth appeared as a small white and blue oasis in the vastness of space. ▼

ENVIRONMENT

Pollution kills Lake Erie

Pollution—from industrial and other waste, vehicle fumes, and litter—is having an increasingly damaging effect on the environment. Now Lake Erie, the fourth largest of the Great Lakes that separate Canada and the United States, is dying. Industrial and local wastes have been discharged directly into the lake for many years, and its waters are now completely polluted. The U.S. Department of the Interior has estimated that pollution is killing 15 million fish each year in Lake Erie.

The first man on the Moon

Neil Armstrong (*above*) was born in Wapakoneta, Ohio, on August 5, 1930. Armstrong took flying lessons as a teenager and earned his flying license before he was legally old enough to drive a car. He studied aeronautical engineering before becoming a naval air cadet. In the 1950s, he flew combat missions in the Korean War. In 1955, he joined the National Aeronautics and Space Administration (NASA) as a high-speed test pilot, and in 1966, he made his first space flight aboard *Gemini 8*.

Superb 3-D images are possible with an SEM. ▼

SPACE EXPLORATION

Man walks on the lunar surface

Two American astronauts, Neil Armstrong and Edwin "Buzz" Aldrin, have landed safely on the Moon inside their lunar module, the *Eagle*—and have walked on the lunar surface. Armstrong was the first to climb out of the lunar module, declaring: "That's one small step for a man, one giant leap for mankind." The men spent two and a half hours outside the lunar module, where they collected more than 48 pounds (21 kilograms) of moon rock, and left a flag and plaque marking their visit.

▲ *Neil Armstrong takes a historic first step on the Moon.*

MEDICINE

Prenatal health check

A new test, called amniocentesis, has been introduced for checking on the health of an unborn child in the early stages of a pregnancy. The test involves inserting a fine needle through the woman's abdomen and the wall of her womb into the sac of fluid (the amniotic sac) that surrounds the fetus. A small amount of fluid is then withdrawn. This fluid contains cells and chemicals from the fetus, and by examining these, doctors can tell whether the child is affected by conditions such as Down's syndrome, a chromosome abnormality.

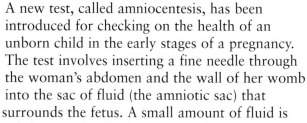

Science News 1969

- Soviet space probe *Venera 5* sends back data about the planet Venus.

- In France, luxury supersonic airliner *Concorde 001* breaks the sound barrier.

- In Texas, the first artificial heart is used to replace a diseased one. The patient lives for three days following the operation.

ENGINEERING

Scanning electron microscope

Electron microscopes have been around since the 1930s, giving scientists the opportunity to look at objects at far greater magnifications than ordinary optical microscopes. However, there has always been a problem with the traditional type of electron microscope—the specimen has to be very thin because a beam of electrons has to be able to pass right through it. Now a new type of instrument, the scanning electron microscope (SEM), is set to change this. With an SEM, electrons are scattered over the surface features of the specimen. Instead of the traditional microscope's flat, two-dimensional images, the SEM produces images that look three-dimensional on the microscope screen.

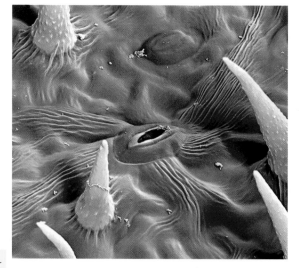

Ionizers improve air quality

HOME APPLIANCES

Scientists claim that a new domestic appliance, the ionizer, will improve the quality of the air we breathe. Manufacturers say that people who install an ionizer in their home feel healthier and happier. An ion is an atom that has gained or lost an electron and therefore contains an electrical charge. An ionizer increases the number of free positive ions of oxygen and nitrogen in the air. It achieves this using a number of pointed electrodes through which the air passes. Not all experts agree with the claim that people feel better with an ionizer in the room, but there is one clear advantage: Particles of pollutant chemicals that are electrically charged are attracted to the ionizer's electrodes. This means that the device cleans the air, and manufacturers are already starting to fit ionizers in air-conditioning units.

◄ *Whether or not an ionizer makes us healthier, it certainly cleans the air.*

First live synthesizer performance

ENTERTAINMENT

Jazz pianist Paul Bley has treated an audience to a new experience at New York City's Philharmonic Hall—he played the synthesizer. This is the first time the electronic instrument has been used in a live performance. We have become used to albums featuring the synthesizer over the past few years, but until now, musicians have avoided using the instrument on stage. This is because it is quite complex to play—all the controls have to be adjusted with great care to get the required sound from the thousands available. Now that Bley has led the way, it is likely that other musicians will follow, and live performances featuring a synthesizer will become as common as those with electric guitar or bass.

What's the time?

ENGINEERING

How accurate is your watch? Does it gain a few seconds a week or a minute a month? Scientists at the U.S. National Bureau of Standards (NBS) in Boulder, Colorado, have built a highly stable "atomic" clock, called NBS-4, that is accurate to around one second in a million years! Clocks like this derive their accuracy from the oscillation (side-to-side movements) of individual atoms that have been exposed to suitable excitation. Various atoms, including nitrogen atoms in the gas ammonia, have been tried before, but at present atoms of the metallic element cesium are favored for these clocks. Excited cesium atoms have been shown to vibrate at a constant frequency of 9,192,631,770 cycles per second. Two years ago, scientists redefined the second as the time taken for a cesium atom to vibrate that number of times.

Atomic clocks are used to define ► *what the time is throughout the world.*

Early gastroscopes

One of the first gastroscopes (tubes for viewing the inside of the stomach) was devised by a London doctor, William Hill, in 1911. This gastroscope was a rigid pipe (like that shown above) and used conventional methods for light transmission. Maneuvering the instrument down the patient's esophagus (throat) was painful for the patient, difficult for the doctor, and time-consuming for both. Consequently, it was not often used and many disorders that would be readily diagnosed and treated today were left unchecked.

MEDICINE

Flexible endoscope finally arrives

Techniques of medical diagnosis and treatment are being revolutionized by the introduction of improved internal viewing tubes, or endoscopes. The new endoscopes are flexible and allow doctors to view body areas that were previously inaccessible. Endoscopes work by carrying light along thousands of optical fibers encased in a tube. Reflected light is returned to the viewer. Small instruments can be passed along the tube, allowing doctors to perform surgery in parts of the body that were once difficult to reach.

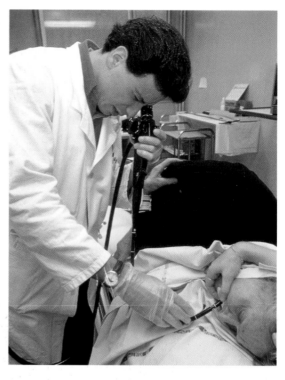

▲ *Flexible endoscopes make it possible to view previously inaccessible parts of the body without causing discomfort.*

TRANSPORTATION

"Jumbo jet" flies across the Atlantic

The largest civilian airplane in the world, the Boeing 747, lumbered across the Atlantic for the first time on January 23 in the service of Pan American Airlines. Nicknamed the "jumbo jet," it flew from New York to London. More people want to fly, but the skies are getting crowded—one answer is to put more passengers on one plane, which will clear the skies and bring down the cost of individual air tickets. The 747 is the result of research and development in military transport. It is 231 feet (71 meters) long, with a wingspan of 196 feet (60 meters), and cruises at 640 miles (1,024 kilometers) per hour.

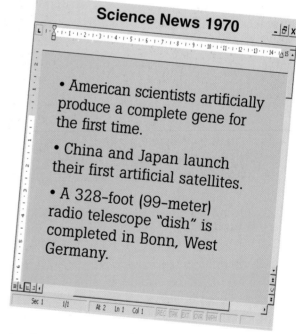

Science News 1970

- American scientists artificially produce a complete gene for the first time.

- China and Japan launch their first artificial satellites.

- A 328-foot (99-meter) radio telescope "dish" is completed in Bonn, West Germany.

A "jumbo jet" can carry up to 490 passengers and 33 crew. ▼

Computer memory set to become floppy

COMPUTERS

It is almost 10 years since magnetic disks were first used for data storage in computers. The speed and ease of access of data stored on disks made them particularly suitable for use as backup memory for the new high-speed computers. As with all aspects of computing, disks are now set to shrink in size. Smaller, 8-inch diameter, versions of these disks, now available at low cost, could make computers accessible to businesses that previously considered them too expensive.

◀ *The new eight-inch diameter disks are flexible, or "floppy," and portable.*

Laser precision with gas

ENGINEERING

Laser technology is only nine years old, but is already being used in industry and medicine. Gas lasers, first introduced in 1961, use gas trapped in a length of quartz tube with mirrors at each end to amplify light rays. Gas lasers are less powerful than crystal lasers but can produce a continuous and narrow beam of light of a precise frequency. This makes them much more useful for very detailed machine work that requires minute, precise measurements, and for building silicon chips used in the electronics and telecommunications industry. The first gas laser used neon and helium, but carbon dioxide is more efficient.

◀ *High-precision gas lasers are ideal for intricate machine work.*

Robot on the Moon

SPACE EXPLORATION

The Soviet Union has delivered an unusual-looking robotic vehicle, named *Lunokhod*, to the Moon by means of the spacecraft *Luna 17*. The spacecraft and its payload successfully landed on the Moon on November 13. *Lunokhod* is a mobile laboratory that crawls over the lunar surface taking photographs, which are returned to Earth using radio signals. The vehicle looks a little like a small bathtub carried on eight strong metal wheels, with various antennae and instruments protruding from it. Its movements are controlled by a team of five Soviet scientists and engineers back on Earth. The vehicle will journey over the Moon's surface for many months and is expected to return thousands of unique photographs.

Lunokhod undergoing tests before its trip to the Moon. ▶

A GLANCE AT THE PAST

The first integrated circuits

In the 1950s, experimental circuit boards were made in which at least one component was contained within the board itself. By the 1960s, early multi-component integrated circuits consisted of 10 individual components on a silicon chip just one-quarter of an inch (6 millimeters) square. By the 1970s, it was possible to pack thousands of components in a chip of the same size.

COMPUTERS

The first true microprocessor

Intel has released a microprocessor, a product that could touch all our lives. While working on the design of a new calculator, engineers realized that the performance of the calculator could be increased for less cost if the 12 chips used to perform all the work were replaced by a single general-purpose chip. The new microprocessor designed by Ted Hoff has been named the 4004 by Intel. Each chip is smaller than a thumbnail, but contains 2,300 transistors and can perform a remarkable 60,000 operations per second.

▲ *The Intel 4004, the most sophisticated computer chip in the world.*

COMMUNICATIONS

Direct transatlantic telephone dialing

Making a transatlantic telephone call has just become easier. Calls across the Atlantic have been possible since the 1920s, but they were connected manually by an operator, and getting a line was not always easy. Now telephone users in Great Britain can dial the United States direct—all they need to know is the number of the person they are calling and the correct international dialing code. When someone in London picks up the phone and dials New York, the call is routed automatically to an international telephone exchange in Cornwall. From there, the call is beamed up to a satellite in space, which bounces it back down to Earth in New Jersey. The call continues on its way by wire to New York. All this happens in a matter of seconds.

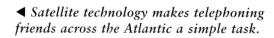

◀ *Satellite technology makes telephoning friends across the Atlantic a simple task.*

MEDICINE

Fractures healed by electricity

Doctors in the United States have shown that fractures (broken bones) heal more quickly by applying tiny electric currents. Since the 1950s, it has been known that pressure generates small electrical currents in bones, and to remain strong and healthy, leg bones require the regular application of stress (from walking, for example). Now it has been realized that electrical currents may stimulate growth and renewal of bone tissue, and so the direct application of a small electric current may help fractures to heal. In trials, a woman whose nine-month-old ankle fracture refused to heal had a metal pin, that was hooked up to a battery, anchored to the broken bone. Within 12 weeks her fracture had healed.

Benefits of vitamin C

MEDICINE

In his book, *Vitamin C and the Common Cold*, the American chemist and double Nobel Prize winner Linus Pauling has supported the benefits of taking a large daily dose of vitamin C, both for fighting colds but also to help prevent more serious diseases such as cancer and heart disease. According to Pauling, vitamin C (or ascorbic acid) has long-term beneficial effects on the body. These benefits arise from its role in the manufacture of collagen, a protein that shapes connective tissues and strengthens skin and blood vessels. Pauling has recommended that people take a daily dose of one-third of an ounce (10–12 grams) of vitamin C every day, which is far higher than the minimum dose recommended by nutritionists.

▲ *Linus Pauling with an orange, an excellent source of vitamin C.*

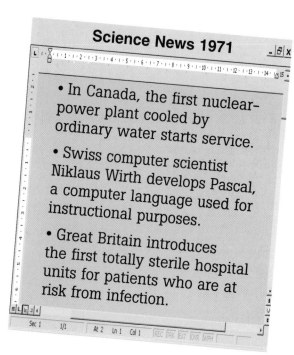

Science News 1971

- In Canada, the first nuclear-power plant cooled by ordinary water starts service.

- Swiss computer scientist Niklaus Wirth develops Pascal, a computer language used for instructional purposes.

- Great Britain introduces the first totally sterile hospital units for patients who are at risk from infection.

Math in the palm of your hand

ELECTRONICS

An American company, Texas Instruments, has succeeded in building the first miniature electronic calculator—it has been called the "Pocketronic." Work began in 1965, and the result is a small calculating machine 6 inches (154 millimeters) x 4.1 inches (107 millimeters) x 1.7 inches (44 millimeters). The calculator is battery-powered, has a keypad for entering numbers, and can carry out basic arithmetic—it can add, subtract, divide, and multiply. Answers are printed on paper tape. Its small size is achieved by packing all the electronic circuitry onto just one silicon chip. The Pocketronic costs $150. Despite its name, the calculator is too bulky to fit in a pocket. It also weighs close to 2.5 pounds (1 kilogram).

Volcanoes and riverbeds on Mars

SPACE EXPLORATION

The American spacecraft *Mariner 9* has become the first human-built object to orbit the planet Mars. Its dual mission is to photomap about two-thirds of the planet's surface and to study changes in the Martian atmosphere. *Mariner 9* is equipped with wide- and narrow-angle television cameras and weighs 1,116 pounds (506 kilograms). The probe is scheduled to circle the Red Planet twice every day for the next twelve months, taking photographs of Mars and gathering data about the composition, density, pressure, and temperature of its atmosphere. When *Mariner 9* first arrived, most of Mars was hidden by dust storms. After the dust cleared, the probe revealed a very different planet—one that boasts huge volcanoes and a canyon system that stretches 3,000 miles (4,800 kilometers) across its surface.

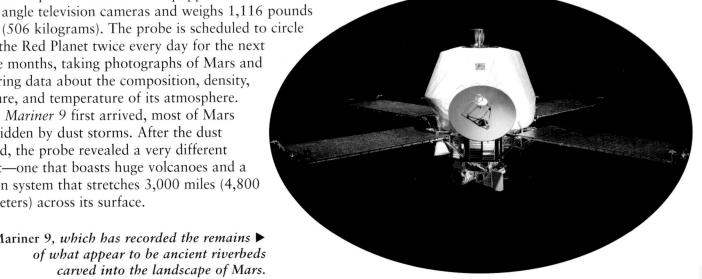

Mariner 9, which has recorded the remains ▶ of what appear to be ancient riverbeds carved into the landscape of Mars.

NEW MEDICINE

In the twentieth century, the overall health and life expectancy of people living in the developed world increased markedly. Initially, this was mainly due to advances against infectious diseases—especially new vaccines and antibiotics. But during the last 50 years, the emphasis switched toward "high-tech" solutions for a much wider range of diseases and disorders.

Developments in electronics, materials science, genetics, laser technology, chemistry, and computers have already contributed to a breathtaking series of medical advances.

Heart pacemaker

The first successful wholly implantable devices for controlling the heartbeat were introduced in the late 1950s. These heart pacemakers, as they were called, were about the size of a large jelly donut. Today's pacemakers are much smaller and weigh just 2 to 3 ounces (55 to 85 grams). A pacemaker is a battery-powered pulse generator that sends electrical impulses to the heart to keep it beating at a regular rate. By the 1990s, tens of thousands of Americans were being fitted with pacemakers each year.

An early pacemaker. ▶

▲ *X ray of original hip joint.*

◀ *Replaced hip joint.*

Joint replacement

Artificial joints are just one of many different types of spare body parts. The first hip replacement operation was performed in 1938, and the operation was improved upon over the following decades, using new materials and better ways of preventing joint infection. By the 1980s, replacement knee, shoulder, finger, and elbow joints had also become available.

Laser surgery

Since lasers were first developed in the 1960s, many different surgical applications have been found for them. A laser ca[n] be used as a "light-knife," cutting cleanly through tissue without causing damage beyond the target area and sealing off all blood vessels as it goes.

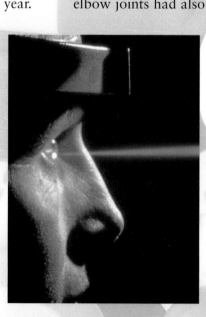

◀ *A laser beam being used in eye surgery.*

▲ *All drugs must pass rigorous tests before they are approved for use.*

Tailor-made drugs

A large part of modern medical treatment involves drug therapy. This was also true back in the 1920s, but modern medicines are far more powerful and specifically targeted than their predecessors. In the past, many remedies were discovered by chance or by systematic observations of the curative effects of various natural substances. By the 1970s, medical understanding of the body's chemistry and the causes of disease had advanced to such an extent that it became possible to "tailor-make," or chemically design, medicines in the laboratory for specific purposes. This often involved the use of computers to visualize the three-dimensional shapes of candidate drug molecules and their intended sites of action within the body.

▲ *Medical pioneer Dr. Robert Jarvik.*

Life saver?

In the 1970s, a young physician from Michigan, Dr. Robert Jarvik, working with the Dutch-born inventor Willem Kolff, built the first "artificial heart." The device, called the Jarvik 7, was made of plastic, aluminum, and an artificial fiber, Dacron®. In 1982, it was implanted into a patient and kept him alive for 112 days. Later, Jarvik 7 devices were used in other heart patients, but many of them died or were harmed by complications, so its use gradually declined. Jarvik, however, continued working on the concept and in 2000 he introduced the Jarvik 2000®.

How a heart-assist pump works

Several different artificial-heart devices appeared during the later years of the twentieth century. Many never caught on, but a new device introduced in 2000, the Jarvik 2000, looks to be the best yet. It should really be called a heart-assist pump as it supplements rather than replaces the natural heart. The silent thumb-sized device is implanted into the lower left-hand heart chamber and pumps blood to the body via a large artery, the aorta. The device is likely to be offered to patients with weakened hearts who are either waiting for a heart transplant or are too old to receive one.

Inside the valveless device ▶ *are tiny rotor blades that work at 10,000 revolutions per minute to pump oxygenated blood from the heart into the aorta via a piece of artificial tubing.*

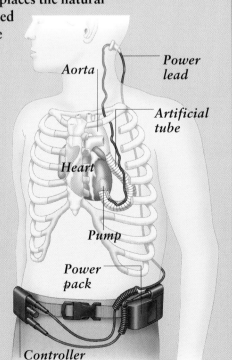

A GLANCE AT THE PAST

History of the black hole

The idea of black holes was first discussed in the 1910s, but it wasn't until 1939 that anyone suggested that such objects might exist. The American physicist Robert Oppenheimer and a colleague, Hartland Snyder, calculated that if a large star ran out of energy, gravity would cause it to collapse into an object so dense, and with such a strong gravitational field, that nothing within a certain distance could escape. In 1968 the term "black hole" was coined to describe this phenomenon.

ASTRONOMY

The amazing phenomenon of "black holes"

Physicists and mathematicians have been developing their ideas on black holes—regions within the universe that are so dense, and have such a strong gravitational pull, that nothing, not even light, can escape from them. Two of those at the forefront of black hole research are the British physicists Roger Penrose and Stephen Hawking. Their ideas imply that inside a black hole, time must come to an end. Hawking has also noted that conditions within a black hole must be similar to what the universe was like when it came into being. However, so far, no black holes have been detected.

▲ *Stephen Hawking believes many black holes exist.*

The ERTS includes two wing-like solar panels, which deliver 1,000 watts of power to its instruments. ▼

HOME APPLIANCES

Salad in a spin!

Washing the salad is easy enough, but you have to wait for the water to drain away. Not anymore! The new salad spinner uses simple, old-fashioned technology to solve an old-fashioned problem. The spinner consists of a container with an inner basket. You simply drop the wet salad into the basket, put on the lid, and turn the handle. A gear connects the handle to the basket, which spins around rapidly, shaking the water off the salad and depositing it in the bottom of the container.

EARTH SCIENCE

First Earth resources satellite

The National Aeronautics and Space Administration (NASA) has launched a new type of satellite called an Earth Resources Technology Satellite, or ERTS. The 1,800-pound (816-kilogram) satellite was launched into polar orbit on July 23 using a Delta Rocket. The satellite will take thousands of photographs of Earth's surface from 500 miles (800 kilometers) up, providing information that will be useful to scientists observing Earth. For example, images from the satellite may be used to help detect mineral deposits, observe population growth in cities, or monitor oil spills or deforestation. The satellite carries a television camera and an experimental sensor called a Multi-Spectral Scanner, which can detect radiation given off by Earth.

SPACE EXPLORATION

Last men on the Moon

Two members of the final Apollo mission to the Moon, *Apollo 17*, have safely landed on the lunar surface. The two men are veteran astronaut Eugene Cernan and geologist Harrison Schmitt. The two astronauts are spending three days on the Moon and exploring the lunar landscape in the Lunar Rover—a lightweight vehicle that was also used during the *Apollo 15* and *16* missions. Schmitt is the first professional scientist to visit the Moon, and his expertise is proving to be a useful asset. In all, he and Cernan have driven more than 21 miles (34 kilometers) over the lunar surface and collected 240 pounds (109 kilograms) of moon rocks, including some of an unusual red color.

◄ *Geologists study moon rocks following the* Apollo 17 *mission.*

ENVIRONMENT

United States bans DDT

Slightly more than 30 years since the insecticide DDT was hailed as a revolutionary advance in pest control, its use has been banned in the United States. The reason is to protect the environment. Using DDT on crops has increased harvests enormously, but the environmental costs are very high, and it is killing wildlife. When DDT is sprayed on crops, it is eaten by creatures, such as mice, and enters the food chain. A bird of prey, such as a hawk, eats the mice, and the DDT builds up inside the bird's body, causing it to produce thin-shelled eggs or deformed chicks.

It has been discovered that DDT has resulted in thin-shelled eggs. ►

MEDICINE

First CAT scanner

A new type of medical scanner has gone into service at a hospital in Wimbledon, England. The device is called a CAT scanner (CAT stands for "computer axial tomography") and it uses X rays and a computer to produce images of cross-sectional "slices" of the body. These images show different tissues and organs in varying shades of gray and can be used to detect abnormalities that are invisible on a conventional X ray. The scanner was developed by a team at the British electronics company EMI, led by engineer Godfrey Hounsfield. The device works by passing X rays through the body at various angles and measuring their absorption, by means of a rotating X-ray source and detector. The data is fed to a computer, which uses complex math to produce an image.

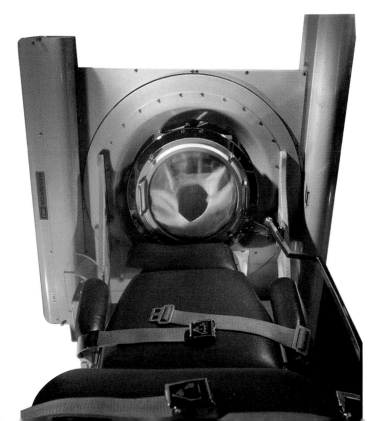

◄ *For CAT scanning, the patient lies on a couch, which slides into the scanning machine.*

165

The first space station

The world's first space station, *Salyut 1* (*above*), was launched by the Soviet Union in 1971 and stayed in orbit for six months. Its main purpose was to study the effects of long-term space flight on the human body and take photographs of Earth from space. It was intended that a series of crews would use *Salyut 1*, but in practice, just one crew of three cosmonauts occupied it for 24 days. Sadly, the three men died when their Soyuz craft depressurized during the return to Earth.

ASTRONOMY

Skylab observatory goes into orbit

The United States has launched its first orbiting space station, which can be occupied by a team of astronauts for months at a time. Named *Skylab*, the observatory was blasted into orbit on May 14 but sustained damage soon after launch. The first crew arrived on May 25 and after making repairs, occupied it for 28 days. *Skylab* is equipped with six telescopes. The crew is conducting astronomical studies of the Sun, Earth resources experiments, and medical studies. Three further crews will stay in the observatory over the coming months, and some of the astronauts will make extended space walks.

▲ *Skylab is made from the third stage of a Saturn V rocket. It is as big as a two-story house, so it provides spacious living areas.*

ENGINEERING

Sears Tower becomes tallest

At 1,461 feet (443 meters), Chicago's new Sears Tower has just become the tallest building in the world. Designed by the architectural firm Skidmore, Owings, and Merrill and masterminded by engineer Fazlur Khan, the building uses a clever new type of structure to resist the huge wind forces that a tall building has to cope with in Chicago. The key to the building's success is its "bundled-tube" structure. The skyscraper is in fact made up of nine separate steel towers, or tubes, which lock together to give the structure added strength.

◄ *Only two of the nine towers reach 1,461 feet (443 meters) in height and have 110 stories—others stop at the 50th, 66th, and 90th floors.*

TRANSPORTATION

NAVSTAR system initiated

The United States Department of Defense has approved an ambitious navigation program known as the NAVSTAR Global Positioning System. A network of 24 satellites will be put into orbit around Earth to provide navigation and timing information to military and civilian users worldwide. A global satellite control network will pick up signals from the satellites and translate them into position information. The satellites will circle at a height of 12,625 miles (20,600 kilometers) above Earth's surface every 12 hours. At any one time, a minimum of four satellites will be visible from any point on Earth. The satellites will continuously broadcast position and time data to users throughout the world.

Skateboards take off

ENTERTAINMENT

The sport of skateboarding has taken off as a result of new wheel technology. Skateboard enthusiast Frank Nasworthy had been unhappy with skateboard wheels for some time. Traditional, roller-skate wheels gave a bumpy ride and skateboards cobbled together with these wheels were often unsafe. Now Nasworthy has adapted urethane wheels, also recently fitted to roller skates, for use on skateboards. Urethane is a good material for wheels because it is both hard-wearing and gives good grip. Skateboarders who use the new wheels enjoy a safer, smoother ride—and this smoothness enables them to achieve faster speeds.

Gene "transfer" engineered

BIOLOGY

Two scientists in San Francisco have shown that it is possible to transfer a gene (a section of the biological "supermolecule," DNA), into the DNA of a second organism. Stanley Cohen and Herbert Boyer took a piece of DNA containing an antibiotic-resistant gene from a bacterium and "spliced" it into a larger piece of DNA from another bacterium. When the altered DNA was reinserted into the second bacterium, the resulting bacterial colony was resistant to antibiotics. The technique of "genetic engineering" is believed to have immense implications for many areas of medicine.

▲ *Skateboarders are enjoying a smoother ride, thanks to new wheels.*

A model of a short section of DNA, the molecule that carries an organism's genes. ▶

Tiny chip contains 10,000 components

COMPUTERS

In the 1950s, G. Drummer, an engineer from England, spent many years working on radar systems. Thanks to the transistor, these systems became smaller and more reliable. Drummer considered the implications of such miniaturization and realized that it would be much better to develop components that already had transistors, capacitors, and resistors built in, rather than individually wiring each separate component to a board. His work led in time to the development of the integrated circuit, or silicon chip. Manufacturer Texas Instruments is now set to mass-produce the first chip that uses large-scale integration (LSI) of thousands of electronic components. Texas Instruments has divided its chip into four units—an arithmetic unit, a register, a control section, and a data path. Altogether, there are more than 10,000 components on a chip just half an inch (one centimeter) square.

Integrated circuits contain all the electronic components ▶ *necessary to run complex machines, such as computers.*

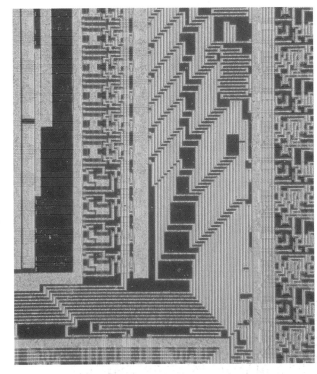

1974

The history of holograms

Hungarian-born British scientist, Dennis Gabor (*above*), came up with the idea of a hologram in 1947 while he was working to improve the electron microscope. Gabor invented the name "hologram" from the Greek words *holos*, meaning "whole," and *gramma*, meaning "message." Making a hologram requires a light source that is "coherent" —that is, constant, and consisting of a single wavelength. This type of light source was not found until 1960 with the invention of lasers.

PHYSICS

Holograms become more widespread

Holograms—three-dimensional images—are becoming widespread in many areas of life. A hologram is made using a special beam of light from a laser, in which light waves of a uniform wavelength travel in phase with one another. This beam is reflected off an object. Then, a second laser beam is made to interfere with the first. This results in a wave interference pattern, which is stored on a photographic plate. Illuminating the plate with a laser or with ordinary light recreates a three-dimensional image of the original object.

▲ *Holograms are beginning to be used for advertising, security devices, and general data storage.*

ELECTRONICS

Improved calculators

Since their arrival on the market, pocket calculators have been a smashing success. Now there are new versions that are smaller, lighter, and cheaper in price. Some new pocket calculators can even be programmed. Manufacturers Hewlett-Packard, for instance, have introduced a pocket calculator that can be programmed using a magnetic card reader. In some ways, it is a type of "personal computer." Users can write programs of up to 100 lines in length and record them on blank cards, or they can buy preprogrammed cards. The cards are magnetic on one side and writable on the other. After a card is passed through the calculator, it can be slid into a slot just above the top row of keys to serve as labels for the keys.

HOME APPLIANCES

Wheelbarrows have a ball

British inventor James Dyson has patented a wheelbarrow like no other. The large-capacity barrow has a body made of molded polypropylene, which is light, tough, and long-lasting. But the most noticeable difference about the barrow is that instead of a wheel it has a ball, made of the same polypropylene material as the body. Dyson claims that there are several advantages to the ball. It runs easily over bumps and works well on soft ground. It is very easy to steer. And because the ball is set well under the body, the barrow is easy to lift (the load is close to the fulcrum, giving good leverage). All this makes for a barrow that promises to be a big hit with gardeners.

◀ *Dyson's ball barrow.*

The first liquid crystals

In 1888, Austrian botanist Friedrich Reisnitzer was examining the melting behavior of an organic substance related to cholesterol. He observed that the substance melted to a cloudy liquid at 294° F (145.5° C) and became a clear liquid at 353° F (178.3° C). Repeating these experiments led to the identification of a new kind of matter, known as liquid crystal (*above*). Because the molecular forces producing these states are very weak, the structures are easily affected by changes in mechanical stress and temperature.

MATERIALS

Liquid crystal displays become common

All of us encounter the three common states of matter—solid, liquid, and gas—on a daily basis. However, there are some substances that act partly like a liquid and partly like a solid. Discovered nearly a century ago, these substances are called "liquid crystals." There are many varieties of these liquid crystals, with several potential uses. This year, the liquid crystal display, or LCD, has become very popular.

Digital watches ▶ with LCD display are a fashion success.

SPACE EXPLORATION

A handshake in space

For the first time, the United States and the Soviet Union have cooperated in space. In July, an orbiting Apollo spacecraft carrying three astronauts docked with a Soviet Soyuz craft carrying two cosmonauts. After successfully docking, two of the U.S. astronauts shared a meal with the Russians. The historic docking lasted two days and is seen by many people as marking the end of the space race between the two superpowers.

◀ Astronaut Tom Stafford (left) *meets cosmonaut Alexie Leonov* (right).

◀ Professor Gould holding the shell of a large mollusk.

PALEONTOLOGY

Species evolved in rapid bursts

Harvard paleontologist Stephen Jay Gould has offered a new slant on the theory of evolution by introducing a concept called "punctuated equilibrium." This proposes that the evolution of new species occurs in rapid bursts, followed by periods of little change. If Gould's idea is correct, then it helps to explain why there are many "gaps" in our records of fossils. For example, if birds evolved from reptiles, why are there not more fossils of animals that are intermediate between birds and reptiles? Gould's explanation for the gaps is that, of all the animals that have ever lived, only a tiny proportion are preserved as fossils. If one group evolves into another very rapidly, there may not be sufficient numbers of intermediate animals for fossils to be left.

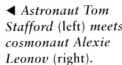

1976

First flight by a supersonic airliner

The world's first supersonic transport (SST) to leave the hangar and head for the skies was the Russian Tupolev Tu-144 (*above*). The aircraft made its maiden test flight in 1968, one year before its commercial rival, the Anglo-French Concorde supersonic jetliner. Designed by the aeronautical engineer Andrei Tupolev, the Tupolev Tu-144 carried 100 passengers and flew at a speed of 1,550 miles (2,494 kilometers) per hour. Various setbacks meant that the Tu-144 never achieved its full potential and it ceased commercial operations in 1978.

TRANSPORTATION

First scheduled supersonic airline flight

The Concorde, the supersonic passenger aircraft developed jointly by France and Great Britain, began scheduled flights on January 21. Two Concordes took off simultaneously from London and Paris. The London aircraft flew to Bahrain, while the Paris plane headed for Rio de Janeiro, Brazil. Concorde is 193 feet (59 meters) long with a wingspan of 84 feet (25.6 meters), and can carry 100 passengers. In May, after a legal battle over landing rights because of the loud engine noise, Concorde was finally given permission to fly over the Atlantic Ocean to New York.

Concorde cruises at ▲ Mach 2.2—more than twice the speed of sound.

MEDICINE

Mystery illness hits American Legion convention

In July of this year, a severe and mysterious illness hit scores of people attending an American Legion convention at a hotel in Philadelphia, killing 29 of them. For the first few days, the convention went normally. Then, large numbers of conventioneers suddenly started feeling unwell, with severe headaches, fever, aching, vomiting, and disorientation. At first, doctors attending the victims, and scientists investigating the cause, were totally baffled. But eventually, the culprit was discovered to be a bacterium, previously unknown to science, that was breeding in the hotel's air-conditioning system and being pumped directly into rooms. In recognition of the Philadelphia outbreak, the bacterium has been named *Legionella pneumophila* and the illness it causes, "Legionnaire's disease."

SPACE EXPLORATION

Spacecraft land on Mars

The United States has landed two space probes—*Viking I* and *II*—on Mars. Photographs taken by the probes of the Martian surface reveal a jumble of reddish boulders in what appears to be a sandy desert, with a pink sky background (caused by red dust particles in the atmosphere). The landers have also tested the Martian soil, which has not revealed any apparent sign of life, and are monitoring the weather on Mars by measuring temperatures and winds. *Viking I* was the first to arrive at Mars on June 19, after a 10-month journey from Earth. *Viking II* followed about seven weeks later.

▼A photograph of the red planet, Mars.

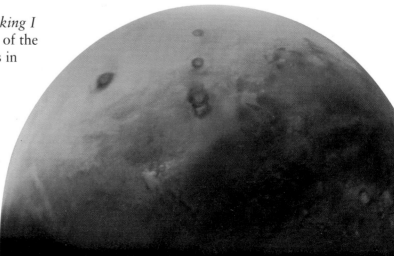

The fastest computer on the planet

COMPUTERS

A new computer has been launched that can perform a staggering 240 million calculations per second. It is a machine that truly deserves the name "supercomputer." Designed and built by Seymour Cray, the Cray-1® is by far the fastest computer on the planet. Cray has an amazing talent for designing circuitry to maximize speed. In order to increase the speed of this system, the Cray-1 has a unique "C" shape that enables the integrated circuits to be closer together. No wire in the entire system is more than four feet (1.2 meters) long. This high-powered machine generates intense heat and has an innovative cooling system using Freon gas. The Cray-1 can be bought for a mere $8.8 million and is primarily aimed at scientific users. The first of these supercomputers is to be installed in the United States at the Los Alamos National Laboratory.

The Cray-1 computer ▲ is designed for use on scientific projects.

▲ *The Konica C35AF is the world's first self-focusing camera.*

Colorful theorem proved

MATHEMATICS

A proof that has eluded mathematicians for decades has finally been found. Mathematicians Kenneth Appel, Wolfgang Haken, and John Koch of the United States have produced a proof for the "four-color theorem." This theorem states that four colors are enough to shade in any map drawn on paper or the surface of a globe, so that no two touching parts of the map are the same color. The proof was extremely complex and needed a computer to examine every possible type of map.

The first auto-focus camera is introduced in Japan

COMMUNICATIONS

The Konica company of Japan has introduced the first camera that focuses itself. Instead of turning a ring on the lens and focusing by eye, with the Konica C35AF® you simply point and shoot. As you press the shutter, the camera's autofocus system takes over. Light rays entering the camera hit a special separator lens that splits the image in two. The camera then calculates the distance between the two images. The camera's processor is programmed to detect that the subject is in focus when the two images are a certain distance apart. If they are not at the right distance, a motor in the camera body adjusts the focusing ring on the lens until they are—then the shutter opens and a perfectly focused picture is taken. The system works well except when lighting levels are very low.

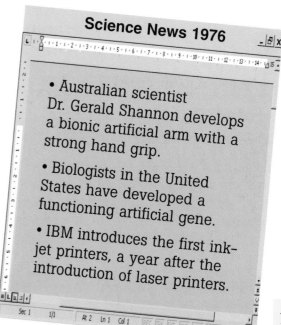

Science News 1976

- Australian scientist Dr. Gerald Shannon develops a bionic artificial arm with a strong hand grip.

- Biologists in the United States have developed a functioning artificial gene.

- IBM introduces the first ink-jet printers, a year after the introduction of laser printers.

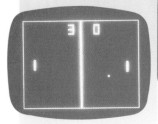

Pong

The first successful video game was Atari's *Pong* (*above*), a version of Ping-Pong that appeared in the early 1970s. There were only three moving elements on the display—the ball, which was a single glowing point of light, and the two "bats," which were short vertical lines at either end of the screen. Each player had a joystick control that allowed the bat to be moved up and down. The aim was to bounce the ball past the opponent's bat and score points.

ENTERTAINMENT

Space Invaders® invade the home

Japanese software company Taito has developed a computer game that is set to take the world by storm. The game is called Space Invaders, and Taito plans to make it available both in amusement arcades and as a console game for home use. The game involves shooting invaders who appear in rows and advance down the screen as a steady beat plays in the background. Space Invaders includes some new game ideas. There are special treats in the form of on-screen fireworks if the last invader you shoot is from the bottom row. In addition, the game saves the highest scores of previous plays, which are displayed on the screen.

▲ *Kids everywhere love Space Invaders.*

Science News 1977

- In California, a human-powered airplane built by Paul Macready flies and wins a $100,000 prize offered in 1959.

- VHS video recorders first go on sale in Europe.

- The Apple® II, the first personal computer that comes fully assembled, is introduced in the United States.

▼ *The preserved body of Baby Dima.*

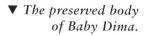

PALEONTOLOGY

Baby mammoth found

An alert bulldozer driver at a gold mine in Siberia has discovered the carcass of a baby mammoth calf buried 6 feet (1.8 meters) deep in the frozen soil. The calf, who is thought to have lived about 40,000 years ago during an ice age, is 46 inches (116 centimeters) long and just 42 inches (106 centimeters) tall, with a trunk 23 inches (58 centimeters) long. The mammoth has been named "Baby Dima," after a stream close to where it was found on a tributary of the Kolyma River. The six-month-old mammoth is almost totally intact and its skin, internal organs, and soft tissues are well preserved.

Small-screen TV

ENTERTAINMENT

The world's smallest television receiver has just been launched. Developed by British inventor Clive Sinclair, it features a tiny screen less than two inches (five centimeters) across and is designed for travelers who never want to miss a program. The set has rechargable batteries but can also be powered by electricity. The small black-and-white picture is best viewed from a distance of one-and-a-half feet (half a meter), and is quite clear in areas with good reception. Perhaps the set's most impressive feature is that it is compatible with television broadcasts all over the world. There are three different TV systems currently in use, which means that sets produced in the United States will not normally work in Great Britain. The Sinclair TV is the first to work with all three television systems.

▲ *The tiny Sinclair TV set.*

It is now possible to deposit ▼ *or withdraw cash at any time of the day or night.*

Coronary balloon angioplasty

MEDICINE

A young German physician, Andreas Gruentzig, has introduced a revolutionary new treatment for coronary heart disease, which is the biggest cause of death in developed countries. Coronary heart disease is caused by narrowing of the coronary arteries—the blood vessels that supply blood to the heart muscle.

Gruentzig's treatment, called balloon angioplasty, involves passing a thin catheter (tube) into a patient's narrowed coronary artery. The catheter has to be maneuvered into the correct position, using continuous X ray viewing. Once the catheter is in place, the surgeon inflates a tiny sausage-shaped balloon at the end of the catheter to open the blockage and restore blood flow to the heart.

First linked automated teller machines

COMPUTERS

Electronic banking has come of age with the introduction of linked automated teller machines (ATMs). ATMs, or cash dispensers, let you deposit or withdraw money from the machine at any time of the day or night. All you need is a plastic magnetic card, which you feed into the machine, using your personal identification number (PIN). The card carries your account number, and the machine, which is linked to the bank's computer system and to other ATMs, dispenses the cash you need. The first cash dispensers date back to 1969, but they used paper vouchers rather than magnetic cards and were unreliable. Electronic cash dispensers appeared in 1972, but were not linked to bank computers.

ANTHROPOLOGY

Footprints in the ash

Anthropologist Mary Leakey has discovered several trails of footprints made by early hominids, preserved in volcanic ash at Laetoli, near the Olduvai Gorge, in Tanzania. Tests indicate that the footprints are about 3.6 million years old, but the contours of the prints are virtually identical to those of modern humans. The find shows that, even at this early stage of human evolution, our ancestors walked upright with a striding gait very similar to our own.

▲ *An early hominid must have walked across the wet ash and left these footprints.*

Lucy's bones

In 1974, Donald Johanson and Maurice Taieb uncovered parts of a complete adult female skeleton at Hadar, Ethiopia. Christened Lucy, the remains were estimated to be three million years old, older than any previously discovered hominid. Lucy was less than 3 feet 6 inches (1.1 meters) in height, and weighed less than 66 pounds (30 kilograms). The find led to the formulation of a new hominid species, *Australopithecus afarensis*.

Science News 1978

- In America, Apple® launches the first floppy disk drive for use with personal computers.

- Sweden becomes the first country in the world to ban aerosol sprays because of damage to the environment.

- In Germany, Wolfgang Paul traps neutrons in a magnetic storage ring and is able to estimate their lifespan.

COMMUNICATIONS

Magnetic phone card

Now there is a fresh use for the plastic card—as a replacement for loose change at a public telephone booth. The new phone card has a magnetic strip on the back, which has information recorded on it. When you buy the card, the magnetic strip indicates that you have purchased telephone calls up to a certain value. You go to a phone booth, put a card in a slot, and make your call. The telephone then subtracts the value of your call from the magnetic strip. The process continues until you have used up all your calls.

TRANSPORTATION

Unleaded gasoline

The United States government has taken the first steps toward banning the use of lead in gasoline. Since 1923, gasoline for autos has contained lead tetraethyl. This is an antiknock agent, which increases the octane level and so the efficiency of the automobile. It also prevents the engine from deteriorating. However, since 1965 scientists have known that lead discharged into the atmosphere via exhaust fumes is dangerous. In humans, for instance, it enters the bloodstream and can damage the brain. Fortunately, new antiknock gasoline additives have now been developed that contain no lead.

Filling up with unleaded gas. ▶

Pluto has a moon

ASTRONOMY

Astronomers Jim Christy and Robert Harrington of the United States have discovered that Pluto, the smallest planet in the solar system, has its own moon. The moon, to be named Charon, is relatively large in relation to the size of its planet—in fact, some astronomers think that Pluto and Charon should be regarded as a double planet. Charon's discovery has forced astronomers to revise their estimate of Pluto's size. Previous estimates were based on blurred images that are now realized to have included both Pluto and Charon.

◀ *An artist's interpretation of how Charon might look as seen from Pluto.*

The first test-tube baby is born

MEDICINE

The first baby conceived outside the human body has been born to a British couple, Lesley and John Brown. The baby, who is to be named Louise, is normal in every respect. Mrs. Brown was unable to conceive in the usual way because of defects in her fallopian tubes, which carry the eggs from the ovaries to the womb. Dr. Robert Edwards and Dr. Patrick Steptoe, two British pioneers of the technique of in vitro (test-tube) fertilization, surgically removed an egg from one of Mrs. Brown's ovaries, and fertilized it with a sample of Mr. Brown's sperm in a laboratory dish. Once a sperm had penetrated the egg and the egg had started dividing, they implanted the embryo in Mrs. Brown's womb, where it developed normally.

▲ *The newborn Louise Brown.*

Remember with the Post-it® note

OFFICE TECHNOLOGY

Some of the most useful inventions are the simplest. A good example is the Post-it note, introduced by the 3M Corporation. There is a thin strip of adhesive along the top of the note that allows it to be stuck to a surface and removed with ease, leaving no mark behind. This makes the Post-it note ideal for marking places in a book or making notes that you eventually want to discard. Curiously, the strong, yet easily removed adhesive used on Post-it notes was invented in the 3M laboratories years ago, but no one could think of a use for it. Art Fry, one of 3M's chemical engineers who sings in his local church choir, saw a use for the adhesive when he wanted removable bookmarks to put in his hymnbook on Sundays.

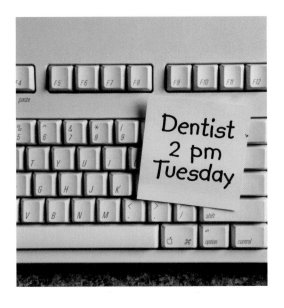

◀ *The simple but effective Post-it note has proved to be an office essential.*

WATER RESOURCES

▼ *Egret flying above a reservoir.*

Human lives depend on a regular source of clean drinking water. And water is needed for food crops, in industrial processes, and for domestic uses such as cooking, cleaning, and carrying waste.

Water resource management is about having a suitable quantity and quality of water in the right place at the right time. This requires extremely careful intervention in the natural cycle of water between land, air, inland waterways, and the sea.

Effects of drought

When rainfall is markedly less than normal for months or years on end, water supplies fail. Rivers run dry, safe drinking water is scarce, the soil becomes parched, and crops die. Even affluent countries with abundant rainfall, such as the United States, sometimes have droughts. In some countries, such as Sudan and Namibia, droughts are a regular feature and cause immense human suffering.

Wildlife reservoirs

In the last century, many natural wetlands were drained to create sites for farms, factories, and towns. The rich mix of wildlife wetlands once supported has largely disappeared. Water storage reservoirs can help fill this gap. By building reservoirs with gently sloping soil banks and leaving them in a natural setting, wetland animals and plants can be encouraged to settle there.

▼ *Shasta Dam, California, and its reservoir in drought conditions.*

▲ **Screening**
Water enters but large items are kept out by a coarse screen.

▲ **Coagulation**
In this tank, a chemical is added to clump particles.

▲ **Flocculation**
Here, particles start clumping together to form a sludge.

1962	**1964**	**1975**	**1980s**	**1990s**
The Delaware Aqueduct starts supplying water to New York City.	*Completion of the Aswan Dam, on the Nile River in Egypt.*	*Record amounts of water used per person in the U.S.A.*	*"Decade of International Drinking-Water Supply and Sanitation" is declared.*	*Scientists believe global warming will affect climate and water supplies.*

A modern "drip-feed" irrigation system. ▲

Watering the land

Worldwide, people use more water for irrigation—for watering crops—than for anything else. There have been major advances in irrigation methods since the 1950s. Modern techniques copy some of the oldest methods, where water is released directly onto plants at the best time of day with little water wastage. In Egypt and Israel large areas of desert have been cultivated using such methods.

Testing purity

Chemists and microbiologists (those who study microbes) regularly check that water supplies are safe to drink. Microbiologists filter the water and grow bacteria and other microbes they find. In this way, they can identify any harmful, disease-causing organisms. Chemists analyze the water for high levels of nitrates (from agricultural fertilizers), heavy metals (from industry), and any other substances that might be harmful if consumed in large quantities.

Water samples being analyzed. ▶

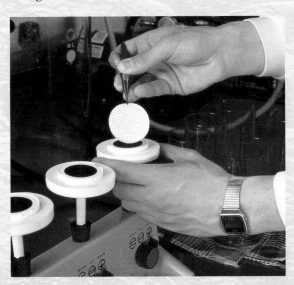

◀ *Churning water to dissolve air in it helps remove bad tastes and odors.*

Water pressure

A pumping station is used whenever water needs to be raised—perhaps to supply a town on a hillside using water from the valley below. Pumping stations are also necessary to maintain high pressure in the water mains system so that water can rise to all parts of a building and still come out of the faucet forcefully.

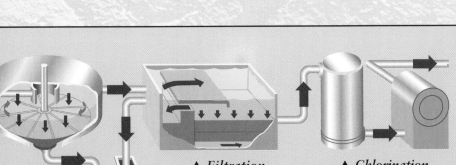

▲ **Sedimentation**
The sludge, containing microbes, is removed.

▲ **Filtration**
The remaining particles are filtered out in a filter bed.

▲ **Chlorination**
In this tank, chlorine is added and kills any remaining microbes.

How water is cleaned

Water from freshwater sources such as lakes and rivers is treated in several ways before it is safe enough to drink. Suspended particles, from large to microscopic, are removed in five stages (*see left*). The clear water is then disinfected—usually with chlorine—and fluoride is commonly added to help combat tooth decay.

Galileo's observation

The Italian astronomer and mathematician Galileo Galilei (*above*) was the first person to observe Jupiter's four largest moons—Ganymede, Callisto, Europa, and Io—in January of 1610. Eight months earlier, Galileo had heard about a new invention, called a telescope, and after testing it, decided to build a better one. Using his telescope, he soon made some important observations of the Moon, Venus, and Saturn, realized that the Milky Way is composed of millions of stars, and discovered Jupiter's moons. Jupiter's four largest satellites are named the Galilean moons in his honor.

Voyager probes arrive at Jupiter

Two United States space probes, *Voyager I* and *II*, have flown past Jupiter, sending back photographs of the planet and its larger moons. *Voyager I* sent back dramatic images showing that Jupiter has at least three distinct rings, which appear to be composed of fine dust grains. It also took photographs of Jupiter's Great Red Spot. *Voyager II* made a close observation of Jupiter's atmosphere and its large moons. Both probes have used Jupiter's gravity to help propel them on course to Saturn, their next destination.

▲ *A photograph of Jupiter's moon, Io, which has many active volcanoes.*

Mandelbrot's fractals

With his book, *Les objets fractals*, and some extraordinary computer-generated graphics, the mathematician Benoit Mandelbrot has raised scientific interest in the geometrical shapes called fractals. These shapes seem infinitely complex and yet are generated by rules that are simple. One of their characteristics is that they are made up of many smaller copies of themselves. On close inspection, the smaller copies consist of yet smaller copies, and so on, to infinity. Mandelbrot is now looking at fractals in nature and the business world. It seems that the shapes of all sorts of things, from cauliflower heads to stock-price graphs, display fractal geometry.

Catalytic converters introduced

Harmful exhaust emissions are being cut down dramatically. The catalytic converter, based on an idea pioneered in France in 1909, has been developed for modern car engines by General Motors. The idea is that a chemical reaction converts pollutants in engine exhaust gases to harmless substances with the aid of one or more catalysts—chemicals that help the reaction take place without themselves being altered. Most converters use the metals platinum and palladium as the catalysts, and they convert gases containing hydrocarbons, oxygen, and harmful carbon monoxide into water and carbon dioxide. It is only a matter of time before catalytic converters are standard equipment on new cars.

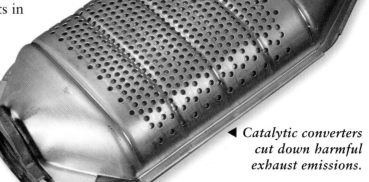

◄ *Catalytic converters cut down harmful exhaust emissions.*

Sony introduces the Walkman®

ENTERTAINMENT

The Sony Corporation of Japan has transformed the way we listen to music. Its latest product is the Walkman, a tiny cassette player that comes with a pair of headphones instead of a loudspeaker. The player is light enough to clip onto a belt or carry in a handbag. Better still, the headphones produce good-quality stereo sound. Now you can listen to music on the train, in the countryside, or walking down the street. And the headphones mean that no one else is disturbed—provided, of course, that you keep the volume at a reasonable level!

Thanks to the battery-operated Walkman, you can listen to music anywhere. ▶

Science News 1979

- Built by Paul Macready, *Gossamer Albatross* is the first human-powered aircraft to cross the English Channel.

- The first flat-screened pocket TV is patented by a Japanese company—Matsushita.

- Two Soviet cosmonauts return to Earth after spending a record 175 days in orbit.

Computer bulletin boards

COMMUNICATIONS

The world's first computer bulletin board system, started last year by Randy Suess and Ward Christensen of Chicago, is now well established. The bulletin board works simply. Users connect to the system by dialing from a computer with a modem. They then leave messages that others who connect to the system can read. Already an on-line community of users has emerged, with people returning regularly to look at messages and post their replies. Elsewhere, other people are setting up their own bulletin board systems, catering to special interests or specific cities or countries. The system is easy to use, puts like-minded people in touch, and allows debate on any topic under the sun.

Now it's the video disk

ENTERTAINMENT

Consumers are puzzled. Just a few years after home video recorders started to become popular, video disk machines are hitting the stores. The new machines play shiny plastic disks that can contain a feature-length movie, including a stereo soundtrack. Manufacturers point to the high quality of both pictures and sound with the new system, and the fact that no rewinding is needed. But buyers are not so sure. You cannot record onto video disks, and so far, only a few movies are available for viewing. It seems likely that few consumers will be prepared to spend money on another video system—especially if they have only recently bought a video recorder.

The new video disk machines offer high-quality ▶ *pictures and sound, but will people buy them?*

Early roller skates

Traditional roller skates, with two pairs of wheels each, first appeared in Great Britain in 1760. They were invented by a Belgian musician, Joseph Merlin, who first used them at a London ball, where he crashed into a large mirror. About 100 years later, roller skates became a hit in both Europe and America. They are still popular today, although now they have plastic wheels instead of the old metal ones, to give a much better ride.

ENTERTAINMENT

Rollerblade® craze hits the United States

American ice hockey player Scott Olson has started a new craze. Olson is the inventor of Rollerblade skates, which have their wheels in a single line, rather than in pairs. Olson, from Minnesota, wanted to work on his ice hockey skills outdoors in the warm summer months. So he developed Rollerblade skates to act in a similar way to ice skates. Already there are signs that the new skates will be popular with many people, not just ice hockey players. Skaters say that they can cruise with ease at around 10 miles (16 kilometers) per hour, which is faster than the usual speed on roller skates. Skilled skaters report speeds of up to 50 miles (80 kilometers) per hour downhill, making padded body protection a must!

▲ *Rollerblade skates enable skaters to reach high speeds.*

ELECTRONICS

Electronic eye at Wimbledon

Some new technology is being introduced at the Wimbledon Lawn Tennis championships this year in an attempt to make the jobs of line judges and umpires easier. It's an "electronic eye" that will survey the service line on some of the courts and make a judgement on whether services are "in" or "out." The system, nicknamed "cyclops," has been introduced because players are now serving at speeds of up to 135 miles (220 kilometers) per hour , making the job of a line judge difficult. The system consists of a series of light beams, projected across the court, about 1.6 inches (4 centimeters) above the surface in the vicinity of the service line; all the beams converge onto a light detector or "eye." When the serve happens, the pattern by which the ball breaks the beams is analyzed by a microprocessor in the "eye," which determines exactly where the ball bounced. If the serve was "out," the device emits a loud beep, but the umpire still has the final word.

▼ *As the patient lies in a water bath, the lithotripter focuses sound waves onto the kidney stone.*

MEDICINE

Shock waves for kidney stones

When a stone (hard mass) forms in a person's kidney it can cause extreme pain. Until recently, the only treatment to relieve this pain was a surgical operation requiring up to six weeks of recuperation. But now a West German aerospace company, Dornier Systems, has introduced an ingenious new machine for dealing with kidney stones without any need for surgery. The machine is named a "lithotripter" (from the Greek words meaning "stone" and "crusher"), and it works by focusing a high-frequency sound shock wave generated outside the body onto the kidney stone. The shock wave causes the stone to break up into tiny fragments, which then pass out of the body painlessly when the person urinates. It is expected that the treatment will be approved for use in the United States within a few years.

Smallpox is eradicated

The World Health Organization (WHO) has declared that smallpox, a devastating infectious disease that has killed hundreds of thousands of people over the ages, has been eradicated. The last naturally acquired case of the disease occurred in the African country of Somalia in 1977. The final two cases in the world resulted from a laboratory accident in 1978. It is the first and only time in history that a disease has been eliminated through planned human intervention. The World Health Organization will continue to maintain stocks of smallpox vaccine and will investigate any rumors of smallpox reappearing anywhere in the world.

Smallpox has been wiped out, thanks to a ▶ worldwide program of vaccination.

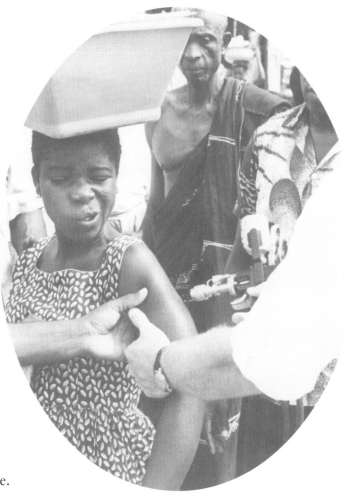

Voice recognition software

Having to type in commands via a keyboard can waste valuable time. A system that could recognize speech would be much more efficient. International Business Machines (IBM) is at the forefront of developing such technology. The two main areas of research are in voice-activated commands and converting speech to text.

The former is by far the more advanced, and systems are already in place where users can input commands over the phone. These systems could soon be common in the workplace.

Science News 1980

- American space probe *Voyager 1* sends back pictures that show the planet Saturn has at least 100 rings.

- The *Pioneer Venus 1* space probe discovers mountains higher than Everest on Venus.

- The world's longest tunnel is completed through Mount St. Gotthard in the Swiss Alps.

Checking out bar codes

Supermarket shopping will never be the same again, as bar codes and scanners come into widespread use. Although bar codes have been used since 1974, they have only been introduced in supermarkets this year. Everything you buy in a supermarket will now carry its own bar code—a set of binary numbers shown as small black-and-white stripes. This identifies the product and shows its price. When you take the item to the checkout counter, the cashier moves the item over a window and a laser scans the bar code, reading it from any angle. The information goes to the store's computer, which instantly displays the price of the product on a screen at the cash register. The computer also adds up your bill. Two American students first dreamed up the idea in 1952, and one of them finally perfected the bar code in 1973.

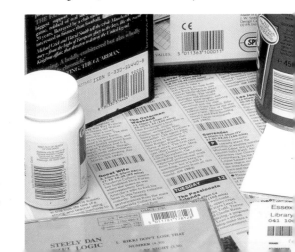

Bar codes will change ▶ the way we shop.

Apple II introduced

The first personal computer designed for anyone to use was the Apple II (*above*), introduced in 1977. Steve Wozniak designed the Apple II with both computing power and appearance in mind. The first Apple II sold for $1,300, had four kilobytes of RAM (built-in memory), and could produce color graphics. Apart from the excellent hardware, it came with VisiCalc, the best spreadsheet package of its day. The Apple II was an instant success. Prior to release, Apple had an annual income of $700,000, while the year after release, the company had a turnover of $7 million.

COMPUTERS

IBM personal computer arrives

Not one to do things by halves, IBM has entered the personal computer (PC) market in a big way, backed by Big Blue's massive sales force. The PC is powered by an Intel 8088 processor and includes an operating system licensed from a tiny Seattle-based company called Microsoft. The machine is no faster than its rivals, but IBM has given it ten times the memory of its competitors. Businesses will be pleased to know that one of the PC's first applications will help with financial planning.

▲ *IBM's PC is expected to be used for financial planning and for editing and storing typed-in letters and documents using specially written software.*

TRANSPORTATION

Bags of safety

Automobile drivers have a new safety measure designed to protect them from the worst effects of a crash. Airbags are now being fitted as standard equipment in private autos. They were first used in the United States in 1974, fitted to the fleet of Mercury autos driven by the sales representatives of Allstate Insurance Company. Later, the Oldsmobile Company offered them as optional extras to buyers of their Delta 88 and Tornado models. Some safety experts are concerned that airbags may be harmful, especially to children riding in the front passenger seat.

ENERGY

Solar-powered plane crosses the Channel

On July 7, *Solar Challenger*, a solar-powered plane, flew from Pointoise Cormeilles airport, near Paris, across the English Channel to the Manston Royal Air Force base in Kent—a distance of 160 miles (260 kilometers). Taking five hours and 23 minutes, the plane had an average speed of 30 miles (48.2 kilometers) per hour and a cruising altitude of 11,000 feet (3,300 meters). American Paul MacCready, who created the human-powered plane *Gossamer Albatross* led the plane's design team.

Airbags will open ▶ at very high speeds.

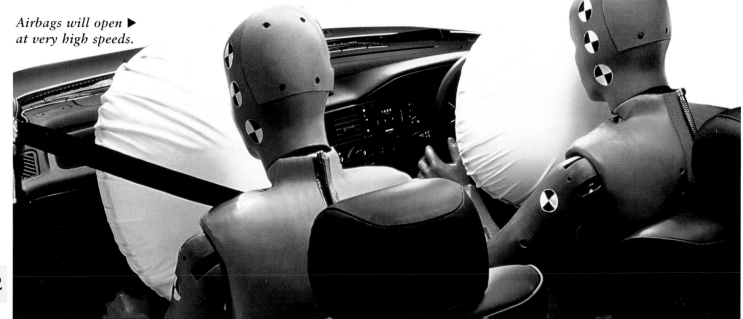

High speed on the rails

On September 27, after almost 15 years' research and development, the first TGV® (*train à grande vitesse*—"train of great speed") pulled out of the Gare du Lyon in Paris and sped off to the city of Lyon. Traveling at around 237 miles (380 kilometers) per hour, it reached its destination in 2 hours 40 minutes, cutting the regular journey time in half. The train is driven by electricity and has a streamlined, bulletlike profile, with engines at both ends. It is designed to be integrated into the existing railway system, running at normal speeds on conventional tracks near its destination. It can run at super speeds on its own specially designed high-speed track, which features curves set at gradients that are slightly steeper than normal.

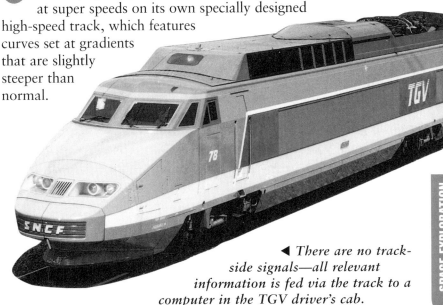

◄ *There are no track-side signals—all relevant information is fed via the track to a computer in the TGV driver's cab.*

Tunneling microscope allows even greater magnifications

A new type of microscope looks set to transform scientific knowledge of the surfaces of substances. Called the scanning tunneling microscope (STM), it is capable of magnifications of up to one million times. To achieve these stunning magnifications, the instrument uses a feature of electrons called the "tunneling effect," in which electrons cross thin barriers to travel very short distances. The result can be images of features less than ten billionths of an inch across—small enough to show individual molecules and even atoms.

Scientists predict that the new ▶ microscope will lead to a break through in the study of substances.

Space shuttle blasts off

Two United States astronauts, John Young and Bob Crippen, have made the first orbital test flight of the space shuttle, the world's first reusable winged spacecraft. The shuttle, named *Columbia*, was blasted into orbit on April 12 and made a two-day flight during which Young and Crippen thoroughly tested its systems. Then they guided it to the first runway landing of a manned spaceship. Special heat-resistant tiles prevented the shuttle from burning up when it reentered Earth's atmosphere. Eventually, a fleet of four shuttles will go into operation.

Science News 1981

• The Very Large Array (VLA), the largest radio telescope in the world, begins operations near Socorro, New Mexico.

• The world's first test-tube twins are born in Melbourne, Australia.

• *Voyager 2* reaches Saturn, providing more information about its rings and moons.

A GLANCE AT THE PAST

CeeFax ON SHOW

GARRY GARRARD of Texas Instruments, Bedford, lectures tonight to S.E.R.T. on the use of LSI circuits in teletext decoding. The lecture is at the University of Aston at 7.30pm.

****

DEREK WRIGHT of the BBC Research Department talks about teletext to the I.E.E.E. tonight at 7pm, at Loughborough University.

(CEEFAX gets green light ... p102)

On-screen information

The use of television screens to carry information began during the early 1970s. This was when broadcasters in Great Britain began to use the airwaves to send text messages to people's screens. This type of service, called videotex, worked by sending out extra electronic pulses along with normal broadcast programs. Users needed a television set with a special decoder in order to view the information, together with a remote control handset to select different items from on-screen menus. Similar services, such as Teletext and Ceefax (*above*), are still providing information about everything from the weather to sports results in Great Britain.

COMMUNICATIONS

The first public on-line service

France Telecom has launched Minitel®, the world's first mass-market on-line information service. Minitel works through the telephone network. Users are given a special terminal by France Telecom, which combines a keyboard, a display, and a modem to connect the user to the large computers that contain all the information. The Minitel terminal acts as a "way in" to data on a wide and growing range of subjects, from train schedules to banking services. The service is available all over France and at the moment the company is giving away terminals to subscribers.

▲ *France Telecom has introduced the Minitel system, which is made up of a keyboard, display, and modem.*

ARCHAEOLOGY

Henry VIII's flagship is raised from the seabed

English king Henry VIII's flagship, the *Mary Rose*, which sunk off the coast of southern England in 1545, has finally been pulled out of the water after years of preparation. The operation was watched by an estimated 60 million television viewers worldwide in the first live broadcast from underwater. The initial lifting took a painstaking eight hours, to avoid any damage to the warship. The ship was carefully transferred underwater by a giant floating crane into a specially built cradle positioned on the seabed. Once secured to the cradle, the 580-ton (526-metric-tonne) structure was raised and towed ashore. Over 19,000 artifacts have been collected, including many of the crew's personal possessions and the ship's stores.

▼ *A new camera and a new film format— Kodak's Disc camera does away with the traditional roll of film.*

COMMUNICATIONS

Kodak gets round to a new camera—and a new film

Camera-makers are always looking for ways to make their products easier to use. Their latest effort is the Kodak Disc camera, which does away with the need to fiddle with rolls of film. Instead of a roll, the film comes on a disk with 15 segments—one frame of film is on each segment. Loading is simple: You just drop the disk into the back of the camera. As you do so, the camera reads a code on the back of the disk that tells it the film speed, so that it can set its exposure meter correctly, another first for Kodak. When you take a picture, the camera's built-in motor winds to the next frame, so that you are always ready to take a shot.

First automatic protein sequencer

The California-based company Applied Biosystems has introduced the first commercial automated gas phase "protein sequencer." This machine can be used to work out the structure of proteins—essential, highly complex molecules like insulin and hemoglobin that play many roles in the body. Every protein consists of a sequence of amino acids, and the machine works by chopping up proteins, then separating and analyzing the chains of amino acids that result. This benefits researchers who are working out how certain gene disorders lead to defective proteins. The machine dramatically reduces the amount of protein sample needed for sequencing.

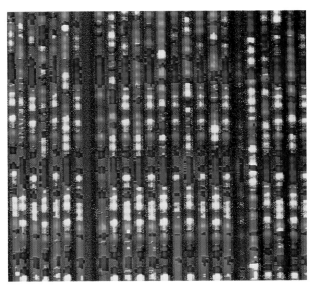

▲ *Proteins viewed through a protein sequencer.*

Science News 1982

- Human insulin made by genetically altered bacteria is approved for marketing in the United States.

- Japanese manufacturer Sony introduces the camcorder.

- At the Utah Medical Center, a man's heart is replaced with a compressed-air driven artificial heart made by Robert Jarvik.

New drug for viral infections

The pharmaceutical company Wellcome has introduced a new type of drug that is effective for treating certain infections caused by viruses—in particular the herpes group of viruses that cause infections such as shingles, chickenpox, and cold sores. The drug is called acyclovir (brand name Zovirax®) and will usually only help with the symptoms of infection rather than cure it. The drug is unusual, however, because previously doctors have been able to offer very little help in the treatment of viral infections. Viruses differ completely in their biology from other infectious organisms, such as bacteria, so antibiotics such as penicillin are completely ineffective against them.

Wind farms are established

A new sight will likely become common across our countryside—giant propellers. These propellers are wind turbines used to generate electricity. Clusters of such generators are to be set up initially in Hawaii and California, but they could appear in any place where there is a prevalent wind. The output of wind generators ranges from 10 to 500 kilowatts and, if forecasts are correct, within two years the annual output from U.S. wind farms could exceed 150 million kilowatt-hours. This sounds colossal, but it will account for less than one hundred-thousandth of the total electricity demand. If more power is to be generated in this way, thousands of wind farms will be needed.

◄ *Wind farms are an environmentally-friendly energy source, but they may have to be established in areas of natural beauty.*

Pioneer of the mouse

The computer mouse was born at the Xerox Research Center where it was used to control a new user-friendly graphical interface (screen icons). This revolutionary system was introduced into a new workstation called the Xerox Star. The mouse became truly popular thanks to a visit by Steve Jobs (*above*), cofounder of Apple computers. When Jobs saw the Xerox system he was so impressed that he decided to spend millions of dollars developing a similar system for home use.

COMPUTERS

A mouse revolutionizes computing

While the computer "bug" is a creature that few of us want to see, the "mouse" may well revolutionize the way we use computers. Apple's latest machine, Lisa, is the first to have a mouse as a standard feature. It has an attractive graphical interface, with icons (representing programs or files) that can be selected using a cursor. The mouse, which fits in your hand and lives on your desk, controls this cursor.

▲ *The Apple Lisa, with its mouse. Underneath the mouse is a ball that rolls as it is moved over the desk. Sensors register movements and move the cursor on the screen.*

MEDICINE

New peptic ulcer treatment

A new drug for peptic ulcers, named ranitidine (Zantac), has been approved for doctors to prescribe in the United States. Ranitidine belongs to a group of drugs called histamine-2 receptor antagonists. This means that it blocks the action of a chemical called histamine at receptor sites on the surface of stomach cells. Because histamine normally stimulates these cells to produce acid, taking ranitidine reduces the amount of acid in the stomach and this helps to heal a patient's stomach or duodenal ulcer. Millions of Americans suffer from peptic ulcers, and therefore ranitidine is likely to bring some welcome relief.

ASTRONOMY

First orbiting infrared telescope

Through international cooperation between the United States, Great Britain, and the Netherlands, the world's first infrared astronomical satellite (IRAS) has been launched into orbit around Earth. The satellite is a telescope, the purpose of which is to search the sky for objects that emit infrared (heat) radiation. Much of this radiation cannot be detected from the surface of Earth because water vapor absorbs it in the atmosphere. In order for the telescope to operate effectively, it is necessary for it to be kept extremely cold, and this is achieved by the evaporation of 127 gallons (481 liters) of liquid helium that are carried on board. The satellite will remain in operation until all the helium has evaporated, which may take about 10 months. The IRAS is expected to detect various types of infrared-emitting objects, including comets and asteroids. It will also attempt to image the core of the Milky Way galaxy and will look for planetary systems forming around distant stars.

◄ *Final preparations are made before the telescope's launch.*

Compact disks arrive

ENTERTAINMENT

The compact disk (CD) is a new way of storing recorded sound that will likely replace long-playing (LP) records in every home. Compact disks have several advantages over other recording media. They are small, only about 4½ (11 centimeters) across, and yet can hold more than one hour of music. They are tough and much less likely to get damaged than LPs. Above all, the sound is stored on CDs as a digital code. This means that superb sound quality is possible. It also makes the disks very easy to use. If you want to play a track in the middle of the disk, you do not need to wind, as with a tape, or aim a pickup arm, as with an LP. You simply key in the track number on the player or remote control and the machine plays the track you want.

▲ *One of the new compact disks.*

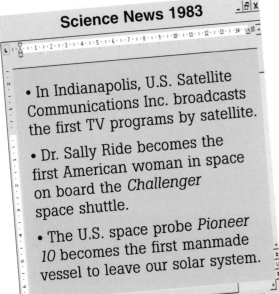

Science News 1983

- In Indianapolis, U.S. Satellite Communications Inc. broadcasts the first TV programs by satellite.

- Dr. Sally Ride becomes the first American woman in space on board the *Challenger* space shuttle.

- The U.S. space probe *Pioneer 10* becomes the first manmade vessel to leave our solar system.

Old minerals discovered

EARTH SCIENCE

Scientists at the Australian National University in Canberra, led by William Compston, have discovered the oldest known materials on Earth. They are tiny 4.2 billion-year-old crystals of the mineral zircon. They were found embedded in some younger sedimentary rocks from the Mount Narryer region of Western Australia. The zircon crystals were dated using the technique of radiometric dating, which involves comparing their content with the radioactive element uranium and its breakdown product, lead. The original rocks the zircon grains came from have either disappeared or have not been found.

Zircon crystals are the oldest material on Earth. ▲

Most powerful particle smasher

PHYSICS

The TeVatron, the world's most powerful particle accelerator, has been built at the Fermi National Accelerator Laboratory (Fermilab) in Illinois. It is the largest of a complex of accelerators that together can accelerate protons to an energy of one trillion (tera-) electron volts (TeV), hence the name. It is a proton synchrotron, meaning it accelerates protons in a long circular path, speeded by huge superconducting magnets. Once energized, the protons are smashed into a target or made to collide with a beam of high-speed antiprotons (the antimatter equivalent of protons). The object is to discover more about the fundamental building blocks of protons and other elementary particles.

The TeVatron accelerator occupies an underground tunnel with ▶ a circumference of four miles (six-and-a-half kilometers). Inside, protons and antiprotons are accelerated close to the speed of light.

1900s
In the U.K. and U.S.A. "rag-and-bone" men collect unwanted items.

1930s
Many "rag-and-bone" men set up businesses, recycling industrial scrap.

1940s
People are encouraged to hand in metal items for the U.S. war effort.

1950s
Scout troops collect newspapers for recycling.

1970s
Health hazards make landfill sites unpopular.

RECYCLING

Recycling means taking waste items and processing them so they can be used again. Yesterday's newspaper can be collected and recycled. Its paper becomes part of next week's comics.

Recycling has a long history dating back to at least Roman times. However, in North America and Europe during the 1960s, consumers had grown used to throwing away household waste and expecting it to be buried or burned. In the 1970s, greater awareness of the hazards and wastefulness of such disposal led to public programs of recycling, many of which began to flourish in the 1980s.

Rags and garbage ▶ recyclers in 1913.

The rag trade

Rags are a valuable commodity. They can be used for stuffing soft furniture and toys, made into patchwork clothes and blankets, or pulped to make paper. Between the 1900s and 1930s, the "rag-and-bone" man with his collecting cart was a familiar sight on the streets of North American, British, and European cities. He would collect almost any unwanted item.

Iron bedsteads collected for the war effort. ▼

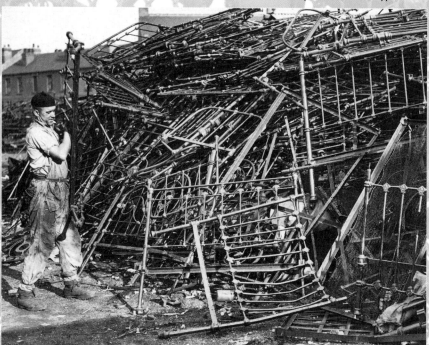

Precious metal

During World War II, raw materials became scarce when the enemy stopped supplies from getting through. In Great Britain and North America, "victory drives" encouraged people to bring old tires and scrap metal to collection points as part of the "winning-the-war" effort. Aluminum pots and pans were melted down and used to make aircraft parts, while iron railings and bedsteads were converted to steel for weapons.

Used cans and plastic

Cans come in two forms: aluminum soda cans and tin cans (steel cans covered in tin plate). For recycling, the two types can be separated magnetically. Recycled tin cans first have their tin separated from the steel and are then crushed into metal blocks. Manufacturers use scrap aluminum to make everything from cans to aircraft parts.

Since the 1980s, there has been an encouraging increase in the use of the recyclable plastic polyethylene terephthalate (PET). This is primarily used to make soft drink bottles but can be recycled into objects ranging from car parts to plastic fence posts.

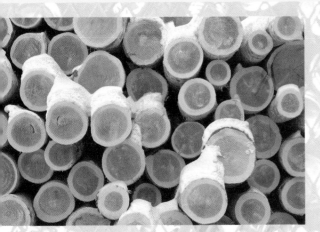

◄ *Softwood logs*
Softwoods, such as pine, are used to make some types of furniture and packaging, or are pulped to make paper.

Wood conservation

The trees that yield hardwoods, such as mahogany and teak, take dozens of years to grow. To help conserve the numbers of both hardwood and softwood trees, unwanted furniture and other wooden items are best recycled and put to other use, rather than being burned or dumped.

Recycling glass

Glass bottles and jars can be broken down, melted, and recycled to make new products. As with most kinds of recycling, sorting is vital. This starts with different colors of glass being collected separately. Later, the glass is separated from any paper labels and metal or plastic tops.

▲ *Used glass bottles have to be sorted according to color—clear, green, or brown.*

▼ *Aluminum soda cans piled up ready for recycling.*

The first space walk

A Soviet cosmonaut, Alexei Leonov (*above right*), undertook the first space "walk" on March 18, 1965. Leonov had to inflate a special air lock attached to his spacecraft, *Voskhod 2*. He then sealed himself in the air lock, depressurized it, and floated off into space for 10 minutes, tethered to the space craft by a safety line. A TV camera relayed the event back to Earth. It took Leonov 12 minutes to get back into the air lock because his suit had expanded, but eventually he rejoined his fellow cosmonaut, Pavel Belyayev (*above left*).

SPACE EXPLORATION

The first untethered space walk

Two space shuttle astronauts have made unattached space "walks" to test a new jet-propeled backpack, known as the manned maneuvering unit (MMU), which has 24 small nozzles that shoot out nitrogen gas. Bruce McCandless propeled himself 160 feet (49 meters) away from the craft before returning to it. Later, Robert Stewart repeated the feat. Astronauts will now be able to perform tasks such as repairing satellites.

▲ *The astronaut can control speed and direction in space by using joysticks.*

ARCHAEOLOGY

Treasures from the seabed

At Uluburun, off the coast of southern Turkey, a team of archaeologists and divers led by George F. Bass and Cemal Pulak have begun to excavate the shipwreck of a vessel thought to date from 1300 B.C. The Phoenician trading ship was first discovered in 1982 in 140 feet (43 meters) of water. It is the oldest shipwreck ever recovered, and Bass and Pulak believe that it will provide substantial historical evidence of trading practices in the late Bronze Age. Divers have begun to bring to the surface a wealth of artifacts and goods, including vast numbers of copper ingots, which match finds made in Egypt, Crete, and Cyprus. Other items recovered include Canaanite pottery, bronze tools and weapons in Greek, Egyptian, and Cypriot styles, and ivory from North Africa.

COMPUTERS

A new variety of Apple®

Imagine a computer that doesn't require you to type in commands in some weird computer language. On the screen there are easy-to-recognize icons representing all your programs and files. If you want to open a program, you simply point and click on it using a mechanical "mouse" that you move on your desk. All this sounds like an experimental vision of the future, and a few years ago it was. Today, this computer, called the Apple® Macintosh®, is released at the "cheap" price of $2,500. Designed and built by the Apple Corporation, the team was led by one of Apple's co-founders Steve Jobs. His dream was to create a computer that was not only great—it had to be "insanely great." Experienced computer experts are already claiming that the Mac is "toylike" and a waste of resources. Only time will tell if the Mac design and format is indeed the future of computing.

◀ *The "insanely great" Apple Macintosh.*

▲ *Laboratory-grown skin preserved in a bottle of formalin.*

Skin is grown in a laboratory

MEDICINE

At the Massachusetts General Hospital, the life of a badly burned boy has been saved by having sheets of his own skin grafted onto the burned areas. The skin was grown in a laboratory from cells taken from unburned areas of his body. It was used to replace coverings of donor skin that had been placed temporarily over the burns. Because the laboratory-grown skin was the boy's own, his body did not reject it. The idea of growing skin came from a discovery by research doctors at Harvard Medical School. While trying to grow mouse tumor cells, they noticed that skin cells could be cultured in a nutrient "broth."

Synthesizers work with computers

COMPUTERS

Musicians, engineers, and computer experts have devised a standard system for allowing music synthesizers to work with computers in an effective and creative way. The system is called Musical Instrument Digital Interface (MIDI). The system allows anyone to record music, played on any of a number of electronic instruments, in the form of coded instructions, which can be stored as small digital computer files. These contain information such as the pitch and length of each note, how hard the notes are struck, and so on. Later, this file can be fed into a music synthesizer, which plays back the music to sound like any chosen instrument, at any desired speed. Software could even be written to go with it, allowing musicians to combine or edit files, or compose music in digital form on a computer screen.

Science News 1984

- At the State University of New York, scientists discover a compound in garlic that is believed to thin blood.

- Genetic fingerprinting is pioneered in Great Britain by Alec Jeffreys.

- Soviet cosmonaut Svetlana Savitskaya becomes the first woman to walk in space.

Chimps are very much like us

BIOLOGY

Two researchers at the Biology Department of Yale University, Charles Sibley and Jon Ahlquist, have developed a method for comparing the DNA (genetic "supermolecule") of different organisms to examine how closely different species are related to each other. The technique is called DNA hybridization and involves mixing together single-stranded DNA from different species and measuring how closely the strands bind to each other. Although most of their work has been concerned with birds, recently Sibley and Ahlquist have compared the DNA of humans and chimpanzees. The results show that human and chimpanzee DNA differs by only about 1.5 to 2 percent—humans and chimps are genetically more than 98 percent alike.

▼ *Our nearest relative?*

Damage to the ozone layer

Scientists first warned that chlorofluorocarbons (CFCs) were depleting the ozone layer in 1974. By that time, up to one million tons of CFCs from products such as discarded refrigerators (*above*) were being released into the atmosphere every year. Environmental groups around the world mounted campaigns for a reduction in CFCs, and in 1985 the United Nations Environmental Program asked governments to reduce CFC manufacture.

ENVIRONMENT

Hole in the ozone layer confirmed

In March, the British Antarctic Survey detected a hole in the ozone layer over Antarctica. Like a protective shield 15–25 miles (24–40 kilometers) above Earth, the ozone layer—ozone is a type of oxygen—blocks out the Sun's ultraviolet rays, which can cause skin cancer. Discovery of the hole confirms that release of chemicals called chlorofluorocarbons (CFCs), used in aerosols, refrigerators, and air-conditioning, is destroying the ozone and letting in deadly ultraviolet rays.

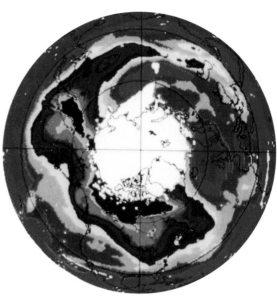

▲ *Satellite image showing the hole in the ozone layer above Antarctica.*

MEDICINE

The implantable heart defibrillator approved

Authorities in the United States have approved the use of an implantable heart defibrillator for people who have repeated episodes of life-threatening tachycardia (rapid heartbeats) or fibrillation (disorganized fluttering of the heart). The device consists of a battery-operated generator, which a surgeon implants in a pocket created under the skin of the abdomen. Three wires lead from the generator and pass up into the chest, where they are attached to different parts of the heart. If the defib-rillator detects the heart speeding up, it administers an electric shock, which for a split second stops the heartbeat. This allows the heart's natural pacemaker tissue to regain control of the heart's rhythm.

Science News 1985

- The Concorde's first commercial flight from London, England to Sydney, Australia, takes 17 hours and 3 minutes.

- The European Space Agency (ESA) launches the *Giotto* spacecraft, aiming to intercept Halley's Comet.

- The wreck of the *Titanic* is found by a joint French-American expedition.

COMPUTERS

Publish your own work

Small businesses and individuals can now produce professional-quality brochures, leaflets, and stationery. The catalyst for this revolution has been the Apple Macintosh® computer. The Mac® was released in January 1984, but sales have been poor, mainly because of a lack of good software. Sales are now likely to rise with the addition of an affordable laser printer and a software package called Aldus PageMaker®. This allows text and graphics to be easily manipulated on-screen and then printed out, and may launch an era of "desktop publishing."

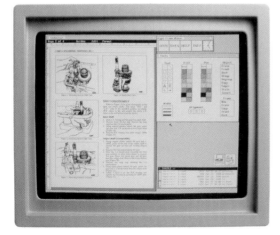

◀ *It is now possible to manipulate page layouts on a computer screen.*

PET scanning

A new medical imaging procedure, known as positron emission tomography (PET) scanning, is starting to be used in some U.S. hospitals. PET scanning is a diagnostic technique based on the detection of positrons (positively charged electrons) that are emitted by radioactively labeled substances introduced into the body. It is a development of radionuclide emission tomography, which was introduced in 1962, and produces images that show variations in chemical activity (for example, breakdown of glucose) through a "slice" of the body. The PET scan is proving to be particularly valuable for studying both the normal functioning of the brain and disorders of the brain.

PET scanning allows chemical activity in the body ▶ to be viewed on a computer screen.

Atomic force microscope

A new microscope has been introduced that allows users to look at objects so closely that separate atoms can be seen. Called the atomic force microscope, it works by scanning an object's surface with a ceramic or semiconductor tip mounted at the end of an arm called a cantilever. As the tip passes over the surface, the cantilever moves up and down. A laser beam is directed at the cantilever and reflects back to a detector. As the cantilever moves, the reflected beam changes its position on the detector, and these movements show the features of the surface. The microscope converts this into an image viewed on a screen.

◀ The new atomic force microscope.

Curious buckyballs

Until recently the only known pure forms of the nonmetallic element carbon were diamonds and graphite. Now U.S. chemists Richard Smalley and Robert Curl, and British chemist Harold Kroto, have discovered a third form. Using a laser, they vaporized graphite rods. The carbon molecule that resulted consisted of 60 carbon atoms (C_{60}), joined together by single or double bonds to form a hollow, sphere-shaped structure. They named the new carbon molecule buckminsterfullerene—buckyball for short—after the architect Buckminster Fuller, who, in the 1950s, designed a geodesic dome with a similar structure.

◀ An array of buckyball molecules.

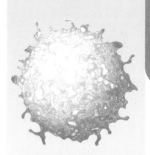

AIDS first recognized

Acquired immune deficiency syndrome (AIDS)—was not recognized as a distinct illness until 1982. In 1981, the United States Center for Disease Control was alerted to a sharp increase in cases of a rare lung infection in the Los Angeles and New York areas. Later, an increase in cases of a rare skin cancer was reported. Soon it was realized there was a group of illnesses caused by the weakening of the body's immune system. The group of illnesses was named AIDS. (The image above shows a white blood cell, part of the body's immune system.)

MEDICINE

Treatment for AIDS introduced

Researchers at the pharmaceutical company Wellcome have created a drug, azidothymidine (AZT), that has some effect in fighting the virus that causes AIDS. This virus has recently been named the human immunodeficiency virus (HIV). A large number of people are infected with HIV and of these many have developed AIDS, which until now has been considered swiftly fatal. For these people, the new drug is timely. It does not cure AIDS, but it does seem to slow the development of the disease.

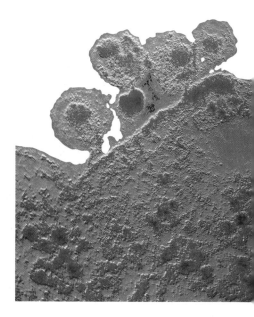

▲ *Electron micrograph of some HIV virus particles.*

ENGINEERING

New underwater robot explores the *Titanic*

New advances have been made in the exploration of the wreck of the passenger liner *Titanic*, which sank after hitting an iceberg on its maiden voyage in 1912. The latest underwater robot, named Jason Jr., will search the wreck, which is some two and half miles (four kilometers) down at the bottom of the Atlantic Ocean. The robot is equipped with high-quality still and video cameras, as well as powerful lighting. Jason Jr. is tethered to the deep-sea submersible vessel, *Alvin*, from which operators can control its every move. So far the robot has brought back pictures of several of the decks of the *Titanic*, as well as the ship's bridge and lookout mast. Explorers are confident that yet more dramatic pictures are possible, and that the robot will help them to understand how the ship broke up and sank.

SPACE EXPLORATION

Giotto's encounter with a comet

A space probe built by the European Space Agency and named *Giotto* has made the first close approach of a human-engineered object to a comet. On March 13, *Giotto* flashed past Halley's comet at a relative speed of 150,000 miles (241,401 kilometers) per hour, coming within 400 miles (644 kilometers) of the comet's surface. It returned some astonishing pictures to Earth, revealing the comet's nucleus to be a dark peanut-shaped body, spewing out 3 tons (2.7 metric tonnes) of gas and dust every second. Just before its closest approach, *Giotto* was struck by a large dust particle that knocked it out of alignment. It took 30 minutes to recover and point its antenna back to Earth. Later analysis showed that most of the material being spewed out by the comet was water. The nucleus of the comet was measured at about 10 miles (16 kilometers) long and 5 miles (8 kilometers) wide.

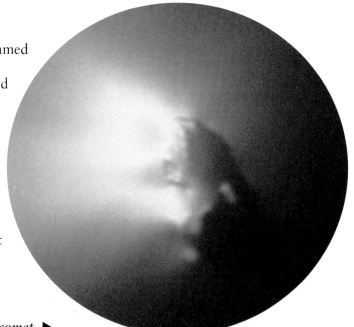

Giotto pictures show gas and dust being ejected by Halley's comet. ▶

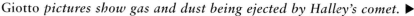

The rings of Uranus

On January 24, the *Voyager 2* space probe flew past the huge gas planet Uranus, coming within 60,000 miles (96,561 kilometers) of the planet's cloud tops, and discovering new rings and moons. Two new rings were discovered in addition to the nine previously known. These rings are made of billions of fragments of rock about three feet (one meter) across. They may be remnants of moons that were broken up by high-velocity impacts or torn apart by gravitational effects. *Voyager 2* has also discovered 10 new small moons circling the planet in addition to the 5 larger ones that were already known. Uranus has a featureless blue appearance and a magnetic field, twisted into a corkscrew shape, behind it.

▲ *The 11 rings of Uranus are extremely thin.*

Science News 1986

• The preserved fossil of a complete frog estimated to be 30 million years old is found in the Dominican Republic.

• Chernobyl, a nuclear reactor in Ukraine, explodes, releasing huge amounts of radiation into the atmosphere.

• U.S. space shuttle *Challenger* explodes after takeoff, killing seven astronauts.

Female *Homo habilis* is found

Anthropologists have uncovered a fossilized skeleton of a female *Homo habilis* ("handy man") at Olduvai Gorge, Kenya. The latest find offers a more complete picture of the 1.8 million-year-old species first uncovered in this area in 1961. The discovery, which consists of a jaw with teeth, parts of the cranium, pieces of right arm, and both legs, is extremely valuable because it includes complete limbs. The skeleton shows that this was a very small hominid—the arm is long relative to the leg length, showing that this individual had body proportions that differ greatly from those of modern hominids. Enough of the face from the shattered skull has been preserved to suggest a resemblance to early *Homo erectus* finds.

Mir takes shape

The Soviet Union has launched the first and main module of a new space station to replace their four-year-old station, *Salyut 7*. The new station is to be called *Mir* (Russian for "peace"). Its main module contains the space station's living area and the station's controls. At one end is a multiple docking adapter, with side-facing ports that will allow additional modules to be added. In this way, the space station can be gradually expanded over time. At either end of the main module there are also docking ports for Soyuz spacecraft and Progress supply ferries. To begin with, *Mir* has a crew of just two people; this will later increase to three.

Mir is in low Earth orbit, circling Earth every 90 minutes ▶ *at an altitude of 190 to 250 miles (300 to 400 kilometers).*

The first find of dinosaur eggs

The first discovery of fossilized dinosaur eggs was made in 1923 by an expedition to Mongolia sponsored by the American Museum of Natural History. The expedition was led by naturalist Roy Chapman Andrews (*above left*). The clutch of 7-inch (18-centimeter) long eggs were estimated to be 80 million years old. These fossilized eggs were found together with more than 70 specimens of a small, four-legged, plant-eating dinosaur called *Protoceratops*, so it was assumed that they were *Protoceratops* eggs. Further examinations, however, suggest that the nests actually belonged to *Oviraptor*, another dinosaur discovered on the expedition.

PALEONTOLOGY

Cache of dinosaur eggs found in Alberta

Paleontologists in Canada have found a nest of fossilized dinosaur eggs, the size of honeydew melons, at Devil's Coulee in southern Alberta. The 75 million-year-old eggs were laid by a dinosaur from a group called the "duckbilled" hadrosaurs—fairly large, plant-eating dinosaurs that walked on either two or four legs. The bones of some unborn baby hadrosaurs were also found. The nest is the first discovered in Canada and only the second in the world with fossilized embryos. The nest and eggs were probably buried by a landslide.

▲ *Examining dinosaur eggs at Devil's Coulee.*

MEDICINE

New antidepressant Prozac® approved in the U.S.

A new drug for treating depression, called fluoxetine (Prozac), has been approved for doctors to prescribe in the United States. It was first produced in 1972 by researchers at the pharmaceutical company Eli Lilly and is acknowledged to be a major step forward in helping people who suffer from chronic depression. Prozac works by increasing levels of a substance called serotonin in the brain. Serotonin plays a part in transmitting messages between nerve cells and is thought to influence sleep, appetite, aggression, and mood. Doctors and patients involved in trials of the drug are enthusiastic about its effectiveness, but doctors warn that it does have side effects in some people.

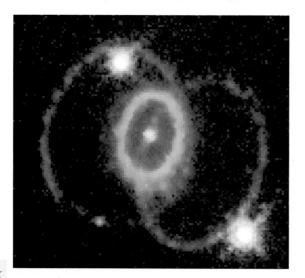

ASTRONOMY

Astronomers witness supernova

Astronomers have witnessed the closest supernova to Earth since the telescope was invented in 1609. A supernova is a gigantic explosion involving the near-total disintegration of a massive supergiant star. The actual explosion happened some 167,000 years ago, but the light from it has only just reached Earth. It occurred in the nearby Large Magellanic Cloud galaxy and catapulted a huge amount of light, radiation, and elementary particles called neutrinos into interstellar space, followed by a fireball shock wave blown out at 10,000 miles (16,093 kilometers) per second. First to see the supernova, on February 24, was Ian Shelton, an astronomer at Las Campanas Observatory in Chile.

◀ *The supernova has rings of ejected material around it.*

DNA evidence convicts criminal

FORENSICS

In Great Britain a serial criminal has been successfully convicted with the use of deoxyribonucleic acid (DNA) "fingerprinting." In 1984, British geneticist Alec Jeffreys discovered that just as everyone has their own individual fingerprints, so each of us has a unique pattern of DNA—the complex substance that the body uses to encode human characteristics. After extensive research, geneticists discovered that DNA could be used for identification purposes. With DNA testing, police investigators can analyze materials found at the scene of a crime, such as blood, hair, and saliva, and use this to establish whether a suspect was present at the crime scene. Since every human cell contains it, DNA is an extremely powerful way to identify a person. The British police intend to set up a DNA database of known criminals, which they hope will dramatically increase the detection of serious crimes.

◀ *A scientist examines several DNA "fingerprints."*

Digital audio tape transforms recording

ENTERTAINMENT

At last it is possible to make recordings at home that are just as good as those made in professional recording studios. The secret is digital audio tape (DAT), which comes in cassettes similar to ordinary analog recording tape but works in a different way. With DAT, sound is stored as a digital code on the tape's magnetized surface. With the right recording equipment, there is none of the distortion that happens with analog tape. Many semiprofessional musicians, who cannot afford time in a commercial studio, are already enthusiastic about the possibilities of DAT for recording their work.

Science News 1987

- Construction work is started on the Channel Tunnel between France and England.

- Soviet cosmonaut Yuri Romanenko returns to Earth after a record 326 days in space.

- Citizen of Japan launches a talking watch that answers when asked the time.

Kevlar® used for bulletproof vests

MATERIALS

A new generation of stronger and lighter bulletproof vests are to be issued to police and armed forces around the world. Previously, protecting an officer from potential attack required the wearing of a vest weighing up to 44 pounds (20 kilograms), and even this did not guarantee survival. Back in the 1970s, DuPont unveiled their latest synthetic fiber, Kevlar. Developed by Stephanie Kwolek, Kevlar displays unprecedented stiffness and tensile strength. The chemical name for Kevlar is poly-p-phenylene terephthalamide. It is actually a type of liquid crystal in which the molecules arrange themselves into rodlike sequences in solution. The resulting fibers can be spun into high-strength cord. Material scientists around the world have now set about finding other uses for this novel fiber.

◀ *Kevlar bulletproof vests are both strong and light.*

Benzene ring

In 1858, German chemist Friedrich August Kekulé von Stradonitz (*above*) worked out that carbon atoms linked together in chains and combined with other atoms to form a huge variety of molecular structures. But this did not explain the structure of benzene, a hydrocarbon liquid that was in itself very stable, but whose theoretical six-carbon, six-hydrogen atom chain was not. It was not until 1865 that Kekulé dreamed of dancing carbon chains linking themselves top to tail to form rings. He had established the concept of the benzene ring.

CHEMISTRY

Benzene ring made visible at last

The ring-like structure of benzene (C_6H_6), envisaged by Friedrich Kekulé, is at last visible thanks to the scanning tunneling microscope—a microscope that is capable of magnifying objects by several million times, producing high-resolution images that show individual atoms. It works by moving the tip of a probe over the surface of a sample, in this case benzene. The tip (only two atoms wide) registers the shape of benzene's molecular structure.

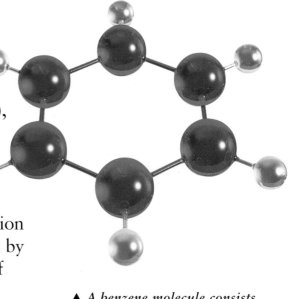

▲ *A benzene molecule consists of a ring of six carbon atoms, with a hydrogen atom attached to each.*

COMPUTERS

Computers learn to read handwriting

In an ideal world, writing by hand would be a natural method of human-computer interaction. Unfortunately, we all have unique handwriting. Therefore, the difficulties in producing a computer that could recognize handwriting are great. Researchers at IBM are currently developing a system that comes close to this goal. Operators simply use a stylus to write on an electronic pad—any text is digitized and sent to the attached computer. The computer then attempts to recognize the text using its stored database of handwriting samples. The operator can teach the computer any text that it cannot recognize, allowing the system to learn at least one person's handwriting.

ENTERTAINMENT

Virtual reality opens up new worlds

The latest in computer technology can take you into an exciting new world. When you put on a virtual reality (VR) headset, you see a world created by the computer. It can take you inside a fantasy game or the cockpit of a plane. As you move along or turn your head, the display alters so that you feel as if you are really there. Some of the first VR systems are games, but there are many other uses—for example, VR could be used to help train people to perform difficult tasks.

◄ *Although used mainly for games, VR may one day be used to teach surgeons how to perform complex operations.*

ENGINEERING

The world's longest tunnel is completed

The world's most ambitious tunnel project, the Seikan Tunnel between the Japanese islands of Honshu and Hokkaido, is complete. This vast engineering task, which was begun in 1971, connects the two islands with a rail link under the Tsugaru Strait. The total length of the main tunnel is 34 miles (54.7 kilometers), but there is also a service tunnel, connected at many points to the main bore, making the total length of undersea tunnels far longer. The tunnel is an engineering triumph.

▲ *The Seikan Tunnel: engineers had to treat the rock, filling its tiny cracks with concrete to stop water pouring through, before each section of the tunnel was drilled.*

Science News 1988

- Physicist Stephen Hawking's book, *A Brief History of Time*, reaches the bestseller list in Great Britain.

- Australia issues the world's first plastic polymer bank note.

- A digitized automatic piano, the Disklavier electronic piano, is introduced by the Japanese company Yamaha.

COMMUNICATIONS

Transatlantic calls made easier

North America and Europe are now linked by the first transatlantic fiber-optic cable. There have been cables under the ocean since the 1950s, but this one is different. Its fiber-optic strands can carry an incredible 37,500 simultaneous telephone conversations along the 4,114-mile (6,620-kilometer) route between the two continents. The cable means that it will be easier to get a line between Europe and North America.

▲ *A ship lays fiber-optic cable in the Atlantic.*

TRANSPORTATION

Traveling by magnet

Train passengers in Japan can look forward to a new kind of railway. Using the repellent forces of superconductive magnets (SCMs), maglev (magnetic levitation) lifts the train carriages about four inches (10 centimeters) above the guideway that replaces conventional steel track. A magnetic linear induction motor (LIM) pushes the train forward.

The MLU001 train reached a top speed of ▶ 220 miles (352 kilometers) per hour on the Miyazaki Maglev test track.

A GLANCE AT THE PAST

Television satellites

Echo I, launched by the National Aeronautics and Space Administration (NASA) in 1960, was the world's first communications satellite. *Echo I* was a balloon with a metallic surface and it soon fell victim to meteorite damage. The first successful communications satellite was *Telstar 1* (above), also launched by NASA, in 1962. It was powered by batteries that were kept charged by 3,600 solar cells. In 1962, *Telstar 1* sent the first direct TV pictures from the United States to Europe. *Telstar 1* and similar satellites continued to send TV signals for several years.

ENTERTAINMENT

Satellites transform television

There is about to be a revolution in European broadcasting. Instead of sending programs straight from ground-based transmitters to people's homes, new companies like Sky TV are using satellites to send out broadcasts. If you subscribe to the new system you get a satellite dish to mount on your home and a receiver to decode the signals. Satellite broadcasting offers more choice than terrestrial TV, and Europe will soon have as many separate channels as the United States, without the need to lay expensive cables under the streets.

▲ *Satellite TV is turning local TV presenters, such as Rita Bilucaglia, into minor celebrities Europe-wide.*

MEDICINE

Scientists of the world unite to work out human DNA

A huge international cooperative effort has begun to determine the complete sequence of human DNA. The Human Genome Project is expected to last 15 years. Its goals include identifying all the 100,000 genes in the human genome (the complete set of chromosomes in each cell of the body) and determining the sequences of three billion chemical base pairs that make up these genes. Teams of scientists throughout the world will painstakingly decode each chromosome.

Science News 1989

- In Great Britain, the first newspapers to be printed with non-rub ink are distributed.

- A 10,180-mile (16,300-kilometer) national highway around the coast of Australia is completed after 15 years.

- American space probe *Galileo* blasts off on a six-year journey to explore Jupiter.

MILITARY TECHNOLOGY

Stealth bomber goes undetected

American aviation contractors Northrop Grumman have tested a revolutionary new aircraft that the United States Air Force claims is immune to the world's radar systems. The uniquely shaped B-2 "Stealth bomber" has an unconventional design: at 69 feet (21 meters), it is the same length as a fighter aircraft, while its wingspan is 172 feet (52 meters), the same as the B-52 bomber. The aircraft's shape consists of a series of smooth, large-radius curves that redirect radar energy.

▼ *The B-2 is piloted by a two-man crew, with an unrefueled range of 6,000 miles (9,656 kilometers). It can reach heights of 50,000 feet (15,240 meters).*

New particle smasher goes into operation

A huge new particle accelerator, the Large Electron-Positron (LEP) Collider, has been opened at CERN (*Centre Européenne pour la Recherche Nucléaire*) near Geneva. The Collider accelerates counter-rotating beams of electrons and positrons (positively charged electrons) almost to the speed of light around a 16.7-mile (27-kilometer) long tube buried 330 feet (100 meters) below ground. The electrons and positrons collide within four huge detecting areas around the ring. When they collide, they turn into pure energy, which turns back into other particles.

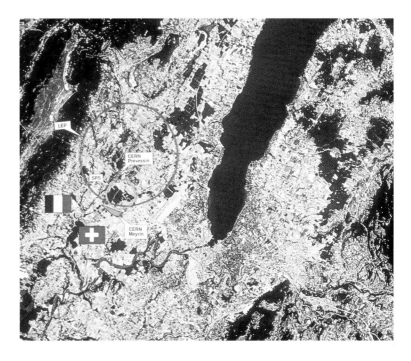

The huge Collider ring can be seen to the left of center on this aerial photograph. ▶

Computer screens can detect touch

People sitting in front of a computer for hours may sometimes hit the screen in frustration. Researchers are developing a screen that can identify where on its surface it has been touched and respond accordingly. Touch-screen technology uses force sensors under the corners of the screen to detect any pressure. When the screen is touched, the forces are measured and used to calculate the touch position. Although it may not take off in the office, its use in interactive displays means it could well have a high-profile future.

◀ *This man is training to use a graphics tablet, a touch-sensitive board closely related to touch screens.*

Last stop for *Voyager 2*

After a 10-year journey, the U.S. space probe *Voyager 2* has flown past the planet Neptune, discovering six new moons (in addition to the two previously known) and the full extent of Neptune's four rings. The planet itself appears to have a more active weather system than was anticipated. Visible on its surface are dark areas that are probably storms and numerous cloud features. The space probe has also taken photographs of Neptune's largest moon, Triton, which has geysers and a thin atmosphere. *Voyager 2* has now completed its tour of the large gas planets of the outer solar system and will head off into outer space.

Neptune's largest moon, Triton, has a cantaloupelike appearance. ▶

1834	1842	1940s	1956	1961
Babbage plans a machine to calculate figures and print results.	Ada Lovelace writes step-by-step instructions for Babbage's machine.	The first electronic computers are built in the U.S.A. and U.K.	IBM develops the first computer-disk storage system.	Fairchild Co. is the first to sell integrated circuits.

HOME COMPUTERS

In 1982, Time magazine took the unusual step of awarding its Man of the Year title to the computer. At the beginning of the 1980s, computers became compact, reliable, and cheap enough for the office, school, or home. Many computers could be bought ready-made from ordinary electrical shops on Main Street.

By 1984, millions were getting excited about the computer's potential as they had their first taste of home computing. Domestic applications included accounting programs, word processing, recipe books, desktop publishing software, and the ever-popular computer games.

Steve Wozniak. ▲

The Apple II ▶ *came in a plastic case and was one of the first computers that could display color graphics. This model, the Apple IIc, was introduced in 1984.*

Brewing apples

Apple Computer founders Steve Wozniak and Steve Jobs built their first microcomputers in the mid-1970s. Along with other members of their local Home-Brew Computer Club in California, they based their computers on small electrical devices called microchips (*see right*). In 1976, they started selling the Apple I, which was just a circuit board in a wooden case. In 1977, they followed up with the highly successful Apple II, a computer that anyone could use.

User-friendly

Computers became much easier to use when they adopted the graphical user interface (GUI). Developed by Xerox, the GUI is a screen display that shows the contents of the computer using icons (mini pictures) rather than typed lists of files. People navigate around a GUI using a device called a "mouse" (*see box on page 203*), which lets them point to, and then click on, icons on the screen.

GUI ▶ *A screen with a graphical user interface is covered with easy-to-understand icons. The trash can icon, for example, is the place to throw away unwanted files.*

1971	**1975**	**1983**	**1988**	**1994**
Intel Co. introduces the 4004 chip, the first microproessor.	*The first home computer, the Altair 8800, goes on sale.*	*Apple introduces the first home computer with a mouse, the Lisa.*	*Tin Toy is the first computer-generated film to win an Oscar®.*	*The first shopping "malls" appear on the Internet.*

▲ *Bill Gates, cofounder of Microsoft.*

Software

Dozens of home-computer manufacturers vied for a share of the market in the early 1980s. But by the end of the decade, only a handful remained. The most popular computers were built in a standard format, using parts that came from a variety of manufacturers. They were designed to run Windows® software, produced by the software leader Microsoft.

How a mouse works

A small rubber ball occupies a socket on the underside of a mouse and rolls when the mouse slides across a flat surface. The ball turns two axles. One moves in response to movements backward and forward, the other in response to movements right and left. Each movement is picked up by sensors and sent along a wire to the computer. A mouse also has one or more buttons. When pressed, the button turns on a circuit that sends a signal to the computer to say the button is in use.

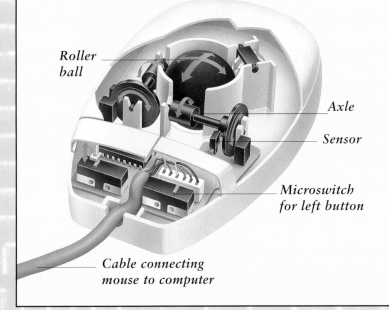

Roller ball

Axle

Sensor

Microswitch for left button

Cable connecting mouse to computer

◀ *A circuit board.*

Chips

Microchips, or silicon chips, enabled people to put computers together swiftly, from just a few standard parts. Complex circuits could be replaced by a single chip. The most sophisticated microchips consist of millions of separate circuit elements, each of which is etched onto a thin layer of silicon.

PCs challenged

As computers become an everyday part of the home, designers are finding ways to make them more attractive. Meanwhile they are facing competition from a new breed of technology: TVs, mobile phones, and other appliances that have built-in computers dedicated to just a few tasks. Some TVs, for example, have built-in computers that can be used to send and read e-mails, while mobile phones are becoming Internet-enabled.

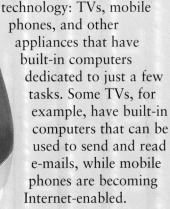

◀ *An iMac™ PC.*

1990

First attempt at a Channel tunnel

The first agreement for a tunnel under the English Channel was signed by the British and French governments in 1875. Work began in 1880 but was soon stopped. In the 1950s the idea was again discussed, and Britain and France announced that work would start in 1968, with a finishing date of 1975. Once again, the task proved too vast, and work was stopped in the early 1970s when costs threatened to spiral. In the mid-1980s, the two countries agreed to begin again with a privately funded project.

ENGINEERING

Hands meet in the Channel tunnel

After four years of work, using specially built tunnel-boring machines, the diggers have finally met in the middle of the tunnel under the English Channel. Now work on finishing the 30-mile (48-kilometer) project will begin. When complete, people will be able to travel by rail from London to Paris, the journey taking little more than three hours. Britain and France have never seemed so close.

▲ Bonjour! *Channel Tunnel construction workers meet after four years' labor.*

COMPUTERS

Microsoft cleans Windows®

In terms of user-friendliness, personal computers (PCs) have been playing catch-up in recent years. The Apple® Macintosh® has captured the public's imagination with its easy-to-use graphical interface, but for the past seven years Microsoft has been trying to develop its own rival interface, Windows, for the PC. Microsoft promised a product that would be easy to use, but the first two versions were painfully slow. This year sees the release of a revamped Windows version 3.0, and Microsoft appears to have gotten it right at last. Independent software developers are jumping on board to create programs for it. Two programs, Microsoft Word® and Microsoft Excel®, are also much improved. With orders already outstripping production, Windows looks likely to dominate the market.

Science News 1990

• Japan launches the first space probe to be sent to the Moon in 14 years.

• NASA launches the Hubble Space Telescope on board the space shuttle *Discovery*. The telescope will probe the outer reaches of the universe from an orbit 372 miles (595 kilometers) above Earth.

ASTRONOMY

The world's largest telescope

The twin Keck telescopes in Hawaii are nearing completion and are about to take over the title of the world's largest optical telescope. Each of the telescopes has a revolutionary primary mirror, 30 feet (9 meters) across, which is made up of 36 individual hexagonal segments, each six feet (1.8 meters) across. Computer-controlled sensors and actuators monitor and adjust the position of each segment to correct the distorting effects of gravity. Keck's two primary mirrors gather 17 times as much light as the Hubble Space Telescope. Keck is scheduled to begin full operation late next year.

◀ *The Keck telescopes on the summit of Mauna Kea in Hawaii.*

First gene replacement therapy

MEDICINE

Doctors and scientists at the United States National Institutes of Health have performed the first gene therapy procedure on a four-year-old girl. Born with a rare genetic disease, she lacked a healthy immune system and was vulnerable to every passing germ. She had a defective gene that normally produces adenosine deaminase (ADA), a key enzyme needed by the immune system. In the procedure, doctors removed white blood cells from the girl's body, grew the cells in a lab, inserted a normal copy of the gene for ADA into the cells, and then put the cells back into her bloodstream. Tests have shown that the therapy strengthened her immune system, and she no longer has recurrent colds.

Genetically treated cells do not work indefinitely, and new ▶ cells must be produced in the laboratory every few months.

▲ *Any solid object, including a person, could have an exact virtual double.*

3-D laser scanners introduced

COMPUTERS

Any object simply scanned by a laser can now have its dimensions accurately input into a computer. This means that every solid object in the real world could soon have its exact virtual counterpart. Once stored on computer, objects can be examined at any angle, have different textures mapped onto them, and could even be stretched in any direction. This degree of control is beyond anything a designer has with a real model. The 3-D scanner works by using a laser source that is sequentially scanned over an object; the scattered laser light is then collected by a sensitive digital camera. The computer translates the reflected light into the object's angles, lengths, and distances.

Is this the end of the dreaded drill?

MEDICINE

In dentistry, a laser-powered device has been developed that uses light instead of a drill to treat cavities. This new device allows tiny layers of tooth to be removed quietly and without discomfort. An incentive for many patients may be the fact that injections would also no longer be required; in a recent trial 98.5 percent of patients said they felt no discomfort. Unfortunately, at present the majority of dental procedures cannot be treated by laser—for example, they cannot be used to remove old or broken fillings and even have difficulty removing soft dental decay. The other major drawback is the cost—a new laser system costs approximately $45,000, beyond the means of most dental practices. However, with many people not visiting a dentist because of a fear of drills, this may yet prove a viable technology.

Patients could very well flock back to drill-less dentists. ▶

The origins of the Web

The World Wide Web was the brainchild of British inventor Tim Berners-Lee (*above*), who began work on the project in 1989. He envisioned that computer users could share information if their machines were connected via the telephone network. He developed a system that enabled computers to be linked up and documents (web pages) to be written in a special computer language called HyperText Markup Language (HTML) for easy transference.

COMPUTERS

World Wide Web introduced

The Internet has been around for years but has been used primarily by academics and the military. It now looks likely to be opened up to mass use, as the World Wide Web—a simple and powerful information retrieval service—is launched. A team led by Tim Berners-Lee at the *Centre Européenne pour la Recherche Nucléaire* (CERN), a scientific organization based in Geneva, has created a computer language that allows communication between all computers connected to the Internet. The Web gives users access to a vast array of documents that are all connected to one another.

▲ *The World Wide Web allows computer users all over the world to communicate and exchange information.*

COMMUNICATIONS

First digital cameras in production

Kodak has announced the world's first digital still-picture camera. The camera works in a similar way to an ordinary camera with one important difference—it stores pictures in memory, as digital code, rather than on film. This means that it is easy to download images from the camera to the computer screen; it also means that wasted film will be a thing of the past—images can be previewed and discarded if they are not required. Altogether, digital photography promises to be a more versatile, easier-to-use system than ordinary film-based photography. For the moment, there is one important drawback. The new camera cannot produce such crisp, high-resolution images as a film-based camera, but this promises to change when cameras with bigger memories come along.

ENVIRONMENT

Biosphere experiment

A privately funded ecological experiment, known as Biosphere 2, has begun. Eight people will live for two years in an air- and watertight enclosure near Tucson, Arizona. Their sealed home, which is dependent on the outside world only for sunlight and electricity, covers two and a half acres (one hectare) of land. As well as the people, the structure contains more than 3,500 plant and animal species and attempts to reproduce five ecosystems—desert, grassland, marsh, ocean, and rain forest. The aim is to test whether a self-sustaining space colony is possible.

◄ *Starting a new life in Biosphere 2.*

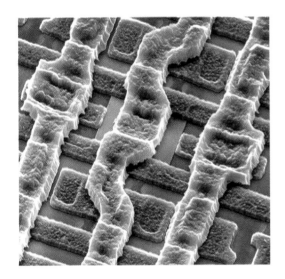

Dynamic memory gets faster

COMPUTERS

Random access memory (RAM) is the best-known form of computer memory, and it has now become even faster. Memory chips are integrated circuits made up of millions of transistors and capacitors. The most common form of this memory is dynamic-RAM, where a transistor and capacitor are paired up to create a memory cell, which represents a single piece of data. This dynamic form of memory has to be constantly refreshed or the data is lost. Unfortunately, this process takes time and slows down the memory. However, the new 64-bit memory chips are much faster than previous memory chips, and have made computer memory much more efficient.

◀ *New, faster dynamic-RAM circuitry.*

Sony launches the Minidisc

ENTERTAINMENT

Another new home-recording format is about to hit the stores, and its makers claim that it is better than anything that has appeared before. It is the Minidisc, launched by Sony, and it combines ease of use with very high recording quality. The Minidisc uses the same digital technology as the compact disk (CD). In other words, the sound is recorded in the form of a digital code, cutting down distortion and providing very high sound quality. Unlike tapes, which you have to wind to find the track you need, Minidiscs allow the user to access tracks instantly at the press of a button. The Minidisc crams up to 74 minutes of music onto a disk measuring only two and half inches (six centimeters) across, and both pre-recorded and blank disks will be available. The new disk may become the ideal format for home recording.

Science News 1991

• The European Remote Sensing satellite (ERS-1), Europe's first environmental satellite, goes into orbit.

• Canadian engineering student Tim Collings develops the V-chip, a system that enables parents to control the content of TV programs by blocking undesirable material.

Neolithic body discovered in melting ice

ANTHROPOLOGY

A perfectly preserved 5,000-year-old human body has been found in the Tirolean Otztal Alps on the Italian-Austrian border. German hiker Helmut Simon was astonished to stumble across the remains revealed by a melting glacier. Radiocarbon dating shows the man, nicknamed "Otzi" after the area where he was discovered, to date from 3300 B.C. His body has been perfectly preserved by the glacial ice. Scientists estimate the man to have been roughly 35 years old when he died, most likely from exhaustion while crossing the Alps. The find is truly remarkable, since it provides comprehensive evidence of the life of Neolithic man. Otzi's hair shows the earliest archaeological evidence of haircutting, while his clothes include an unlined fur robe made from the skins of ibex and deer, a furry cap, and leather shoes stuffed with grass for padding. He was carrying a few tools and food supplies.

◀ *Otzi's body was perfectly preserved by the glacier.*

A GLANCE AT THE PAST

The first videophone

The history of the videophone began with the first television systems, in 1927. That year Herbert Hoover, then American Secretary of Commerce, had a telephone conversation with Sherman Gifford, president of AT&T, during which the two men could see each other. Experiments were continued in Germany in 1936. This time, a system of videophone booths was proposed, with video conversations possible from one booth to another. Between the 1950s and 1970s, AT&T developed various videophones, such as the videophone 2500 (above), but none proved widely popular.

COMMUNICATIONS

Enter the videophone— the telephone is transformed

Telephone users have long dreamed of a phone that allows you to see the person you are talking to. The technology to scan and display the image of a person making a call has existed for years. The problem has been sending the pictures down a standard telephone line. But now British Telecom has come up with the Integrated Services Digital Network (ISDN), with which both voice and picture can be sent as digital code, before being decoded at the other end.

▲ *Now that telephones are better able to handle image data, videophones may gain in popularity.*

ENGINEERING

The leaning tower of Pisa gets a corset

The famous leaning tower of Pisa has been given a helping hand. Constructed in the twelfth century as the bell tower of the nearby cathedral, it was built on soft soil with poor foundations. It leans to the south and the amount of lean is steadily increasing—it is already over 16 feet (five meters) off center. Engineers have been worried for some time that the huge compression forces on the outer walls would make the stones crumble. So they have given the tower a "corset," made up of 12 plastic-coated steel bands wrapped around the structure at the second-floor level. The bands have closed up some of the existing cracks in the masonry and, it is hoped, will prevent more cracks from forming.

ENVIRONMENT

UN Earth Summit

An Earth Summit—the United Nations Conference on Environment and Development —was held in June in Rio de Janeiro, Brazil. Its aim was to look at the negative impact of worldwide economic development on the environment. With 117 heads of state and representatives of 178 nations attending the meeting, it was the largest gathering of world leaders in history. Issues discussed include global warming and the mass destruction of the Amazonian rainforest, home to nearly half the world's species. Countries attending the summit agreed to protect endangered species and reduce carbon dioxide emissions.

Since 1945, nearly half the Amazonian rainforest ▶ *has been cleared for timber or cattle farming.*

Nicotine patch now available

A new method to help smokers kick their habit has become available by prescription in the United States. The system, called the nicotine transdermal system, consists of a patch that the would-be nonsmoker applies to a different area of skin each day. The patch contains some nicotine—the active, addictive, substance in cigarettes. The nicotine diffuses through the skin into the person's bloodstream and then travels to the brain, reducing his or her craving for a cigarette. Sold under a number of brand names, such as Nicoderm® and Habitrol®, the system does not cure nicotine addiction. However, by using it to give up smoking, the addict does at least avoid one of the main health risks of cigarettes, which comes from the tar in cigarette smoke entering the lungs.

The nicotine patch is applied to the skin. ▶

▲ *The MHD-driven* Yamoto 1 *is 98 feet (29.4 meters) long, and holds 10 passengers and crew.*

Silent running

Japan has begun sea trials of a prototype magnetic ship. *Yamoto 1* is propelled by two MHD (magnetohydrodynamic) thrusters that run without any moving parts. When completed, the MHD ship should be able to attain speeds of more than 100 knots (125 miles or 200 kilometers per hour), with little noise. This is several times the top speed of today's ships, which are slowed down by turbulence created by the ship's propellers. MHD works by applying a magnetic field to an electrically conducting fluid. The electrically conducting fluid used in the MHD thruster of the *Yamoto 1* is seawater.

Mobile phones enter the digital age

The Swedish Ericsson Company has launched the first digital mobile phone. Like other digital equipment, the new telephone changes the user's voice signal into a code that can be understood by a computer. There are many benefits. Digital telephone systems can handle many signals at once—a number of users can share the same radio channel without interference or loss of voice quality. Sound on the whole is better than with normal phones. There is better security, and the digital system allows facilities like caller identification and voice mail to be built in. Most telecommunications experts are convinced that the future for mobile phones is digital. But during the changeover period, telephones will be available that can switch over to normal operation if no digital service is available.

Experts predict that the future of the mobile phone is digital. ▶

Early bathyscaphes

Swiss scientist August Piccard devised the prototype bathyscaphe in 1948, and in 1953 took one to a depth of 10,300 feet (3,140 meters). In 1960, he designed an improved model, the *Trieste* (*above*), with his son Jacques. Jacques and his colleague, Donald Walsh, reached a depth of 35,800 feet (10,910 meters) in the Pacific Ocean. The Piccard bathyscaphes were essentially underwater balloons; seawater was pumped in or out to make them rise and fall, and propellers provided horizontal motion underwater. They were always attached to a mother ship on the surface.

OCEANOGRAPHY

Submersibles roam the sea bed

Since the record-breaking dive of the *Trieste* in 1960, engineers and oceanographers have been making progress on self-propelling submersibles that can prowl the ocean bed independent of a mother ship. Some of them have room for one or two researchers, but this is very expensive and risky, so unmanned submersibles—ROVs (Remotely Operated Vehicles) or RCVs (Remote Controlled Vehicles)—have been developed to handle the difficult work done at dangerous depths.

▲ *In 1985, an RCV named* Jason, *complete with TV cameras, explored the sunken wreck of the* Titanic.

The Pentium ▶ is set to power the next generation of PCs.

COMPUTERS

Pentium® processor

Intel®—the company at the forefront of the silicon revolution—has launched the Pentium, the fastest microprocessor chip on the market. The Pentium processor is impressive—it has 3.1 million transistors and can carry out an amazing 90 million instructions per second. The new chip promises a fivefold increase in performance over Intel's previous chip, the 486. This makes it 1,500 times faster than the first Intel microprocessor introduced in 1971.

ASTRONOMY

The very long baseline array

A network of 10 identical radio dishes—spread from the state of Washington to the U.S. Virgin Islands in the Caribbean and from Hawaii to New Hampshire—has been set up to help gain more accurate images of radio wave-emitting celestial objects. The network of radio dishes is called the Very Long Baseline Array (VLBA). By combining signals from two or more of the radio antennae using a method called interferometry, it is possible to produce better pictures of radio wave sources than are obtainable by using any one dish on its own.

The Hawaiian antenna of the VLBA. ▶

10 million watts for a second!

ENERGY

An experimental fusion reactor at Princeton University has succeeded in generating 10 million watts of power for a single second of operation. This is a landmark in the development of what many proclaim to be a virtually inexhaustible source of power. A fusion reaction occurs when two lighter atomic nuclei fuse to form a nucleus of a heavier element. As the nuclei fuse, a small amount of mass is converted into a large amount of energy.

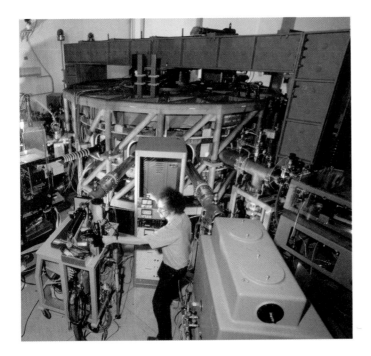

◀ *Experimental fusion reactors aim to imitate the process that powers the Sun.*

Science News 1993

• Astronauts make a record five-hour space walk from the U.S. space shuttle *Endeavor*.

• The first passenger trains travel through the Channel Tunnel between England and France.

• The first voice-operated TV/radio remote control is launched worldwide.

Anti-RSI ergonomic keyboard

MEDICINE

The modern office brings with it new health risks. One of the most debilitating is Repetitive Strain Injury (RSI), which can leave sufferers crippled with pain. These injuries occur after many years working with ordinary keyboards. The sustained strains required by the use of a standard flat keyboard lead to fatigue, pain, and sometimes disability. Researchers at Apple® computers have developed a fully ergonomic keyboard that fits both the shape of hands and different finger lengths to reduce movement and tension. This new keyboard is split up into separate sections to eliminate twisting of the wrist; the keys are also tilted to further reduce muscle tension.

Virtually dead

MEDICINE

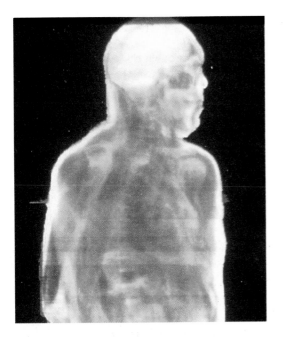

The Visible Human Project is set to revolutionize medical teaching, making it possible to explore structures in the human body as never before. A team of scientists has imaged an entire fresh cadaver (dead body) using Magnetic Resonance Imaging. The cadaver was frozen in gelatin and very finely sliced; each slice was then photographed by a high-resolution digital camera. A second team has developed software to either display each slice individually or create 3-D images of internal structures. The first cadaver used was male; however, the team is about to repeat the procedure on a female body. This valuable reference is initially to be distributed on CD-ROM, but the team is about to announce plans to make all its data freely available on the Internet, where the information will be available to medical students and researchers the world over.

◀ *Virtual cadavers provide valuable data for medical research.*

Fermat's theorem

Pierre de Fermat (*above*), a French lawyer and amateur mathematician, proposed his infamous "last" theorem in 1637. It was one of a series of mathematical observations and is called the "last" theorem because it was the last to be proved. When Fermat first wrote down the theorem in a book, he also wrote a note (in Latin) saying that he had worked out a wonderful proof of his theorem, which "the margin is too small to contain." Whether he was joking or really had a proof is not known, since no written evidence was ever found.

MATHEMATICS

Fermat's "last" theorem proved

British mathematician Andrew Wiles has demonstrated the first proof of Fermat's last theorem—a math problem that has defeated the world's finest minds for over 350 years. The theorem proposes that there is no solution to the equation $x^n + y^n = z^n$, where x, y, z, and n are all positive whole numbers and n is greater than two. Demonstrating this is true has been very difficult. Wiles has been working in secrecy for eight years, and his final proof is hundreds of pages long.

▲ *Andrew Wiles has devoted many years of his life to proving Fermat's famous theorem.*

ANTHROPOLOGY

Missing link found?

American paleoanthropologist Tim White has discovered what he believes to be the missing link between early hominids and apes. White and his team have unearthed a new kind of hominid, calculated to be 4.4 million years old, in the Awash region of central Ethiopia. He has named the new species *Australopithecus ramidus*, since he believes it may be the potential root species of the *Australopithecus* family and therefore the link between apes and hominids. Excavations have uncovered pelvis, leg, ankle, and foot bones; this follows fragments that were discovered in 1992, consisting of teeth, pieces of skull, jawbone, and arm bones. However, other anthropologists have expressed grave doubts about White's claims.

Science News 1994

- The Hubble Space Telescope provides convincing evidence of the existence of a black hole in a distant galaxy.

- American astronaut Mark Lee makes an untethered space walk using a jet pack.

- A new interactive TV system allows viewers in America to select from a choice of hundreds of individual programs.

ASTRONOMY

Comet fragments crash into Jupiter

Twenty-one fragments of a comet have been seen crashing into the huge gas planet Jupiter. As each piece of comet Shoemaker-Levy entered Jupiter's atmosphere at some 135,000 miles (217,000 kilometers) per hour, it caused a huge explosion, resulting in plumes thousands of miles high, and hot "bubbles" of gas. This was the first collision of two solar system bodies ever observed. The fragments were first spotted from Earth over a year ago.

◀ *The bright spots show where the fragments entered Jupiter's atmosphere.*

Eurofighter flexes its wings

The long-awaited test flight of the prototype Eurofighter 2000 has taken place, with German test pilot Peter Weger flying the new fighter-bomber over Bavaria. The Eurofighter has been built by a consortium of German, British, Italian, and Spanish aircraft manufacturers, the product of a new defense initiative in Europe. The Eurofighter is far superior to prior aircraft of its type—two Eurojet EJ200 engines provide 20,250 pounds (9,185 kilograms) of afterburner thrust, which gives it plenty of power to spare.

◀ The single-seater plane can reach speeds of 1,280 miles (2,060 kilometers) per hour.

Airport on a manmade island

A new airport in Japan has solved the problem of aircraft noise for those who live nearby. The new terminal at Kansai is built on an artificial island some three miles (five kilometers) offshore. Creating the island was one of the greatest engineering projects ever. A seawall was built around the site. The area inside the seawall was filled with rock. Next, the engineers built the vast terminal building, which is designed to flex slightly during earthquakes so it will not break up.

▼ Kansai airport can take 25 million passengers a year.

Genetic tomatoes

Flavr Savr™ tomatoes, which have been genetically modified (GM) to last longer, have gone on sale. In GM foods, genes are taken from the cells of one plant and inserted into another to produce crops that grow better and have more flavor. However, some argue that GM foods are dangerous.

▲ GM foods could solve world food shortages.

1995

A GLANCE AT THE PAST

The first evidence of meteorite impact

The first evidence that a large meteorite hit Earth some 65 million years ago came during the 1970s when an American geologist, Walter Alvarez, found a puzzling dark layer of clay within some beds of rock (*above*) in Italy. Analysis results showed that the clay was rich in the rare metallic element iridium, which is found in meteorites. This iridium-rich layer, which can be detected in many parts of Europe and North America, coincided with a time in Earth's history when the dinosaurs and other animal groups died out. Alvarez speculated that a huge meteorite impact was the cause of the iridium layer and had sparked catastrophic environmental effects that led to worldwide extinctions.

EARTH SCIENCE

Is this what destroyed the dinosaurs?

Geologists in Mexico have discovered a buried crater, an estimated 60 miles (96.5 kilometers) wide, caused by a meteorite impact some 65 million years ago. Scientists think the environmental catastrophes the impact must have caused—including earthquakes and tidal waves—probably contributed to the extinction of the dinosaurs. The meteorite that caused this crater must have been approximately six miles (10 kilometers) in diameter.

▲ *This image of the crater was generated by a computer from geological data.*

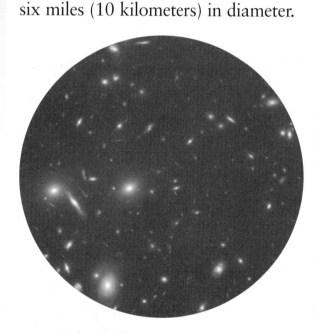

▲ *Galaxies distant in space and time.*

ASTRONOMY

Galaxies detected 15 billion light-years away

This year, American and European astronomers have detected galaxies at just about the farthest distances possible in the universe—about 15 billion light-years. Because the universe is believed to be not much older than 15 billion years, the light has been traveling toward us from these galaxies for most of the lifetime of the universe. So, the galaxies should give an idea of what the universe looked like when it was young. Surprisingly, the galaxies have a fairly mature structure. They also provide evidence that stars started forming soon after the beginning of the universe.

MEDICINE

Laser treatment for near sight

A new laser treatment has been approved for permanent correction of myopia (nearsightedness). The treatment is called photorefractive keratectomy (PRK). It involves the use of a computer-controlled laser to reshape the front of the cornea of each eye by sculpting a thin layer of tissue off its surface. (The cornea is the clear, front part of the eyeball and plays a major part in focusing light rays into the interior of the eye.) Normally, people who have had the treatment no longer need to wear glasses or contact lenses. Although the longterm effects of PRK are not yet known, the side effects seem to be mild, with some discomfort and blurring of vision for a few days.

The PRK treatment for ▶ myopia only takes a few minutes.

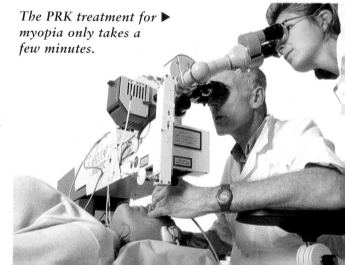

SPACE EXPLORATION

Galileo probe arrives at Jupiter

A NASA space probe, *Galileo*, has arrived at the planet Jupiter after a six-year journey. In July, it separated into an orbiter, which will circle the planet, and an atmospheric probe. In December, the atmospheric probe began to parachute down into Jupiter's atmosphere, returning data to the orbiter about the chemical composition and physical state of the atmosphere. After 57 minutes, the probe was crushed by Jupiter's atmosphere. The *Galileo* orbiter then went into orbit around Jupiter and, beginning next year, will start to study Jupiter's four largest moons and its constantly changing cloud patterns.

◄ *A photograph of Jupiter's largest moon, Ganymede, taken by the* Galileo *probe.*

Science News 1995

- Scientists reveal that a huge iceberg has broken away from the Antarctic continent.
- Russian cosmonaut Valeri Polyakov lands after spending a record 438 days in space.
- New technologies for use on the World Wide Web appear, including Netscape Navigator® and the first search engines.

COMPUTERS

Microsoft® launches Windows® 95

August will see the release of the latest Windows version, Windows 95. Microsoft is already talking up Windows 95, claiming it will make everything you do on a PC faster and easier. It has completely changed the look of the graphics and has finally added a trash can to the desktop, like the Apple® version that has existed for years. Apart from its new look, Windows 95 will allow the user to have a number of programs open simultaneously, offer easier Internet access, and permit longer file names. Windows 95 also signals the death of the disk operating system (DOS), as it takes over from DOS as soon as the computer is switched on.

Windows 95 will ▶ *revolutionize PC use.*

COMPUTERS

Biometric access systems

Security devices such as door keys, and personal identifiers such as credit cards and passports, could one day be things of the past due to a new type of security technology called biometrics. Biometrics is all about recognizing people from characteristics such as their fingerprints, hand shapes, or irises (colored areas of the eyes). These characteristics don't change during your entire life, so they can be used as very effective personal identifiers or as "keys" for gaining access to buildings, bank accounts, or computer networks. All biometric access systems depend on a scanning device linked to a computer running special image-processing software.

GENETICS

No area of science has grown faster over the last half century than genetics. Until the 1950s, little was known about genes, except that they resided in cell structures (chromosomes) and determined the characteristics of living organisms.

This all changed following the discovery of the structure of DNA—the physical basis of genes—in 1953. Research into genes took off, culminating in 2000 with publication of the first draft of the human genome—the complete sequence of human DNA.

So far the main results of the gene revolution are products of genetic manipulation or "engineering," such as genetically modified crops and medically useful proteins made by bacteria that have been modified with human genes. In addition, more is known about the genetic causes of disease, and this should lead to improved treatment and detection of illness.

▲ *Two sets of twin sisters.*

Twins studies

Knowledge of human genetics in the twentieth century greatly benefited from studies on twins. Identical twins are of great interest to geneticists because they have exactly the same genes. This means that any differences between them must be caused by external factors. Through studies on twins reared together and others reared apart, it has been possible to discover which human traits are caused by genes and which are not.

Chromosomes

During the 1880s, biologists noticed some curious dark structures inside the nuclei of living cells. They called these structures chromosomes but were uncertain of their function. Later, they realized that most cells contained paired chromosomes, but egg and sperm cells contained only one of each pair, which indicated that chromosomes had a role in heredity. By the early 1900s, scientists were suggesting that chromosomes carried hereditary units called "genes" that determined the characteristics of plants and animals.

◀ *DNA loops*
The threads in this electron micrograph are plasmids, each of which may contain hundreds of genes.

Chromosome pairs
Pairs of human chromosomes can be seen in this microscope image. ▶

Plasmids

All organisms, even bacteria, have genes. Some of the genetic material in bacteria comes in the form of circular loops of DNA, called plasmids. A huge amount of current genetic knowledge derives from studies on bacterial DNA. In the 1940s, for example, it was shown that genes could be passed between different organisms by plasmids.

1960s
The code by which DNA directs protein synthesis is cracked.

1970s
Basic techniques of genetic manipulation are developed.

1982
Eli Lilly produces the first genetically engineered insulin.

1990
Gene replacement therapy is performed for the first time.

2000
The first draft of the human genome is completed.

How DNA works

One of the most important scientific breakthroughs of the twentieth century occurred in 1953 with the discovery of the structure of DNA (deoxyribonucleic acid), the physical substance of genes. Previously it was known that DNA contained sugar, phosphate, and four substances known as nucleotide bases—adenine (A), thymine (T), cytosine (C), and guanine (G). But scientists didn't know how these fitted together in a DNA molecule. Whatever structure existed, it had to be capable of storing information in a coded form, and there had to be an obvious mechanism by which it could be copied. The "double helix" structure proposed by Watson and Crick fulfilled both of these criteria.

◄ **Base sequence**
Since the 1980s, machines have been available for "reading" the sequence of bases (A, T, C, and G) in any piece of DNA.

◄ **Double helix**
DNA consists of two intertwined sugar and phosphate strands, joined by pairs of nucleotide bases (A-T and C-G). The order of the bases along one of the strands carries coded information for making proteins.

◄ **Replication**
To copy itself, a double helix splits into strands. Individual bases (A, T, C, and G), floating in the cell nucleus, bind to complementary bases on the single strands (A with T and C with G), forming two new, identical double helixes.

◄ **Two new double helixes.** ►

Genetic modification

Since the 1980s, scientists have been able to perform genetic modification or "engineering." This means introducing a gene from one organism into the DNA of another. For example, a bacterial gene might be inserted into the DNA of a plant to make the plant more resistant to insects. There is no evidence that eating genetically modified foods poses a risk to health. But there are concerns that genetic engineering might produce harmful organisms that escape and breed in the wild with unpredictable consequences.

▲ *Genetically modified tomatoes are claimed to have an improved flavor.*

▲ **Dolly, the cloned sheep.**

Animal cloning

In 1996, Scottish scientists generated a genetically identical copy or "clone" of an adult ewe (female sheep) from a single cell taken from the sheep. The clone was called Dolly. The experiment showed that the adult cells of an animal contain workable versions of all the genes necessary to produce an entire animal. In the future it might be possible to clone people. An obvious concern is that this technology might be used for unscrupulous reasons.

1996

A GLANCE AT THE PAST

Channels on Mars

In 1877, the Italian astronomer Giovanni Schiaparelli saw some markings on Mars which he named *canali* (meaning channels), and he drew a map of their distribution. *Canali* was unfortunately mistranslated into English as "canals," leading some people to believe they were constructed by intelligent beings to distribute water around the planet. This was not Schiaparelli's belief at all. It is now known that the channels are an optical illusion.

BIOLOGY

Life from Mars, our neighboring planet

National Aeronautics and Space Administration (NASA) scientists have found strong evidence suggesting that primitive life-forms existed on Mars over three and a half billion years ago. This comes from studying a large meteorite fragment in Antarctica, known to have come from Mars. Mineral features indicating biological activity and fossils of primitive organisms were found inside the meteorite.

▲ *Scientists examine earlier images of Mars to compare them with the meteorite find.*

Science News 1996

- In the U.S., world chess champion Garry Kasparov beats the computer Deep Blue®.

- French marine biologists find the remains of *Alexandria,* which sank beneath the Mediterranean in A.D. 335.

- The World Health Organization announces a birth-control injection for men.

SPACE EXPLORATION

Water on the Moon

NASA has confirmed there is water on the Moon—although not much, and frozen—but possibly enough to support a sizeable Moon colony sometime in the future. The water has been detected by NASA's Lunar Prospector spacecraft and is scattered in thin concentrations over a large area, mostly in the Moon's polar regions. It is estimated there could be several trillion gallons of frozen water on the Moon—the equivalent of a moderate-sized lake. The water probably reached the Moon from icy comets hitting it. As well as providing something to drink and wash with, water can be broken down into hydrogen and oxygen, which might be used for rocket fuel.

BIOLOGY

Sheep cloned in Scotland

Scottish scientists have created a genetically identical copy, or "clone," of a sheep from a single cell taken from it. They transferred the nuclei from various sheep cells into unfertilized eggs from which the natural nuclei had been removed. The eggs were placed in the wombs of ewes and one resulted in the birth of a lamb, called "Dolly." This proves that adult cells contain workable versions of all the genes needed to produce an entire animal.

Dolly is an exact genetic copy of the sheep ▶ *that provided the transferred nucleus.*

Tagging with the implantable electronic microchip

Microchips are everywhere and before long they could also be inside the human body. Implantable microchip units have been developed that can store, record, and transmit information uniquely associated with an individual item, animal, or human. The main thrust of this research is in the field of animal tagging, where chips can be used to store a unique identification number. Each chip is sealed within a bio-compatible glass capsule. The size of this capsule is similar to that of a grain of rice. It does not take a great deal of imagination to extend this use to humans. Researchers are already claiming that it can be used as a tamperproof method of identification and for locating lost or missing people.

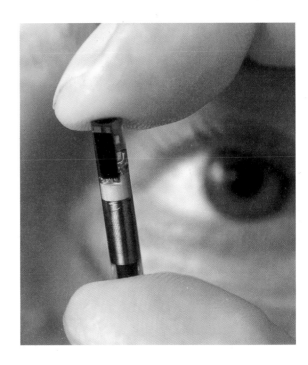

This tiny electronic tag can be used ▶ to identify both people and animals.

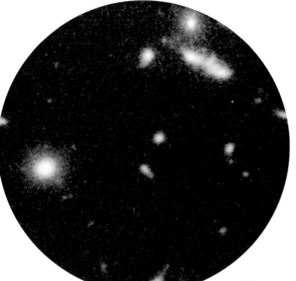

Photographs of galaxies forming

Images taken by the Hubble Space Telescope have revealed objects billions of light-years from Earth, which astronomers think are the early building blocks of galaxies or "galaxy precursors." The small blue objects are visible in images taken of a tiny region of the sky that also contains many fully formed galaxies. Because light from the distant objects has taken 11 billion years to reach Earth, the images show what was happening 11 billion light-years ago, when the universe was only a few billion years old. The objects seem to be close to one another, and each is thought to contain several billion stars, together with dust and gas. Astronomers believe that many such objects have collided and merged over time to grow into the giant and luminous galaxies seen today. The telescope needed more than one day of exposure time for each photograph.

◀ Distant galaxies as seen by the Hubble Space Telescope.

Speeding up game play

Intel has been producing successful microprocessors (chips that perform all the instructions in a computer) for over 20 years, and has now launched a new series of Pentium® processors that include MMX® (MultiMedia eXtensions) technology. This series contains 5.5 million transistors, and a high-speed memory area to accelerate performance. It is capable of performing up to 300 million instructions per second. The addition of MMX technology means that the chips also contain a new set of instructions designed to enhance multimedia performance. The processors will be included in high-performance computers used in the rapidly expanding Internet.

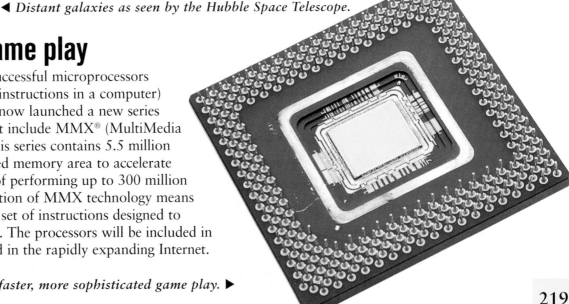

The MMX technology will allow faster, more sophisticated game play. ▶

The first computer chess

The first mechanical chess player was not a computer, but a machine that was made of simple electrical circuits and used a gramophone to say "check" or "mate." Built in 1912 by Spanish engineer Leonardo Torres, this chess machine was limited to performing one simple endgame scenario. Later, in 1956, Stanislaw Ulam programmed a computer to play chess on a 6 x 6 board. Called *MANIAC I* (*above*), it became the first computer to beat human opposition in a game.

COMPUTERS

Kasparov gets the Deep Blues

In 1985, student Feng-hsiung Hsu began to develop a chess-playing computer. Twelve years later this computer—IBM's Deep Blue®—has stunned the world by beating the world chess champion Garry Kasparov. The most amazing fact about Deep Blue is its sheer speed: it is able to examine 200 million different chess positions per second.

▼ *World chess champion Garry Kasparov takes on Deep Blue.*

GARRY KASPAROV

DEEP BLUE

PALEONTOLOGY

Ancient embryos found

Fossil evidence has been found in China to support the idea that complex animals must have begun to appear on Earth as long ago as 600 million years. Clusters of tiny balls, less than one-twentieth of an inch (1.3 millimeters) in diameter, have been discovered in 570 million-year-old rocks. The balls have a delicate cellular structure that has never been seen before in fossils of this age. Astonishingly, the fossils appear to be preserved animal embryos, caught by the process of fossilization just after fertilization. How they were turned into fossils, however, remains a mystery.

TRANSPORTATION

Beating traffic jams

British motorists need never find themselves in traffic jams again. The Trafficmaster route-planner, an in-car computer device, uses information from a network of sensors situated along highways to warn a driver of traffic build-up and suggest an alternative route. It can also be used to plan trips. The driver simply punches in the starting point and destination and the route-planner does the rest. It also automatically tunes the car radio into each local station as the car drives through different regions.

▼ *The Trafficmaster system takes the stress out of road travel.*

High-definition television arrives

TV station WFAA of Dallas and Fort Worth, Texas, is the first to broadcast high-definition television (HDTV) to a mass audience. Although the new HDTV receivers are high-priced, many people are already enthusiastic about the new service, which gives a picture that is crisper and clearer than anything they have seen before. This is because the signal is digital and the pixels that make up the screen image are smaller, closer together, and greater in number than on ordinary TV sets. There is digital sound, which is as clear as sound from an audio compact disc—with the bonus of up to five channels—for a movie-quality, surround effect. Another movielike feature is the wide screen, in the same proportions as a movie screen.

Viewers can now recreate a movie-theater effect in their own homes with HDTV. ▶

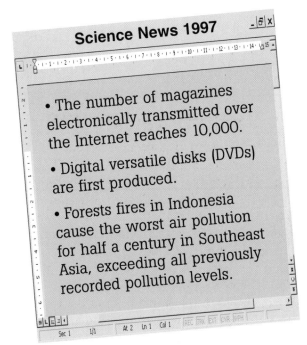

Science News 1997

- The number of magazines electronically transmitted over the Internet reaches 10,000.

- Digital versatile disks (DVDs) are first produced.

- Forests fires in Indonesia cause the worst air pollution for half a century in Southeast Asia, exceeding all previously recorded pollution levels.

Transitional species or dead end?

An international team led by anthropologist Tim White has discovered fossilized, skeletal remains of what they believe to be a new species of hominid. The find was made in the Awash valley in central Ethiopia, and has been christened *Australopithecus garhi* by researchers (in Afar, the local language, *garhi* means "surprise"). The remains include part of a skull, with a complete upper jaw and unusually large teeth, estimated to be 2.5 million years old. The combination of teeth and bones is more primitive than the earliest humans and yet more advanced than the most modern australopithecines. *Australopithecus garhi* appears to fall somewhere between *A. afarensis* (3.6–2.9 million years old) and *Homo erectus* (1.7 million years old). Experts think this could have been the crucial transitional species that led directly to the *Homo* lineage, or it could be a branch of the tree that died out.

Roving vehicle on Mars

Pathfinder, a United States space probe, has landed on Mars and released a vehicle, *Sojourner*, to explore the surface. *Sojourner* is controlled by an Earth-based operator, who uses images obtained by cameras on both *Pathfinder* and *Sojourner* to maneuver the rover over the rocky terrain. *Pathfinder* landed on Mars on July 4, bounced several times, then rolled, before coming to rest. Two days later the six-wheeled *Sojourner* moved out onto the Martian surface. One reason for the mission is to demonstrate the feasibility of low-cost landings on Mars.

Sojourner is providing vital information about the nature of the surface of Mars. ▼

1998

A GLANCE AT THE PAST

A GLANCE AT THE PAST

The first mobile phones

The first mobile phones were developed during the 1940s and 1950s, when engineers came up with the cellular system—a network of antennae, each of which could both transmit and receive radio signals with a limited range. Signals could be picked up from the nearest antenna and transmitted to the one nearest the person being called. The system was developed gradually over the following decades, with the cellular system being linked by computer.

COMMUNICATIONS

Explosion in mobile phone use

This year has seen an explosion in the use of mobile phones. Telecom company Nokia® has sold 100 million phones and many people are now using their mobile phones in preference to "landline" phones. The units are cheaper than ever before and small enough to carry in a pocket or handbag; they have features, such as built-in directories and automatic voice mail, that make them easy to use. Mobile phones have also gone global and can be used virtually anywhere in the world.

▲ *Modern mobiles are much lighter and more compact than the original, chunkier handsets.*

COMPUTERS

Apple launches iMac™

Think of a computer and you'll inevitably think of a beige box. With the release of the iMac, Apple has decided it's time to think again. The iMac looks like no other computer; housed in translucent plastic, it comes in six different colors. The iMac has power as well as beauty with a processor that is a match for any PC. Apple describes the iMac as their computer for the new millennium, so it comes as little surprise to find that the "i" stands for Internet. Designed with the Internet fully in mind, users should be "surfing" as soon as the computer is plugged into a phone line. With their stock selling at a five-year low, Apple is pinning its hopes on this attractive little computer.

COMMUNICATIONS

Now you need never get lost again!

You can now carry a small, handheld device that will tell you exactly where you are in the world. This is made possible by the global positioning system (GPS), a network of 24 satellites orbiting Earth. The GPS unit that you carry with you receives radio signals from these satellites, calculates how long the signals take to reach it, and works out how far it is from the three or four nearest satellites. From this information, it calculates its precise position on Earth. There are already many users lining up to try the system, ranging from people involved in surveying and mapping, to travelers and explorers.

◄ *The new GPS can be accessed via a small, neat, handheld unit like this.*

Science News 1998

- The Sandia National Laboratories in Texas produce the first photonic crystals, devices that will bring rapid advances in optical computing.

- In the United States, widescale installation begins of ADSL (Asymmetric Digital Subscriber Line), a technology for increasing digital data transmission over phone lines.

Loudspeakers disappear

COMMUNICATIONS

For years in the world of loudspeakers, it has been "big is best." But the latest generation of speakers makes stereo sound with units so flat they can be hung on the wall like pictures. These fit well into modern rooms and are ideal in home movie setups, where up to five speakers can be used. They also have potential in portable products such as laptop computers. The new technology, pioneered by the British company NXT New Transducers, replaces the big cones of conventional, bulky speakers with components called "exciters" that make the flat panel move in a rippling motion to create the vibrations that produce sound.

◄ *Speakers today come in many shapes and sizes.*

World's tallest office building completed in Malaysia

ENGINEERING

The Petronas Towers, in the Malaysian capital of Kuala Lumpur, are complete and they form the tallest office building in the world. The twin 88-story towers are 1,483 feet (452 meters) tall. Among self-supporting structures, only the CN Tower in Toronto is taller, at 1,814 feet (553 meters) high. The towers contain some 7.5 million square feet (697,000 square meters) of space, which accommodates a museum, a concert hall, shops, and parking for 4,500 cars, as well as offices. Architect César Pelli based the intricate shapes of the towers on patterns found in Islamic art to create a building that combines cultural identity with modern steel and concrete technology. The tallest structure of all in the world is a tethered television mast in North Dakota, at a height of 2,063 feet (629 meters).

The Petronas Towers in ▶
Kuala Lumpur, Malaysia.

The very versatile disk—DVD

COMMUNICATIONS

It looks like an ordinary audio compact disc (CD), but the digital versatile disk (DVD) can do much more. The main difference between the two is that the DVD can store many times more data than a CD—anything that has been "translated" into digital, computer-readable code, such as computer files, software, audio, still pictures, and movies. The disks are being produced in several forms: read-only disks, suitable for computer games or movies; blank disks for copying; and rewritable disks that can be recorded over again and again.

The new DVD players are likely ▶
*to prove much more versatile than
audio CD players.*

First evidence of extrasolar planets

The first evidence of the existence of planets beyond the solar system emerged in the late 1980s. Small, periodic changes were observed in the light coming from certain stars, then "wobbles" were detected in the motions of other stars, suggesting that they were being orbited by large planets. Scores of planets have now been detected in this way. Most are larger than Jupiter.

ASTRONOMY

Remote planet photographed

Astronomers are beginning to discover direct evidence of planets beyond our solar system. Recently, astronomers at the Keck Observatory in Hawaii have observed light from a star 153 light-years away being dimmed by a planet passing in front of it. This follows a photograph taken last year by the Hubble Space Telescope, which shows a faraway giant gas planet being ejected from a young, double star system.

▲ *The Keck Observatory enables scientists to see far into outer space.*

PALEONTOLOGY

Earliest reptile fossil

A fossil of the oldest known vertebrate (animal with a backbone) to have lived on dry land has been unearthed in Scotland. The 340 million-year-old fossil is also, arguably, the earliest known reptile. The remnants of the six-inch (15-centimeter) long headless fossil (named *Casineria*), which would have looked like something between a newt and a lizard, was originally spotted by an amateur collector on the shore of Cheese Bay in the county of Lothian in 1992. This year, paleontologists discovered it had five fingers (a pattern that has continued through all reptiles, birds, and mammals), simple claws, a stiff backbone, and a forearm structure that indicated it was a reptile and lived on land.

Science News 1999

- The extremely powerful Chandra X-ray Observatory—which can take highly magnified photos of distant stars and galaxies—has been launched into space on board the space shuttle *Columbia*.

- Anthropologists in Portugal unearth the complete skeleton of a four-year-old child buried 25,000 years ago.

COMMUNICATIONS

Enter the Web cam

Everyone is talking about Web cams. Like most computer equipment, a Web cam has two parts—hardware and software. The hardware is a digital camera, which you connect to your computer. The software takes a picture from the camera every so often, turns it into a standard file format, and uploads it to the server (computer) where your Web site is stored. The picture can be viewed by anyone visiting your site, and visitors can return to see how the image has changed. Already people are thinking up many uses for Web cams, ranging from the silly to the serious.

◄ *A Web cam enables you to put pictures on a website, refreshing them at regular intervals as the scene changes.*

Handheld Internet access

COMMUNICATIONS

Gone are the days when you needed a large, powerful personal computer to give you access to the Internet. The latest generation of handheld personal organizers has wireless Internet access built in, to give truly modern computing on the move. There is no bulky keyboard—instead, you input all your information and commands via the touch-sensitive screen. Useful functions such as a diary, address book, and to-do list are all available, as are scaled-down versions of regular computer programs such as word processing software. E-mail can be written, sent, and received through the personal organizer, and you can access websites, although web browsing is not as rich an experience as it is with a desktop computer.

◀ *The latest way to connect to the Internet.*

Human chromosome decoded

BIOLOGY

Scientists in the United Kingdom, Japan, and the United States have announced that, for the first time ever, a human chromosome has been completely decoded, as part of the Human Genome Project. The decoded chromosome is one of the smallest of the human chromosomes, number 22 (there are 23 pairs of chromosomes altogether). The researchers have worked out the sequence of 33.5 million nucleotide bases that make up the chromosome, and so far have found over 500 genes on it, though with further analysis this number could rise to over 800 genes. The function of some of the genes is already known, but researchers say that the chromosome also contains a surprising number of genes that appear to have no function whatsoever.

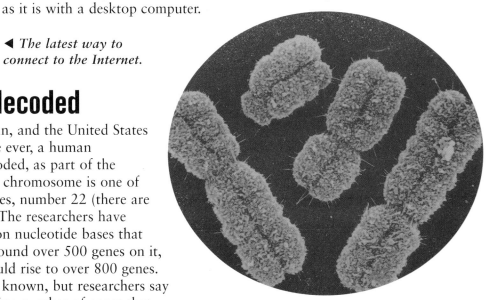

▲ *Human chromosomes.*

Space station being built

SPACE EXPLORATION

Way above the surface of Earth, a new space station is taking shape. It is the International Space Station (ISS), which is being built by 11 European Union countries, the United States, Canada, Russia, Brazil, and Japan. The first module, called *Zarya*, the station's early propulsion and power module, was launched from Russia's Baikonur Cosmodrome in November of 1998. Soon after, the space shuttle *Endeavor* linked America's *Unity* module, a passageway and docking port module, to *Zarya*. This year, more than 2,000 pounds (900 kilograms) of supplies and hardware were delivered, and tons more equipment, further modules, and living quarters will arrive next year.

◀ *The ISS is a result of international cooperation.*

1960s
Modems are invented, allowing telephone transfer of digital data.

1970s
The first image scanners become available.

1982
Digital sound is introduced in the form of compact disks.

1987
Desktop publishing of magazines and books takes off.

1988
MPEG method is devised for compressing digital video.

DIGITAL AGE

Toward the end of the twentieth century, everything was going "digital," meaning that many different types of information—text, pictures, sound, video, even 3-D shapes and patterns—started being stored as numbers.

The ever-increasing global importance of computers was the main force behind this change. Using modern computer hardware and software, it has become easy and inexpensive to store, edit, and combine information in various ways. It is also possible to compress it and transmit it across the world at high speed and without any loss of data. But to do so, the data must first be turned into a form that computers can understand—that is, into numbers.

▲ *Magnified image showing pixels.*

Pixel magic

An image can be digitized by dividing it up into millions of tiny squares (called pixels), measuring the relative amount of each of the three primary colors of light (red, green, and blue) in each pixel, and recording these measurements in computer memory.

Publishing by numbers

Since the mid-1980s, desktop publishing has grown to become the most popular way of producing printed material. Desktop publishing means assembling all the words and images for a publication as a set of digital computer files in preparation for printing. For example, although the book you are reading is not digital, all the words and pictures were assembled in digital form during its production.

Page design ▶
Special software has been available since 1985 for laying out book and magazine pages on a computer screen, using digital text and images.

MAX!

Digital recognition

The digitization of information is extending into many diverse areas of life, such as security recognition systems. For example, scanning devices are now available for recording the pattern of a person's iris (the colored area of the eye) as a 4,096-digit code. A person's iris pattern stays the same throughout life, and the digital code that can be generated from it is so unique that it can be used as a personal identifier to a high degree of accuracy.

▲ *Tim Berners-Lee.*

World Wide Web

One of the most significant inventions of the 1980s was made by a British computer specialist, Tim Berners-Lee. He devised a system for linking computer files so that he could jump between them. Then he made an addressing scheme for files on a computer network, allowing anyone to freely access, or "link in," to them. In 1991, Berners-Lee's invention, which has since spawned the World Wide Web, debuted on the Internet.

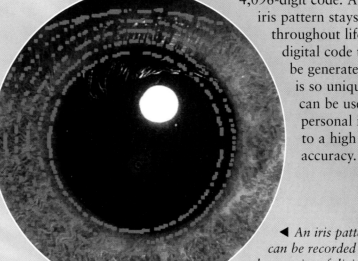

◄ *An iris pattern can be recorded as a long series of digits by computer software, which first breaks down an image of the iris into concentric rings.*

Digital sound

A sound carried in a wire as an electrical waveform can be turned into a string of numbers and thus made digital through the process known as "sampling." Sampling involves measuring the amplitude (voltage) of the waveform at regular intervals and then converting these measurements into binary numbers. In the example shown here, the sample values can be any number between 0 and 255. In binary computer code, any number within this range can be expressed as a string of eight digits or "bits," each of which is either a 1 ("on" signal) or a 0 ("off" signal). For example, the number 108 can be recorded in binary form as 01101100.

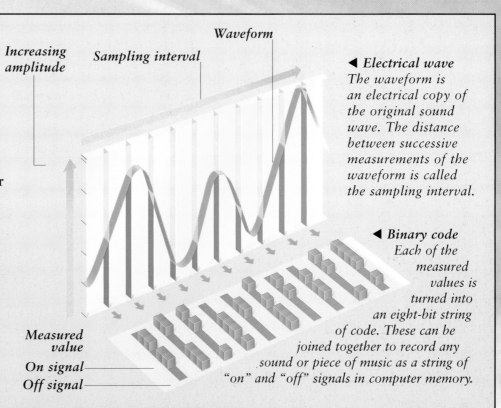

Increasing amplitude

Sampling interval

Waveform

Measured value

On signal

Off signal

◄ **Electrical wave**
The waveform is an electrical copy of the original sound wave. The distance between successive measurements of the waveform is called the sampling interval.

◄ **Binary code**
Each of the measured values is turned into an eight-bit string of code. These can be joined together to record any sound or piece of music as a string of "on" and "off" signals in computer memory.

2000

The original artificial heart

The original artificial heart (*above*), developed by American physician Robert Jarvik, was a metal and plastic device that almost completely replaced the patient's weakened or diseased heart. Introduced in 1985, the Jarvik 7 was sewn to parts of the two upper chambers remaining from the original heart, and to the two main arteries supplying blood to the lungs and to the rest of the body. It was powered by an external machine connected to the device by air tubes passing through the chest wall.

MEDICINE

New thumb-sized artificial heart

Heart patients in Texas have received a new type of thumb-sized artificial heart pump called the Jarvik 2000®. On April 2, this heart-assist pump was implanted in an American woman who was suffering from an enlarged heart. Jarvik Heart, Inc. and the Texas Heart Institute have been developing the Jarvik 2000 for more than 10 years. The new device does not replace the natural heart, but supplements it. It is implanted in the heart, from which it pumps blood into the body's main artery, the aorta.

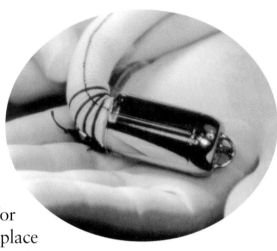

▲ *The heart-assist pump.*

Science News 2000

- Two Russian cosmonauts and an American astronaut become the first occupants of the International Space Station.
- Trials of a revolutionary new anti-malaria vaccine start in Gambia in Africa.
- American astronomers find the exact location of a black hole at the center of our galaxy.

BIOLOGY

First draft of human genome

Researchers for the Human Genome Project in the United States and Great Britain have revealed that they already have a "working draft" of the human genome—the entire sequence of 3.1 billion chemical bases that make up human DNA. It has been a huge task: written down on paper, the base sequence would fill one hundred thousand pages. Within the genome, scientists have identified some 38,000 sequences of bases that are definitely genes. The achievement is expected to revolutionize medical science, forging a new era of gene-based treatments that can be tailored to each individual's genetic makeup.

SPACE EXPLORATION

Personal satellite assistant

Engineers at the Ames Research Center in California are developing an intelligent flying robot, about the size of a softball, for use in future space missions. The device will act as another set of eyes and ears for spacecraft crew and support personnel. Called the Personal Satellite Assistant (PSA), the device contains advanced sensors for monitoring conditions in a spacecraft (such as the level of oxygen in the air), a computer for analyzing data, camera and wireless equipment for handling communications between astronauts and support staff, and its own propulsion components (for independent movement). Two or more PSAs may even be able to conduct combined troubleshooting activities, such as detecting pressure leaks.

◄ *The compact design of the PSA allows it to reach otherwise inaccessible areas of a spacecraft.*

PALEONTOLOGY

Fossilized dinosaur heart found

Scientists at the North Carolina State University have announced the discovery of a fossilized dinosaur heart— the first one ever found. The 66-million-year-old dinosaur fossil, belonging to a plant-eating species called *Thescalosaurus*, was found in 1993 in South Dakota. It has taken years of investigation to prove that a grapefruit-sized object within its chest is a heart. The object is not completely visible but can be seen in a three-dimensional model of the dinosaur's chest cavity built from X-ray scans. Investigators became convinced it was a heart when they found high concentrations of iron, which they believe originated in the dinosaur's blood, within the object.

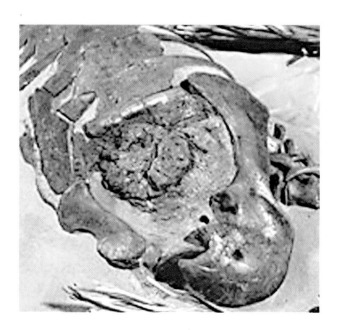

The dark object at the center of this photograph ▶ of the dinosaur fossil is the partially-visible heart.

▲ *Bluetooth handset with earpiece.*

COMMUNICATIONS

Bluetooth™ connects the world

A revolutionary new radio technology called "Bluetooth" is likely to have a big impact on our lives. The new technology allows different electronic devices, such as computers, phone handsets, and CD players, to communicate and share data without any wires. Bluetooth communication is limited to a 33-foot (10-meter) radius, but can go through walls. When Bluetooth-capable devices come within range of one another, they have an electronic conversation to determine whether they have data to share. The user doesn't have to press a button or give a command—it all happens automatically. The system operates on a radio frequency of around 2.45 gigahertz, which is also used by devices such as baby monitors. To prevent interference, Bluetooth transmitters switch their operating frequency 1,600 times a second.

MEDICINE

This won't hurt!

Avoiding vaccinations for fear of needles could be a thing of the past with the development of a painless new drug delivery system by a British company, PowderJect®. The novel "powder injection" technique works by accelerating fine particles of a drug to such a high velocity that they can pass straight through the outer layers of skin and into the bloodstream. The injection delivers the dose of a drug over a skin area about the size of a thumbnail and works by using pulses of compressed helium gas to accelerate the drug particles.

The head of the device does not ▶ penetrate the skin, so it does not have to be discarded after each use.

Index

Index

Index

Index

Index

Index

Index

Acknowledgments

Marshall Editions would like to thank the following for their kind permission to reproduce their pictures. If the publishers have unwittingly infringed copyright in any illustration reproduced, they would pay an appropriate fee on being satisfied to the owner's title.

t= top; b=bottom; l=left; c=center; r=right

SM/SSPL = Science Museum/Science & Society Picture Library;
SPL = Science Photo Library

1 Daimler-Chrysler; 3 bl Digital Vision; c NASA/SSPL; br Courtesy of Samsung Electronics; 4/5 Novosti (London); 6 Digital Vision; 8 c Holt Studios International/Nigel Cattlin; 8 tl Cavendish Laboratory; 8 tr SM/SSPL; 9 br Max Planck Institut; 9 c Ancient Art and Architecture Collection; 9 tr Royal Free Hospital of Medicine, Wellcome Trust; 10 br SPL; 10 tl Marconi; 10 tr SM/SSPL; 11 br The National History Museum, London; 11 tr The Advertising Archive; 12 c Novosti (London); 12 tl SM/SSPL; 12 tr SM/SSPL; 13 br Hulton Getty; 13 c SM/SSPL; 14 bl Carrier Corporation; 14 c SPL; 14 tl Wellcome Library, London; 14 tr Department of Clinical Radiology, Salisbury District Hospital/SPL; 15 br Hulton Getty; 15 c SM/SSPL; 15 tr Corbis; 16 c Robert Opie; 16 tl Holt Studios International/Nigel Cattlin; 16 tr Corbis; 17 br Hulton Getty; 17 c SM/SSPL; 17 tr Manfred Kage/SPL; 20 bl GSF Picture Library; 20 c SPL; 20 tl Corbis; 20 tr SPL; 21 br American Museum of Natural History; 22 bl TRH Pictures; 22 c Maltings Partnership; 22 tl Hulton Getty; 22 tr Corbis; 23 br Hulton Getty; 23 c SM/SSPL; 23 tr SPL; 24 c SPL; 24 tl Daimler-Chrysler; 24 tr Daimler-Chrysler; 25 c The Natural History Museum, London; 25 tr Corbis; 28 bl GEC Archives; 28 c Corbis; 28 tl The Natural History Museum, London; 28 tr The Natural History Museum, London; 29 br Mary Evans Picture Library; 29 tr TRH Pictures; 30 bl Hulton Getty; 30 tl Hulton Getty; 30 tr Corbis; 31 br Ancient Art and Architecture Collection; 31 c SM/SSPL; 31 tl Cavendish Laboratory; 31 tr Corbis; 32 bl GSF Picture Library; 32 c SM/SSPL; 32 tl Corbis; 32tr Bettmann/Corbis; 33 br SM/SSPL; 33 c SM/SSPL; 33 tr Mary Evans Picture Library; 34 bl Hulton Getty; 34 tl Mary Evans Picture Library; 34 tr Mary Evans Picture Library; 35 tr Ford Motor Co; 38 bl Hulton Getty; 38 tl SM/SSPL; 38 tr Galaxy Pictures; 39 bl Michael Fogden/Oxford Scientific Films; 39 c Hulton Deutsch Collection; 39 tl TRH Pictures; 40 bl SM/SSPL; 40 tl Nigel Cattlin/Holt Studios International; 40 tr J L Carson/Custom Medical Stock Photo/SPL; 41 bl SM/SSPL; 41 c SM/SSPL; 41 tl SM/SSPL; 42 c Wessex Regional Genetics Lab./Wellcome Centre Photo Library; 42 tl SM/SSPL; 42 tr Henning Christoph/Katz Collection; 43 br Ishihara Foundation; 43 tr Hulton Getty; 44 c AKG Berlin/IMS; 44 tl SM/SSPL; 44 tr TRIP/Eric Smith; 45 br Hulton Deutsch Collection/Corbis; 45 c SM/SSPL; 45 tl Hulton Getty; 46 bl Schenectady Museum; Hall of Electrical History Foundation/Corbis; 46 tl AKG/Cambridge Univ; 46 tr SM/SSPL; 47 c Hulton Deutsch Collection; 47 tr Hulton Getty; 50 bl Bettmann/Corbis; 50 tl Corbis; 50 tr Bettmann/Corbis; 51 bl Laura Dwight/Corbis; 51 c Jan Butchofsky-Houser/Corbis; 51 tl SPL; 51 tr Bettmann/Corbis; 52 bl Ancient Art and Architecture Collection; 52 tl Hulton Deutsch Collection/Corbis; 52 tr National Oceanographic Library; 53 br Carl Zeiss; 53 tl Mary Evans Picture Library; 53 tr Mary Evans Picture Library; 54 bl SPL; 54 tl SM/SSPL; 54 tr The Advertising Archives; 55 bl SM/SSPL; 55 c SM/SSPL; 55 tr Henning Christoph/Katz Collection; 56 bl SM/SSPL; 56 c The Natural History Museum, London; 56 tl SM/SSPL; 56 tr SM/SSPL; 57 bl SM/SSPL; 57 tr Wellcome Trust Photo Library; 58 bl SM/SSPL; 58 tl SM/SSPL; 58 tr SM/SSPL; 59 bl SM/SSPL; 59 tl Michael Holford; 62 bl SM/SSPL; 62 tl SM/SSPL; 62 tr SM/SSPL; 63 bl Rolex; 63 tr Rolex; 64 br Johnson & Johnson; 64 tl SM/SSPL; 64 tr SM/SSPL; 65 br SM/SSPL; 65 c SM/SSPL; 65 tl Mary Evans Picture Library; 65 tr NASA; 68 bl Michael Yamashita/Corbis; 68 c SM/SSPL; 68 tl AKG; 68 tr SM/SSPL; 69 bl Minnesota Historical Society/Corbis; 69 tl GSF Picture Library; 70 br SM/SSPL; 70 tl SM/SSPL; 70 tr SM/SSPL; 71 bl SM/SSPL; 71 tr SM/SSPL; 72 bl The Advertising Archives; 72 c Royal Astronomical Society; 72 tl Mary Evans Picture Library; 72 tr Mary Evans Picture Library; 73 br SM/SSPL; 73 tl SM/SSPL; 74 c Hulton Getty; 74 tl SM/SSPL; 74 tr SM/SSPL; 75 b SM/SSPL; 75 tl SM/SSPL; 75 tr SM/SSPL; 76 bl Mary Evans Picture Library; 76 tl SM/SSPL; 76 tr SPL; 77 br SM/SSPL; 77 tr The Culture Archive; 78 br Bettmann/Corbis; 78 tl SM/SSPL; 78 tr SM/SSPL; 79 br SM/SSPL; 79 c SM/SSPL; 79 tl The Advertising Archives; 80 bl Corbis; 80 tl Balafon Image Bank/Outline Press; 80 tr Gruhn Guitars; 81 br The Natural History Museum, London; 81 tl SM/SSPL; 81 tr Alison Wright/Corbis; 84 br SM/SSPL; 84 tl Mary Evans Picture Library; 84 tr Hulton Getty; 85 bl Mary Evans Picture Library; 85 c SM/SSPL; 85 tl The Natural History Museum, London; 86 bl SM/SSPL; 86 tl Du Pont; 86 tr SM/SSPL; 87 br Bettmann/Corbis; 87 cr SM/SSPL; 90 bl Ancient Art and Architecture Collection; 90 tl SM/SSPL; 90 tr SM/SSPL;

91 b Underwood & Underwood/Corbis; 91 tl The Culture Archive; 92 bl SPL; 92 tl SPL; 92 tr Bettmann/Corbis; 93 br National Renewable Energy Lab.; 93 tl The Culture Archive; 94 bl London Features International/Fermi Enrico; 94 tl SPL; 94 tr TRH Pictures; 95 bl Imperial War Museum; 95 tr Schenectady Museum; Hall Of Electricty History; 96 br Hulton Getty; 96 tl TRH Pictures/Carina Dvorak; 96 tr SM/SSPL; 97 br Bettmann/Corbis; 97 c Bettmann/Corbis; 98 bl SM/SSPL; 98 tl SM/SSPL; 98 tr SM/SSPL; 99 bl Daniel Heuclin; 99 tr Sikorsky; 100 bl Bettmann/Corbis; 100 tl SPL; 100 tr SPL; 101 br Archive Photos; 101 l Art and Architecture Collection; 104 br Schenectady Museum; 104 tl Hall Of Electricty History; 104 tr CERN; 105 br SM/SSPL; 105 c South Australian Museum; 106 br SM/SSPL; 106 c Ancient Art and Architecture Collection; 106 tl Bettmann/Corbis; 106 tr Hulton Getty; 107 br American Museum of Natural History; 107 tl TRH Pictures; 108 bl Lambert/Archive Photos; 108 tl SM/SSPL; 108 tr Hulton Deutsch Collection/Corbis; 109 bl Hulton Getty; 109 tr Science & Society; 110 bl The Culture Archive; 110 tl Galen Rowell/Corbis; 110 tr Archive Photos; 111 br NASA; 111 c SM/SSPL; 114 bl Ralph White/Corbis; 114 tl Robert Opie; 114 tr Roger Ressmeyer/Corbis; 115 bl Hulton Getty; 115 tl SPL; 115 tr SPL; 116 bl The AC Long Health Science Library, Columbia University; 116 tl SM/SSPL; 116 tr Royal National Institute of the Deaf; 117 br Bettmann/Corbis; 117 tl Hulton Getty; 118 bl SM/SSPL; 118 tl Mary Evans Picture Library; 118 tr CERN; 119 tl SM/SSPL; 120 bl SM/SSPL; 120 tl NASA; 120 tr SM/SSPL; 121 bl Hulton Getty; 121 tl Robert Opie; 124 br SPL/Eye of Science; 124 c Robert Opie; 124 tl The Advertising Archives; 124 tr The Advertising Archives; 125 br Hulton Getty; 125 c Lego Systems-AS; 126 bl Hulton Getty; 126 tl GSF Picture Library; 126 tr Bettmann/Corbis; 127 br Hulton Getty; 127 tr SM/SSPL; 128 bl Novosti Photo Library; 128 tl Corbis; 128 tr SM/SSPL; 129 tr Hulton Deutsch Collection Ltd; 130 br M Wyndham; 130 tl The Associated Press; 130 tr SM/SSPL; 131 br Marshall Editions; 131 tr SM/SSPL; 134 c SPL; 134 tl Xerox Photographic Office; 134 tr Xerox Photographic Office; 135 bl TRH Pictures/USAF; 135 tr Robert Weight; Ecoscene/Corbis; 136 br Gordon Greene; 136 c Michael Holford; 136 tl Bettmann/Corbis; 137 br Environmental Images/Herbert Girardet; 137 tl Novosti (London); 137 tr Novosti (London); 140 br SPL; 140 c The Advertising Archives; 140 tl Tibet Images/Robin Bathy; 140 tr GSF Picture Library; 141 br SM/SSPL; 141 tl Charles O'Rear/Corbis; 142 bl SM/SSPL; 142 tl Minnesota Historical Society/Corbis; 142 tr The Advertising Archives; 143 br TRH Pictures/Volvo; 143 c NASA; 143 tr Duomo/Corbis; 144 br Hulton Getty; 144 tl SM/SSPL; 144 tr Corbis; 145 br TRH Pictures; 145 c FAO; 145 tl SM/SSPL; 146 br Sony United Kingdom; 146 tl Bettmann/Corbis; 146 tr Roger Ressmeyer/Corbis; 147 b Michael Holford; 147 tr NASA/SSPL; 148 bl John Novis; 148 c Bettmann/Corbis; 148 tl Cameragraphic; 148 tr Roger Ressmeyer/Corbis; 149 c TRH Pictures; 149 tr Novosti (London); 152 bl Bettmann/Corbis; 152 tl Bettmann/Corbis; 152 tr SM/SSPL ; 153 c Bettmann/Corbis; 153 tl SM/SSPL; 154 b Corbis; 154 tl SM/SSPL; 154 tr TRH Pictures/Westland Aerospace; 155 b Corbis; 155 t, TRH Pictures; 156 bl SPL; 156 br Bettmann/Corbis; 156 tr NASA; 157 br Bettmann/Corbis; 157 tl Roger Ressmeyer/Corbis; 158 b Museum of Flight/Corbis; 158 tl SM/SSPL; 158 tr BSIP/SPL; 159 br Bettmann/Corbis; 159 c Hulton Deutsch Collection/Corbis; 159 tr IBM; 160 bl Hulton Getty; 160 tl IBM; 160 tr Intel; 161 br NSSDC/NASA; 161 tl Roger Ressmeyer/Corbis; 164 bl NASA/SSPL; 164 tl SM/SSPL; 164 tr Bettmann/Corbis; 165 bl SM/SSPL; 165 c FLPA/Roger Tidman; 165 tl SPL; 166 bl Hulton Getty; 166 tl Novosti (London); 166 tr NASA/SSPL; 167 br SPL; 167 c SPL; 167 tl Rex Features; 168 br Dyson Press Office; 168 tl SM/SSPL; 168 tr The Purcell Team/Corbis; 169 br Wall McNamee/Corbis; 169 c Novosti (London); 169 tl SPL; 169 tr SM/SSPL; 170 br SM/SSPL; 170 tl Corbis; 170 tr Novosti (London); 171 c The Advertising Archives; 171 tr Roger Ressmeyer/Corbis; 172 bl Staffan Widstrand/Corbis; 172 tl The Culture Archive; 172 tr The Advertising Archives; 173 bl Bettmann/Corbis; 173 tr The Advertising Archives; 174 br Trip; 174 tl The Natural History Museum, London; 174 tr Bettmann/Corbis; 175 bl W.Cody/Corbis; 175 c Rex Features; 175 tl SPL; 178 br SPL; 178 tl SM/SSPL; 178 tr NASA/SSPL; 179 br The Advertising Archives; 179 tr Bettmann/Corbis; 180 bl SPL; 180 tl Bettmann/Corbis; 180 tr The Culture Archive; 181 br SPL; 181 tr Bettmann/Corbis; 182 b TRH Pictures/Ford; 182 tl SM/SSPL; 182 tr IBM; 183 bl SM/SSPL; 183 t TRH Pictures/SNCF; 184 bl SM/SSPL; 184 tl BBC; 184 tr SM/SSPL; 185 SPL; 185 SM/SSPL; 186 bl SPL; 186 tl Corbis; 186 tr SM/SSPL; 187 b SPL; 187 c GSF Picture Library; 187 tr SM/SSPL; 190 bl Dorling Kindersley; 190 tl SPL; 190 NASA; 191 br Goodall Institute; 191 tl SM/SSPL; 192 bl Roger Ressmeyer/Corbis; 192 tl Robert Brook/Environmental Images; 192 tr NASA; 193 br IBM/Jim Girmzewski; 193 c SM/SSPL; 193 tr Roger Ressmeyer/Corbis; 194 br SPL; 194 tl Martin Sanders; 194 tr SPL;

195 br SM/SSPL; 195 tl NASA; 196 bl Corbis; 196 tl The Natural History Museum, London; 196 tr Layne Kennedy/Corbis; 197 bl SM/SSPL; 197 tl Hoechst; 198 bl SPL; 198 tl SM/SSPL; 198 tr SPL; 199 br SM/SSPL; 199 c Corbis; 199 tl Frank Spooner Pictures/GAMMA; 200 bl TRH Pictures/USAF B-2; 200 tl SM/SSPL; 200 tr SM/SSPL; 201 br NASA; 201 c New Scientist; 201 tr SM/SSPL; 204 bl NASA; 204 tl Hulton Deutsch Collection/Corbis; 205 br SPL; 205 c SPL; 205 tr National Medical Slide Bank; 206 br SPL; 206 tl SPL; 206 tr Hannah Gal/Corbis; 207 br The Associated Press; 207 tl SPL; 208 br Environmental Images; 208 tl Bettmann/Corbis; 208 tr SPL; 209 br SM/SSPL; 209 c Japan Ship Centre; 209 tr SPL; 210 br Roger Ressmeyer/Corbis; 210 c Intel Corp.; 210 tl Hulton Getty; 210 tr ORCV Hydro Products; 211 bl Created by the University of Colorado Health Sciences Center, Center for Human Simulation. Using images from The National Library of Medicine's Visible Human Project®; 211 tl Corbis; 211 tr Ed Young/Corbis; 212 bl NASA; 212 tl SM/SSPL; 212 tr Corbis; 213 bl Environmental Images/Robert Brook; 213 br FSP; 213 t TRH Pictures/Dasa; 214 br SPL; 214 tl SPL; 214 tr SPL; 214c Dan Lamont/Corbis; 215 tl Galaxy Picture Library; 218 br SPL; 218 tl US Geological Survey/Corbis; 218 tr Corbis; 219 br SM/SSPL; 219 c NASA/Roger Ressmeyer/Corbis; 219 tr SPL/James King-Holmes; 220 br TRH Pictures; 220 tl Texas Instruments; 220 tr Popperfoto/Reuters; 221 br SM/SSPL; 221 tr Roger Ressmeyer/Corbis; 222 bl SPL; 222 tl Doug Wilson/Corbis; 222 tr Dave.G. Houser/Corbis; 223 br Sony United Kingdom; 223 c John Dakers; Eye Ubiquitous/Corbis; 223 tl Bang & Olufsen; 224 bl Tony Stone; 224 tl Corbis; 224 tr Roger Ressmeyer/Corbis; 225 bl SPL/NASA; 225 c SPL; 225 tl Palm Inc; 228 bl SPL; 228 tl SPL; 228 tr Bettmann/Corbis; 229 br SPL; 229 c Ericsson; 229 tr JP/NC Museum of Natural Sciences.

Special Focus Topic pages

18/19 background Mehau Kulyk/SPL; 18 t SM/SSPL; 18 c National Museum of Photography, Film & TV/SSPL; 19 t SPL; 19 bl ER Productions/Corbis; 19 br Wellcome Dept. of Cognitive Neurology; 26/27 background Giles Chapman Library; 26 t Topham Picturepoint; 26 c, b Hulton Getty; 27 t Giles Chapman Library; 27 b Newspress; 36/37 background Bob Rowan/Corbis; 36 t Corbis; 36 bl AT & T Archives; 36br Topham Picturepoint; 37 tl John Barlow; 37 tr Courtesy of Samsung Electronics; 48/49 background Digital Vision; 48 t SM/SSPL; 48 b BBC Library/Hulton Getty; 48/49 t SM/SSPL; 48/49 b Popperfoto; 60/61 background Digital Vision; 60 t Underwood & Underwood; 60 c Arthur W.V.Mace; Milepost 92/Corbis; 60/61 Hulton-Deutsch Collection/Corbis; 61 NASA/SPL; 66/67 background Geoge Lepp/Corbis; 66 l Simon Harris/Robert Harding Picture Library; 66 r Peter Mauss ESTO/Arcaid; 67 tl Richard A.Cooke/Corbis; 67 tr Michael Busselle/Corbis; 67 b Rosie Atkins/Gardens Illustrated; 82/83 background Tek Image/SPL; 82 t, c, b NMPFT/SSPL; 83 t Polaroid UK. Ltd; 83 b Andrew Sydenham; 88/89 background Digital Vision, 88 b Grundig UK, 89 cl www.dolby.com, 89 cr Dr. Jeremy Burgess/SPL; 89 b Damien Lovegrove/SPL; 102/103 background Roger Ressmeyer/Corbis, 102 t Bettmann/Corbis, 102 c, b Novosti (London), 103 t, b Corbis; 112 t Françoise Sauze/SciencePhoto Library, 112 c Popperfoto, 112 b John Walmsley, 113 Iain Bagwell; 112/113 background Patrice Loiez, Cern/SPL, 122 Bettmann/Corbis, 122/123 Jurgen Scriba/SPL, 123 Yann-Arthus Bertrand/Corbis, 132 background ibt Amadeus/Britstock-IFA, 132 t Princess Margaret Rose Orthopaedic Hospital/SPL, 132 Bettmann/Corbis, 132/133 Tony Latham, 133 Philips Research Laboratories; 138/139 background Chinch Gryniewicz/Corbis, 138 t UPI/Corbis-Bettmann, 138 b National Museum of Photography, Film & TV/Science & Society Picture Library, 139 Philips Images; 150 t, bl NASA/SPL, 150 br, 151 t, b NASA; 162/163 James King-Holmes/SPL, 162 t Princess Margaret Rose Orthopaedic Hospital/SPL, 162 bl SPL, 162 br NIH/Custom Medical Stock Photo/SPL, 163 t Geoff Tompkinson/SPL, 163 b Bettmann/Corbis; 176/177 Bill Varie/Corbis, 176 t Philip Marazzi, Papilio/Corbis, 176 b Ted Spiegel/Corbis, 177 t Chris Mattison; Frank Lane Picture Agency/Corbis, 177 c Simon Fraser/SPL, 177 b Jim Sugar Photography/Corbis, 188/189 background Joseph Sohm; Chromo Sohm Inc./Corbis, 188 t Bettmann/Corbis, 188 b Hulton-Deutsch Collection/Corbis, 189 tl Photodisc, 189 tr Charles O'Rear/Corbis, 189 b James L.Amos/Corbis; 202/203 background John Walsh/SPL, 202 t Roger Ressmeyer/Corbis, 202 b Adrian Weinbrecht, 203 t Steve Schnieder/SIPA PRESS/Rex Features, 203 bl Adam Hart-Davis/SPL, 203 br courtesy of Bite Communications; 216/217 background Chris Knapton/SPL, 216 t De Keerle/Frank Spooner Pictures, 216 c Dr. Gopal Murti/SPL, 216 L.Willat, East Anglican Regional Genetics Service/SPL; 217 t Philippe Plailly, 217 c Ph.Plailly/Eurelios/SPL, 217 b Laura Wickenden; 226/227 background Digital Vision, 226 Adrian Weinbrecht, 227 l Hank Morgan/SPL, 227 r IriScan